COMMON SENSE

AND

GENESIS

COMMON SENSE
AND
GENESIS

PHILLIP M. BRANSON

WESTBOW
PRESS®
A DIVISION OF THOMAS NELSON
& ZONDERVAN

WestBow Press books may be ordered through booksellers or by contacting:

WestBow Press
A Division of Thomas Nelson & Zondervan
1663 Liberty Drive
Bloomington, IN 47403
www.westbowpress.com
1 (866) 928-1240

ISBN: 978-1-5127-3103-3 (sc)
ISBN: 978-1-5127-3104-0 (hc)
ISBN: 978-1-5127-3102-6 (e)

Library of Congress Control Number: 2016902250

Print information available on the last page.

WestBow Press rev. date: 3/25/2016

AUTHOR'S NOTE

The purpose of this book is to offer a logical, commonsense translation of Genesis. I did not write it to be a dogmatic statement of absolute authority but as a translation that conforms to its literal writing. I'm aware that this book differs widely from conventional teachings.

When I first read Genesis, I didn't have much formal religious training, so I wasn't influenced by the opinions and interpretations of others. From the outset, I formed the theories stated here based on the words I read, and further study has strengthened them. This is what Genesis says to me. I offer it as a possible alternative to the interpretations that have been handed down unquestioned and unchallenged for several hundred years.

This book is not a work of apologetics. I began with the assumption that the Bible says what it means and means what it says. I recommend that readers who are uncomfortable with this premise read, among others, Josh McDowell's *Evidence That Demands a Verdict,* volumes 1 and 2. For a scientific commentary, I recommend *The Genesis Record* by Henry M. Morris. I suggest sincere students start with a prayer for understanding and read the Bible so they can see what it says to them without the encumbrance of someone else's interpretation.

And please don't bother me with the triviality of the J, E, D, P, etc., authors. We know the Bible is a compilation of the records of many men over many centuries; just how many centuries in fact is open to debate. But if the Bible is truly the Word of God except when it explicitly quotes someone else, what difference does it make who or how many editors or cowriters God used to record His Word?

It seems much more logical that the accounts were written whenever possible by eyewitnesses. Some of the facts undoubtedly were passed on through several generations verbally before being written by a chosen scribe. So what? Is it so difficult to believe these accounts were watched over and their integrity protected? If in fact this is the Word of God, it's much more of a stretch to believe otherwise.

So if the Bible as written is truth, where is there room for such wide differences in its interpretation? Once an incorrect interpretation has been made and accepted as fact, a great many other passages must be interpreted in a manner to accommodate that assumption. This leads to some illogical, far-fetched explanations that cause doubt and make the Bible—the Creation story in Genesis in particular—difficult for many to accept.

I have chosen to work from the King James Version of the Bible, but the various translations—while in some cases mildly discordant—are generally in agreement insofar as the literal translation is concerned. But the King James Version is over 400 years old. It was preceded by several other versions—to name two, the Great Bible of 1535 and the Bishop's Bible of 1568. Some of these early versions were translated from the original Hebrew and Aramaic, while others were not. This book deals with the interpretation of the words with an emphasis on logic and common sense.

The theory of evolution is just that - a theory; it hasn't been proven no matter what you may have been told by those whose agendas say otherwise. But if you choose to believe it, you have chosen a religion totally apart from Judaism and Christianity, both of which accept Genesis as truth. If you believe in evolution, you have chosen an atheistic belief that is separate from virtually every other major religion of today. Christianity by definition means following the teachings of Jesus Christ, and Jesus believed and often quoted Genesis, as did Paul and other writers of the New Testament.

I hope this book will offer alternatives to conventional doctrine and thus lead readers to a clearer understanding of what may have been intended as it was written. I also hope this work will help readers to accept the historicity of Genesis. Archaeology is proving every day that the geographical facts in Genesis are accurate. Once you realize the towns and cities are where they were said to have been, that a well is still where it was said to have been, that the mountains and plains, even the weather patterns, are correct, it becomes less daunting to accept the rest of the book on faith. Paul says in Romans 10:17, "So then faith *cometh* by hearing, and hearing by the word of God." I believe that Genesis is the Word of God, and my sincere desire is that each reader of Genesis will be blessed with faith and the peace of understanding that comes with it.

—PHILLIP M. BRANSON

It is very pious to say and prudent to affirm that the holy Bible can never speak untruth— whenever its true meaning is understood. But I believe nobody will deny it is often very abstruse, and may say things which are quite different from what its bare words signify.

—GALILEO GALILEI

I never guess. It is a capital mistake to theorize before one has data. Insensibly one begins to twist facts to suit theories, instead of theories to suit facts.

—SIR ARTHUR CONAN DOYLE

CHAPTER ONE

In the beginning God created the heaven and the earth.

(Note that this verse does not begin, "In the beginning bang." Common sense tells us it could never be "In the beginning bang" because *bang* could never be the beginning of anything. What material was there to go bang? How long had it been there? Where did it come from? Did it carry its age with it after the bang?

What caused it to go bang? And on and on, ad infinitum. It's now even been suggested that there may have been a series of bangs with the universe expanding until it finally implodes in on itself and starts the whole process all over again with yet another bang. But still no explanation of what caused the first bang or where or how the material originated.)

The word used throughout the first chapter for *creation* is *bâhrâh* (sometimes spelled *bârâ*), a word meaning "created from nothing" (*creatio ex nihilo*).

We are told in many places in the Bible that in creating the universe, God spoke it into existence. Hebrews 11:3 is the most definitive; there are also references such as Psalm 33:6 and 33:9. He didn't use existing materials for any of the things He created in the first chapter. Therefore, from the beginning of the account of Creation and reaffirmed repeatedly, whatever exists today does so because God spoke it into existence. Whatever characteristic or peculiarity it may have (such as the semblance of age) is a result of God's having created it with those qualities. A method of determining age such as carbon dating might indicate that a rock appears to be a certain age. Although there are some problems with the dating process, for the most part, the dating is accurate. A rock does have those characteristics, but its carbon dating just shows the way God made it!

Everything spoken into existence was just a day old when it was created, but it would be absurd to suggest all these things were created in their absolute infancy; rather, they all had the semblance of age to one degree or another. Surely it can't be a stretch of faith to believe that if He could speak something into existence, He could also give it the qualities He chose.

VERSE 2

And the earth was without form, and void; and darkness *was* **upon the face of the deep. And the Spirit of God moved upon the face of the waters.**

This is the first mention of the Holy Spirit. Actually, the Trinity, the triune God, is variously credited with different parts of Creation. This doesn't mean the tasks were divided but rather that all three were present at any given time.

VERSE 3

And God said, Let there be light: and there was light.

The first item to be created specifically to combat the void and darkness was light. This is significant because it came on day one, while the creation of the sun and stars (the light givers) didn't come until day four. This, in my opinion, is the explanation of how light apparently traveled many light-years in less than the actual number of years indicated. The whole light path was created at one time, and it was spoken into place first.

It's unfortunate that whenever a passage such as this troubles some scholars, they immediately assume the passage must be at fault and try to interpret it according to their understanding. They will shrug it off with an explanation such as, "The Bible isn't concerned with chronology," "The Bible wasn't written by a scientist," or some other lame phrase that does nothing but undermine the confidence of the student. Better to consider the fact that maybe the Bible was concerned and maybe it does mean what it says; maybe the interpretation is at fault.

VERSE 4

And God saw the light, that *it was* **good: and God divided the light from the darkness.**

VERSE 5

And God called the light Day, and the darkness he called Night. And the evening and the morning were the first day.

Is there any reason for assuming this is anything other than a twenty-four-hour period? We're talking about God speaking creation into existence, and nothing was said about some heavenly stammer or stutter! Common sense dictates here.

VERSE 6

And God said, Let there be a firmament in the midst of the waters, and let it divide the waters from the waters.

VERSE 7

And God made the firmament, and divided the waters which *were* **under the firmament from the waters which** *were* **above the firmament: and it was so.**

The word *made* is not the same word as the previous word used to mean "to create from nothing." In this instance, the substance already exists, having been spoken into existence in the previous verse. The distinction is not important here, but it's very important later. (It's interesting that the concept of the atmosphere containing water seemed to be fully understood and taken for granted.)

VERSE 8

And God called the firmament Heaven. And the evening and the morning were the second day.

Originally, and in some cultures still, a day was reckoned from sunset to sunset, thus the expression "evening and morning" as compared to our day and night.

VERSE 9

> **And God said, Let the waters under the heaven be gathered together unto one place, and let the dry** *land* **appear: and it was so.**

This indicates to me that in the beginning, there was only one ocean and one body of land. That could well have been the case until the flood or even later, when the continents began to separate and drift apart.

VERSE 10

> **And God called the dry** *land* **Earth; and the gathering together of the waters called the Seas: and God saw that it** *was* **good.**

VERSE 11

> **And God said, Let the earth bring forth grass, the herb yielding seed***, and* **the fruit tree yielding fruit after his kind, whose seed** *is* **in itself, upon the earth: and it was so.**

VERSE 12

> **And the earth brought forth grass,** *and* **herb yielding seed after his kind, and the tree yielding fruit, whose seed** *was* **in itself, after his kind: and God saw that** *it was* **good.**

VERSE 13

> **And the evening and the morning were the third day.**

The third day is significant because it not only continued the pattern of speaking the components of creation into existence; it also introduced a phrase repeated three times on that day that was repeated twice more on day five and another five times on day six. That phrase is of course "after his kind." It's an early and direct refutation of the theory of evolution, and by virtue of the ten repetitions, it must be considered as having been deemed very important even then.

VERSE 14

And God said, Let there be lights in the firmament of the heaven to divide the day from the night; and let them be for signs and for seasons, and for days, and years:

VERSE 15

And let them be for lights in the firmament of the heaven to give light upon the earth: and it was so.

VERSE 16

And God made two great lights; the greater light to rule the day, and the lesser light to rule the night: *he made* **the stars also.**

VERSE 17

And God set them in the firmament of the heaven to give light upon the earth,

VERSE 18

And to rule over the day and over the night, and to divide the light from the darkness: and God saw that *it was* **good.**

VERSE 19

And the evening and the morning were the fourth day.

Verses 14–19 describe the creation of the sun, moon, and stars as mentioned previously, three days after the creation of the light they provide.

VERSE 20

And God said, Let the waters bring forth abundantly the moving creature that has life, and fowl *that* **may fly above the earth in the open firmament of the heaven.**

VERSE 21

And God created great whales, and every living creature that moveth, which the waters brought forth abundantly, after their kind, and every winged fowl after his kind: and God saw that *it was* **good.**

Here we see the simple answer to an age-old question. For while we are told that fowl (including chickens) were spoken into existence, no mention was made of eggs!

VERSE 22

And God blessed them, saying, Be fruitful, and multiply, and fill the waters in the seas, and let fowl multiply in the earth.

VERSE 23

And the evening and the morning were the fifth day.

The word translated as "whales" (*tannîyn*) included all things that lived in the water such as sharks, crocodiles, and fish. The word translated as "fowl" (*ôwph*) included every living thing that flew, including birds and insects.

VERSE 24

And God said, Let the earth bring forth the living creature after his kind, cattle, and creeping thing, and beast of the earth after his kind: and it was so.

VERSE 25

And God made the beast of the earth after his kind, and cattle after their kind, and every thing

**that creepeth upon the earth after his kind: and
God saw that** *it was* **good.**

I assume that "cattle" (*behêmâh*, from a root originally meaning
"dumb" or "mute") referred to all herbivores, while "beasts" (*chay*)
included all meat eaters, and "creeping things" (*remes*, from a root
meaning "to crawl" or "glide") included everything that crawled such
as caterpillars and spiders and such up to and including large, land-
based reptiles.

Verse 25 is almost a repetition of verse 24, thereby lending even
more emphasis to the fact that each animal produced its own young
and none was the result of having developed from something else,
the process commonly known as evolution.

VERSE 26

**And God said, Let us make man in our image, after
our likeness: and let them have dominion over the
fish of the sea, and over the fowl of the air, and
over the cattle, and over all the earth, and over
every creeping thing that creepeth upon the earth.**

This is the first mention of "us" and the first mention of "man."
The word for "make," *asâh*, as used here meant "to bestow or endow
with the qualities of," but the word for create in the next verse was
still *bahrah*. The word for "God" was the same as was used from the
beginning—meaning three in one. The word for "man" is in the plural,
as in "mankind," and the use of the word *them* instead of a singular
"him" is significant.

VERSE 27

So God created man in his *own* **image, in the image
of God created he him; male and female created
he them.**

Both male and female were very specifically said to have been
spoken into existence. The word for "man" is *'âdâm*, a generality
meaning "mankind." The fact that it can also be used for Adam's name
certainly adds to the confusion.

VERSE 28

And God blessed them, and God said unto them, Be fruitful, and multiply, and replenish the earth, and subdue it: and have dominion over the fish of the sea, and over the fowl of the air, and over every living thing that moveth upon the earth.

We aren't told how many people were created here. These first men were created as hunters, gatherers, and fishermen. God commanded them to multiply and fill the earth while ruling over all other living things. Evidence shows that early man did inhabit nearly all points of the earth, so there must have been a great many at the beginning to be able to survive.

VERSE 29

And God said, Behold, I have given you every herb bearing seed, which *is* upon the face of all the earth, and every tree, in the which *is* the fruit of a tree yielding seed; to you it shall be for meat.

Here is still more repetition of the theme of each entity reproducing its own kind. It's amazing to realize that evolution was acknowledged as a threat that far in advance and that so many times it was refuted. This, to me, is further proof that the Bible is the inspired Word of God.

VERSE 30

And to every beast of the earth, and to every fowl of the air, and to every thing that creepeth upon the earth, wherein *there is* life, I *have given* every green herb for meat: and it was so.

Interesting that God took time to explain the flora had been created to feed the fauna. But of course, without grasses and other natural feed, none of the animals would have survived.

VERSE 31

And God saw every thing that he had made, and behold, *it was* very good. And the evening and the morning were the sixth day.

CHAPTER TWO

VERSE 1

**Thus the heavens and the earth were finished, and
all the host of them.**

Chapter and verse divisions may not always seem appropriate,
but the divisions in no way change or affect the meaning of what
was written. When reading the Scriptures, please keep in mind that
the chapter and verse separations were added much later, and
sometimes, the continuity seems to be interrupted. Here as always,
common sense will serve as the best guide.

VERSE 2

**And on the seventh day, God ended his work
which he had made; and he rested on the seventh
day from all his work which he had made.**

So concluded the seven days of Creation. This account was
quoted and referenced many times in the Old and New Testaments.
There are nearly two hundred in the New Testament alone, many
by Jesus Himself. So rejecting the biblical account of Creation in
Genesis destroys the credibility of Jesus and the teachings of the
New Testament.

As mentioned earlier, there's no logical reason to assign more
than twenty-four hours to a day, nor is there any logical explanation for
a pause or gap between any of the consecutive days of Creation. The
theory that has been advanced to advocate such a pause (usually put
between verses 1 and 2), the so-called gap theory, came much later
in history. It was put forth largely as a means of conciliation toward
those who were being swayed by evolution and its teaching that vast
amounts of time were necessary for the development of the world as
it is today.

There's nothing wrong with the gap theory in itself, and there
undoubtedly has been a great deal of time that has passed since

Creation. The gap was just put in the wrong place because of incorrect interpretations of chapter 2. At the end of the first chapter, after Creation was complete, it makes sense for there to have been a time lapse of perhaps several million years.

The theory of evolution is constantly being revised and updated, argued, and changed by its proponents as new discoveries are made, whether in space or through archaeology, and yet it's being taught as fact in our schools as though it were complete, perfected, and proven. There cannot be conciliation or compromise between the scriptural account of Creation and the theory of evolution; each precludes the other. Any attempt at coexistence, dual acceptance, or equal credence is doomed to failure on both sides.

Those who teach evolution should also teach atheism, the total rejection of all religion as we know it, and teach evolution as the only true religion. Then at least there would be a clear choice between the two. Unfortunately, many well-meaning but misguided thinkers have tried to avoid a direct conflict and have inadvertently aided in the acceptance of evolution by muddying the waters of creation. The serious student is left with nothing tangible to hold onto except faith.

VERSE 3

And God blessed the seventh day, and sanctified it: because that in it he had rested from all his work which God created and made.

This is where the story of the original Creation ended and would have been a more logical end to chapter 1. It is also, as mentioned before, where the gap should go. As far as I know, no one has ever advanced the theory that a gap in time could have taken place at this point, mainly because it doesn't fit with the accepted theory that Adam and Eve were the people created in chapter 1.

However, it seems much more logical here than anywhere else, especially between any of the seven days. It would also make moot the debate about how old the earth actually is. Many devout creationists believe the earth is only about four thousand years old give or take a few thousand. If Adam and Eve had been created on the sixth day, that would indeed be the case. Yet we know that science is continually making discoveries concerning the age of the earth and especially the length of time man has been living here.

Recently, it was shown that Neanderthal man could well have lived in a period that overlapped that of present-day humanity and perhaps even intermarried with them. Well, what do you know? That's exactly what the Bible says was happening before the flood. It's now speculated that Neanderthals were more intelligent than first believed, and the question of the day is what could have caused them to disappear. Of course, no one has mentioned the possibility of a catastrophe such as a universal flood because that would be heresy for the preachers of evolution.

But a long time gap here would not be a concession to evolution; rather, it would confirm God's Word. God completed Creation before the gap began. The Bible certainly says nothing to preclude this, and in fact, there are many reasons to accept there was a considerable time lapse at that point. But for that argument to have any validity, we must accept the interpretation of verse 7 as it's presented here.

VERSE 4

These *are* the generations of the heavens and of the earth when they were created, in the day that the Lord God made the earth and the heavens,

VERSE 5

And every plant of the field before it was in the earth, and every herb of the field before it grew: for the Lord God had not caused it to rain upon the earth, and *there was* not a man to till the ground.

"A man to till the ground" is an idiom; it means "farmer." While that may seem a trivial point, it's very important because without farmers there could not be civilization. We know that God created hunters, gatherers, fishermen, and presumably herdsmen from the descriptions given in Genesis 1:27–29. But as we know, this is essentially an aboriginal society without the characteristics of civilization. It was not until someone could produce more food than he and his family required that others would be free to make the sophisticated and humane advancements in culture and society we consider requisites of civilized living and behavior.

VERSE 6

But there went up a mist from the earth, and watered the whole face of the ground.

Prior to the flood, we are told it had never rained. The earth was a greenhouse of sorts without any of the climate zones and geographical problems (deserts, mountains, polar caps, etc.) that exist today.[1]

VERSE 7

And the Lord God formed man *of* the dust of the ground, and breathed into his nostrils the breath of life; and man became a living soul.

The word for "formed" used here, *yâtsar* (the first time it appears in the Bible) is not the same word for "create" that was used throughout chapter 1. Whereas *bahrah* in chapter 1 meant to create from nothing or speak into existence, here we are told dust was used to form Adam in the same manner a potter would mold or form clay. Since the two methods of Creation were different and since this act was described in detail, it is illogical to assume this was a recounting of the creation of humanity as it was told in chapter 1. However, virtually every biblical scholar today makes that assumption.

Adding to the confusion unfortunately is the fact that the word for "man" and "Adam" are the same—*ahdahm*. The same word is used elsewhere to denote humankind and the generality "men." I believe this coincidence is what contributed to the mistaken notion that Adam was the first man.

There are references in the New Testament to Adam as the first man and Christ as the last, but we cannot take these out of context because the subject was sin and the meaning was clear—that Adam was the first man to sin and that sin ended with Christ. It would be as illogical to assume that the passage meant Adam was the first man created as to assume that it meant Christ was the last man born. It is always important to translate biblical passages in context.

Once the erroneous assumption is made that 2:7 was a recap of 1:26 and the equally confusing translation of 5:1–2, all sorts of questions come forth that should never have been raised or that have obvious answers. Already mentioned was the age of the earth. Other questions raised ask about the origin and development of the races, whether angels cohabitated with humans to produce giants, and the always popular, "Where did Cain get his wife?" The attempts to answer these questions have contributed to the confusion and doubt of the serious student because they have to be skewed to conform to the original erroneous translation.

The second part of this verse is also significant. The "breath of life" (literally "breath of lives") that was breathed into Adam seems to refer to a spiritual as well as a physical life; it is the earliest reference to man's soul. Of course, we aren't given the details of the composition of those who were spoken into existence in the first chapter other than that they were created "in the image of God." However, Paul wrote of Adam as the first man to possess a living soul in 1 Corinthians 15:45, so perhaps there were differences.

VERSE 8

And the Lord God planted a garden eastward in Eden; and there he put the man whom he had formed.

This should certainly prove that the subject of this chapter is one man only, Adam. The word for "formed" is again *yâtsar*. It cannot be argued that God put all humanity in the garden of Eden. Furthermore, the singular "the man" combined with the same word for "formed" makes it self-explanatory that this was the intended translation.

VERSE 9

And out of the ground made the Lord God to grow every tree that is pleasant to the sight, and good for food; the tree of life also in the midst of the garden, and the tree of knowledge of good and evil.

A description of the Garden of Eden. Apparently, there were no weeds, thistles, or thorns there and everything that grew was either good to eat or beautiful to see.

VERSE 10

And a river went out of Eden to water the garden; and from thence it was parted, and became into four heads.

The question of how the rivers could flow and replenish themselves without evaporation and rain is interesting. The fact that they did so is indicative that there were apparently vast amounts of water underground before the flood.

VERSE 11

The name of the first *is* **Pison: that** *is* **it which compasseth the whole land of Havilah, where** *there is* **gold;**

VERSE 12

And the gold of that land *is* **good: there** *is* **bdellium and the onyx stone.**

VERSE 13

And the name of the second river *is* **Gihon: the same** *is* **it that compasseth the whole land of Ethiopia.**

VERSE 14

And the name of the third river *is* **Hiddekel: that** *is* **it which goeth toward the east of Assyria. And the fourth river** *is* **Euphrates.**

There has been much speculation as to the exact location of the Garden of Eden and where these rivers were. Archaeologist Dr. Juris Zarins has devoted much of his life in an effort to definitively pinpoint its location. The reason his and others' efforts haven't been more successful is because the location was described before the flood and before the continents were separated.

However, since rivers flow downhill, we at least know Eden was in an elevated location and encompassed a large enough area to form the mouths of four rivers feeding in four different directions. Eden may well have been very large indeed.

VERSE 15

And the Lord God took the man, and put him into the garden of Eden to dress it and to keep it.

While it was not written in so many words, it's safe to assume either the instructions for this "dressing and keeping" were given by God or the knowledge of how to do so was imparted when Adam was formed. As noted earlier, Adam was created because "there was not a man to till the ground." That being so, gardening and farming can truly be said to be godly activities.

VERSE 16

And the Lord God commanded the man, saying, Of every tree of the garden thou mayest freely eat:

VERSE 17

But of the tree of knowledge of good and evil, thou shall not eat of it: for in the day that thou eatest thereof thou shalt surely die.

Literally, "dying, thou shalt die." The passage doesn't mean that Adam would drop dead immediately but that the aging process would begin and end in his death. Here is the evidence that Adam was the first man to face a choice between good and evil, righteousness and sin. And the rest, as they say, is history.

VERSE 18

And the Lord God said, *It is* not good that the man should be alone; I will make an help meet for him.

VERSE 19

And out of the ground the Lord God formed every beast of the field, and every fowl of the air; and

brought *them* unto Adam to see what he would call them: and whatsoever Adam called every living creature, that was the name thereof.

VERSE 20

And Adam gave names to all cattle, and to the fowl of the air, and to every beast of the field; but for Adam there was not found an help meet for him.

It is not meant here to imply that God first tried to find a companion for Adam among the animals. If anything, it is meant to show that such couldn't have been the case. It also serves to establish Adam and subsequently humanity (remember that *Adam* and *mankind* are the same word) as superior to—and therefore apart from—all the animals, with dominion over them as set forth in 1:28. We aren't told whether the names Adam gave the animals were a result of divine inspiration or from his own imagination.

VERSE 21

And the Lord God caused a deep sleep to fall upon Adam, and he slept: and he took one of his ribs, and closed up the flesh instead thereof;

VERSE 22

And the rib, which the Lord God had taken from the man, made he a woman, and brought her unto the man.

This is certainly a different account from that of 1:26–27, in which God spoke men—both male and female—into existence. The word used for "made" here is *bânâh*, the only time it's used in Genesis. The connotation is, among other things, one of making children. The question now becomes how much difference if any there was between those spoken into existence (in God's image, after His likeness) and Adam, who was formed from the soil, and Eve, who was formed from Adam's rib. I personally believe there were differences as discussed in verse 7 above. One is obvious. The early men (Homo habilis, Cro-Magnon, Neanderthal, etc.) all lived and died, but Adam's line didn't

COMMON SENSE AND GENESIS | 17

experience death until after he and Eve had eaten from the Tree of Knowledge of Good and Evil.

Second, we know there were giants produced as a result of unions between the descendants of the two, the sons of God (presumably sons of Adam) - and the daughters of man (those who were created if the first chapter.) These genes later again produced giants at the time of Goliath and others unusually gifted in physical stature. Some other physical variations may also have existed that through genetic recurrence account for the distinctions between people today.

The different races were undoubtedly included in the original Creation of chapter 1. Therefore, many subtle differences could have existed as well as perhaps greater differences that didn't survive the flood.

VERSE 23

And Adam said, This *is* now bone of my bones, and flesh of my flesh: she shall be called Woman, because she was taken out of man.

VERSE 24

Therefore shall a man leave his father and his mother, and shall cleave unto his wife: and they shall be one flesh.

As we saw in 2:5, Adam was the beginning of civilization. That scenario was completed with the creation of Eve, his wife, and the institution of marriage. It is interesting that the word *wife* here is synonymous with "helpmeet" with no further elaboration. Also, *father* and *mother* are used even though neither Adam nor Eve had parents. But the descendants of the people who were spoken into existence in chapter 1 would have been fathers and mothers, multiplying and producing children as directed by God in 1:28 and of course all succeeding generations.

The emphasis this account puts on the first marriage and the detail in which it is described are testimony to the importance God placed on it. These five verses should put it to rest any doubt about the sanctity of marriage in the Bible.

VERSE 25

And they were both naked, the man and his wife, and were not ashamed.

Did this condition last a while, or did the serpent appear right away? We aren't told, but it's not unreasonable to believe Adam and Eve enjoyed at least some period of happiness and peace before the temptation and fall from grace. In fact, they could have had a considerable amount of time together.

CHAPTER THREE

VERSE 1

Now the serpent was more subtil than any beast of the field which the Lord God had made. And he said unto the woman, Yea, hath God said, Ye shall not eat of every tree of the garden?

VERSE 2

And the woman said unto the serpent, We may eat of the fruit of the trees of the garden.

VERSE 3

But of the fruit of the tree which *is* in the midst of the garden, God hath said, Ye shall not eat of it, neither shall ye touch it, lest ye die.

VERSE 4

And the serpent said unto the woman, Ye shall not surely die:

VERSE 5

For God doth know that in the day ye eat thereof, then your eyes shall be opened, and ye shall be as gods, knowing good and evil.

VERSE 6

And when the woman saw that the tree *was* good for food, and that it *was* pleasant to the eyes, and a tree to be desired to make *one* wise, she took of the fruit thereof and did eat, and gave also unto her husband with her; and he did eat.

VERSE 7

And the eyes of them both were opened, and they knew that they *were* naked; and they sewed fig leaves together, and made themselves aprons.

VERSE 8

And they heard the voice of the Lord God walking in the garden in the cool of the day; and Adam and his wife hid themselves from the presence of the Lord God amongst the trees of the garden.

VERSE 9

And the Lord God called unto Adam, and said unto him, Where *art* thou?

VERSE 10

And he said, I heard thy voice in the garden, and I was afraid, because I *was* naked; and I hid myself.

VERSE 11

And he said, Who told thee that thou *wast* naked? Hast thou eaten of the tree, whereof I commanded thee that thou shouldest not eat?

VERSE 12

And the man said, The woman whom thou gavest *to be* with me, she gave me of the tree, and I did eat.

I remember listening to tapes on this section by Pastor Chuck Smith of Calvary Chapel in Costa Mesa, California. He pointed out that this was the origin of "passing the buck." Adam first passed it to God, stating it was God's fault because He had given Eve to Adam. Then he passed it to Eve because she had given him the fruit to eat. Not to be outdone, Eve passed the buck to the serpent that had beguiled her. Reading this passage always brings back the humor and simplicity of that wonderful teaching.

VERSE 13

And the Lord God said unto the woman. What *is* this *that* thou hast done? And the woman said, The serpent beguiled me, and I did eat.

VERSE 14

And the Lord God said unto the serpent, Because thou hast done this, thou *art* cursed above all cattle, and above every beast of the field; upon thy belly shalt thou go, and dust shalt thou eat all the days of thy life:

VERSE 15

And I will put enmity between thee and the woman, and between thy seed and her seed; it shall bruise thy head, and thou shalt bruise his heel.

The generally accepted interpretation here is that the reference to the woman's seed was either Jesus Christ or His church and the seed of the serpent was Satan. While Satan would inflict some sorrow and hurt along the way, in the end, he would be fatally wounded.

VERSE 16

Unto the woman he said, I will greatly multiply thy sorrow and thy conception; in sorrow thou shalt bring forth children; and thy desire *shall be* to thy husband, and he shall rule over thee.

The woman was reduced from a position of helpmeet, equal partner, to a subservient role. This condition remained pretty much unchanged until the nineteenth and twentieth centuries, when women regained some of the equality they had lost in the garden. In many parts of the world, however, women are still very much less than equal to men.

VERSE 17

And unto Adam he said, Because thou hast hearkened unto the voice of thy wife, and hast

eaten of the tree, of which I commanded thee, saying, Thou shalt not eat of it: cursed *is* the ground for thy sake; in sorrow shalt thou eat *of* it all the days of thy life;

VERSE 18

Thorns also and thistles shall it bring forth to thee; and thou shalt eat the herb of the field;

The job of farming and tending the garden got a lot tougher. After that, the farmer had to contend with weeds and presumably other pests and hardships, and, after the flood, with inclement weather conditions as befall the modern farmer.

VERSE 19

In the sweat of thy face shalt thou eat bread, till thou return unto the ground; for out of it wast thou taken; for dust thou *art*, and unto dust shalt thou return.

He was made mortal with the inevitability of death at the end of his life. Although he did not suddenly drop dead after eating the fruit, his aging process began and his days became numbered.

As we shall see in chapter 5, the life expectancy was a great deal longer than it is today. With the flood, God set the life span of man at 120 years. However, as noted in chapters 9 and 10, Noah and his descendants still had rather long lives. Apparently, the aging process that limited man to 120 years developed gradually, most probably in conjunction with the changes in the earth's atmosphere brought about by the flood and perhaps to facilitate the repopulation of the earth by the first few generations following Noah.

VERSE 20

And Adam called his wife's name Eve; because she was the mother of all living.

This is another passage that can be easily misinterpreted to suggest Eve was the first woman. In Hebrew, the translation is, "And

Adam called his wife's name Eve, because she became the mother of all living." The context here is that she became the matriarch or grandmother of all succeeding generations.[2] Of course that was true since all future generations came from the line of Noah, who was directly descended (tenth generation) from Adam and Eve.

VERSE 21

Unto Adam also and to his wife did the Lord God make coats of skins, and clothed them.

The word for "make" here is again *âsâh*, indicating he used existing material, namely, animal skins. However, no mention was made of the animals having first been sacrificed as is sometimes suggested.

VERSE 22

And the Lord God said, Behold, the man has become as one of us, to know good and evil: and now, lest he put forth his hand, and take also of the tree of life, and eat, and live forever:

VERSE 23

Therefore the Lord God sent him forth from the garden of Eden, to till the ground from whence he was taken.

Thus began the civilization of humanity. Records indicate that farming began about 9500 to 10,000 BC or perhaps a bit earlier, and the domestication of animals about 9000 BC, which would put Adam's creation possibly between 12,000 and 15,000 years ago. These estimates are of course very rough and speculative.

The time gap from the earliest records of prehistoric man to the advent of farming and civilization is estimated at anywhere from 1.5 to 2.5 million years. However, most of the advancement in tool making occurred in the last 100,000 years or so.

We aren't told how many people were created in chapter 1. We know they were commanded to "multiply and replenish the earth," so it can be assumed the earth wasn't filled at Creation; there could have been a great many or relatively few at first. My belief is that there were enough to ensure they would survive and fulfill that command and, as will be discussed later, enough to represent all three major races—Caucasoid, Negroid, and Mongoloid—that would descend from these original people.

It would then have taken a considerable amount of time for the populations to spread to all corners of the world. The fact that they did spread is a given in view of archeological evidence as well as the fact that the flood was universal, not just local. If the estimates for the time men have inhabited the earth are accurate, that would be the length of time of the gap after chapter 1. The Bible says nothing to dispute this, and I see no reason not to accept the scientific estimates of the time man has inhabited the earth as relatively accurate.

VERSE 24

So he drove out the man; and he placed at the east of the garden of Eden Cherubims, and a flaming sword which turned every way, to keep the way of the tree of life.

Because of their sin, Adam and Eve were forever cut off from the eternal life they had expected. It is interesting that somehow this mention of a Tree of Life became twisted into a myth of a fountain of youth that has been sought in vain by men throughout various times and in many locations.

CHAPTER FOUR

VERSE 1

And Adam knew Eve his wife; and she conceived, and bare Cain, and said, I have gotten a man from the Lord.

VERSE 2

And she again bare his brother Abel. And Abel was a keeper of sheep, but Cain was a tiller of the ground.

The wording here suggests that Cain and Abel might have been twins since the word for "conceived" is used only once. At any rate, the first two offspring of Adam and Eve represented two opposite types—the herdsman and the farmer. The feud between these two has been ongoing for many centuries; it was very prevalent in the days of the Wild West and is still evident in parts of the world.

VERSE 3

And in process of time it came to pass, that Cain brought of the fruit of the ground an offering unto the Lord.

VERSE 4

And Abel, he also brought of the firstlings of his flock and of the fat thereof. And the Lord had respect unto Abel and to his offering:

VERSE 5

But unto Cain and to his offering he had not respect. And Cain was very wroth, and his countenance fell.

So both brothers made an offering, and one was accepted, while the other wasn't. We're not told why Cain's offering was unacceptable, whether it was due to the quality of what he offered, what was in his heart at the time of the offering, or how the offering was prepared. Paul wrote, "By faith Abel offered a more excellent sacrifice than Cain" in Hebrews 11:4. The important point is that because Cain's offering was unacceptable, it caused contention between the brothers. Also important is the fact that both brothers obviously recognized the need to worship God, with each making an offering.

VERSE 6

And the Lord said unto Cain, Why art thou wroth? And why is thy countenance fallen?

VERSE 7

If thou doest well, shalt thou not be accepted? And if thou doest not well, sin lieth at the door. And unto thee *shall be* **his desire, and thou shalt rule over him.**

In *Commentary on the Whole Bible* by Jamieson, Fausset, and Brown, Zondervan Publishing House, Grand Rapids, Michigan, 1979, it's suggested,

> The purport of the divine rebuke to Cain was this: "Why art thou angry, as if unjustly treated? If thou doest well (i.e., wert innocent and sinless) a thank offering would have been accepted … But as thou doest not well (i.e., art a sinner) a sin offering is necessary, by bringing which thou wouldest have met with acceptance and retained the honors of thy birthright."

This language implies that previous instructions had been given as to the mode of worship. I make no comment on this interpretation other than that it seems logical and helps clarify an otherwise confusing passage, but it requires the presumption of prior instructions from God regarding the offerings and the different types of offerings and therefore the method of worship God had previously mandated. While this may be the case, it's an assumption not confirmed by the text.

VERSE 8

And Cain talked with Abel his brother; and it came to pass, when they were in the field, that Cain rose up against Abel his brother, and slew him.

VERSE 9

And the Lord said unto Cain, Where *is* Abel thy brother? And he said, I know not: *Am* I my brother's keeper?

VERSE 10

And he said, What hast thou done? The voice of thy brother's blood crieth unto me from the ground.

VERSE 11

And now *art* thou cursed from the earth, which hath opened her mouth to receive thy brother's blood from thy hand;

VERSE 12

When thou tillest the ground, it shall not henceforth yield unto thee her strength; a fugitive and a vagabond shalt thou be in the earth.

VERSE 13

And Cain said unto the Lord, my punishment *is* greater than I can bear.

No sign of regret or plea for pardon from Cain. Much like the criminals of today, he seemed sorry he'd been caught and regretted his sentence but didn't show much remorse for having committed the crime. After initially denying knowledge of Abel's whereabouts, his focus switched to his punishment, and he decried its severity.

VERSE 14

Behold, thou hast driven me out this day from the face of the earth; and from thy face shall I be hid; and I shall be a fugitive and a vagabond in the earth; and it shall come to pass, *that* **every one that findeth me shall slay me.**

Here is where common sense dictates that many people must already inhabit the world. Since he was the oldest sibling (probably the only remaining child since no mention was made of any other children being born until Seth, who was sent later to replace Abel), Cain wouldn't have had much to fear from remaining close to home and certainly nothing to fear from leaving.

Banishment became unbearable when he was forced to go forth among strangers. He even stated, "Every one that findeth me shall slay me." It is illogical to assume that these strangers were all part of the family of Adam and Eve. But if one accepts the premise that Adam and Eve were the first and only male and female created by God in chapter 1, then only this illogical interpretation is possible.

VERSE 15

And the Lord said unto him, Therefore whosoever slayeth Cain, vengeance shall be taken on him sevenfold. And the Lord set a mark upon Cain, lest any finding him should kill him.

We aren't told what the mark was, and there is speculation as to whether it was a visible mark or perhaps some change in his appearance that kept people away. Whatever the mark was, it was successful in preventing him from being killed. We learn in the next few verses how Cain not only survived but also founded a family and a city and prospered.

VERSE 16

And Cain went out from the presence of the Lord, and dwelt in the land of Nod, on the east of Eden.

Nod's location is open to speculation. Since this occurred before the flood, it's a moot point; the earth was so drastically changed by that event. According to most generally accepted models of the world before the flood, there weren't any really desolate areas such as deserts because of the greenhouse effect encompassing the planet. So wherever Cain chose to settle would have most probably been fertile and prosperous.

Remembering that Cain was a farmer, a possible location for Nod is the Fertile Crescent, in the Middle East, often called the "cradle of civilization." The Fertile Crescent is also one of the suggested locations for the garden of Eden.[3] And as stated here, Nod was adjacent to Eden.

VERSE 17

And Cain knew his wife; and she conceived, and bare Enoch: and he builded a city, and called the name of the city, after the name of his son, Enoch.

This is the passage that prompts the question of where Cain got his wife. As mentioned before, there really is only one logical explanation: there were other people in the world besides those in Adam's family.

VERSE 18

And unto Enoch was born Irad: and Irad begat Mehujael: and Mehujael begat Methusael: and Methusael begat Lamech.

Thus did the line of Cain prosper. We aren't told of any contact with his parents or siblings, but it is presumed that due to his banishment, there was none. We can also assume, however, that some progress toward civilization was taking place, since Cain was also a farmer. His descendants had time for music and metallurgy among other pursuits. This all took place, though, outside the presence of the Lord and apparently didn't include godliness, and any form of worship would have been nonexistent or to a heathen god. This would be consistent with Cain's taking a wife from an aboriginal people and adopting his wife's beliefs and methods of worship.

VERSE 19

And Lamech took unto him two wives: the name of the one *was* **Adah, and the name of the other Zillah.**

This is the first mention of polygamy in the Bible, although the practice might well have been commonplace among those who were created before Adam and Eve. This is further evidence that the line established by Cain was not living in accordance with the wishes of God.

VERSE 20

And Adah bare Jabal: he was the father of such as dwell in tents, and *of such as have* **cattle.**

VERSE 21

And his brother's name *was* **Jubal: he was the father of all such as handle the harp and organ.**

The word used here for "harp" is *kinnôwr*, from a root meaning "to twang." I suspect the first instruments more closely resembled those we associate with mountain music or oriental music than an actual harp. The word for organ is *ûgwâb* or *ûggâb*, which is derived from the root meaning "breathing" or "producing sound from breathing" such as with a reed instrument or horn.

VERSE 22

And Zillah, she also bare Tubal-cain, an instructor of every artificer in brass and iron: and the sister of Tubal-cain *was* **Naamah.**

The mention of working with metals is made so offhandedly that it seems almost taken for granted. We aren't told if the process was invented there or was already being used. We don't know if the words for iron (*barzel*) and brass (*nechôsheth*) refer to the metals we know today or simply to some other form of metal such as copper. We only know for sure that it was an improvement over stone tools.

Of course, it's possible that this earliest knowledge was lost with the flood and had to be relearned or rediscovered. However, it's obvious that the knowledge of the knowledge, that is, the awareness of the art of metallurgy, existed and had been handed down with the rest of biblical writings.

It becomes even more difficult to establish a date for the flood. The *Encyclopedia Britannica* lists the approximate dates for the Iron Age depending on the particular geographical area as beginning as early as 3000 BC, with the Bronze Age and its use of copper dating back as far as 6500 BC. Before that came the Stone Age, which is divided into Paleolithic, Mesolithic, and Neolithic periods. These periods include all the prehistoric time in which man had inhabited the earth, which in estimates varies from 120,000 years up to 600,000 or 700,000 years. The estimate is "approximate and conjectural, obtained through Anthropology, Archaeology, Genetics, Geology, or Linguistics. They are all subject to revision due to new discoveries or improved calculations," which means they don't know. The last Stone Age period, the Neolithic, dates to approximately 8,000 BC.

If we accept that the first men created in chapter 1 were the hunters, gatherers, herdsmen, and fishermen who may have inhabited the earth for however long was necessary to comply with the above time estimates, and we accept that Adam was created as the first farmer (because "there was not a man to till the ground") to begin the process of civilization, we can then place Adam's creation at somewhere perhaps between 15,000 and 12,000 BC. This would agree with the changes known to have taken place at about that time.

It is known from archaeological evidence that the change from a hunting-gathering existence to an agrarian economy occurred in a gradual movement coming out of the Fertile Crescent beginning about 9000 BC. And the Fertile Crescent is exactly where we would expect to find the Garden of Eden, which could very well have included all or most of what is now the Fertile Crescent, from which the art of farming is said to have originated.

Remember that naming the animals was also one of Adam's first duties; is it unreasonable to speculate this process could also have included the domestication of some of the animals?

Some of these changes would have occurred between the creation of Adam and the flood, but most wouldn't have become apparent (as far as the archeological evidence is concerned) until the repopulation of the earth through the sons of Noah. So although we know from the genealogies in the next chapter that the flood took place 1,576 years after God created Adam, establishing a date for it is still difficult. Adam could have been created much earlier than the time listed above.

Archaeological discoveries such as the Kennewick man, the Anzick boy, and others from the Clovis Era, Cactus Hill in Virginia, the Paisley Caves in Oregon, the Topper site in South Carolina, Curva Fell and Monte Verde in Chile, and many others indicate that man had been in North and South America for many thousands of years. Whether these findings date back to antediluvian times has not been established primarily because of the non-acceptance of the concept of a worldwide flood and the established date for it. The fact that men were here that long ago proves that the world population was indeed spread out over the entire earth at a very early time.

If we could establish a definite time for the flood, we would know whether these were people whom God had created in the first chapter or were descendants of Noah and his family after the flood. Since every bit of evidence indicates these early people were hunters, gatherers, fishermen, and such, it's reasonable to assume these people may have been here before the flood.

Reconciling the biblical account with what's known from other sources can be frustrating, but they do fit together, and much of the difficulty disappears when we consider the semblance of age with which all things in creation were endowed.

VERSE 23

> **And Lamech said unto his wives, Adah and Zillah, Hear my voice; ye wives of Lamech, hearken unto my speech: for I have slain a man to my wounding, and a young man to my hurt.**

VERSE 24

> **If Cain shall be avenged sevenfold, truly Lamech seventy and sevenfold.**

We don't know the circumstances of this killing, but it might be presumed that it was either accidental or in self-defense inasmuch as Lamech seemed distraught and believed his protection should be eleven times that of Cain. It also shows that Cain's transgression and subsequent punishment was common knowledge some five generations after the fact.

VERSE 25

> **And Adam knew his wife again; and she bare a son, and called his name Seth; For God,** *said she,* **hath appointed me another seed instead of Abel, whom Cain slew.**

It cannot be logically argued that Adam and Eve had any children after Cain and Abel until Seth, or at least any other sons. We are told in the next chapter they had sons and daughters after Seth, and probably quite a few, but this verse doesn't translate comfortably if one assumes there were sons other than Cain and Abel before Seth. This then is another strong argument for the world being populated at the time by people other than the descendants of Adam and Eve. Otherwise, again, Cain's protest at his banishment and fear of being slain makes no sense. And again, there is no logical explanation for Cain's wife.

VERSE 26

> **And to Seth, to him also there was born a son; and he called his name Enos: then began men to call upon the name of the Lord.**

Unlike the line descending from Cain, this family was worshipful and walking with God.

CHAPTER FIVE

This *is* the book of the generations of Adam. In the day that God created man, in the likeness of God made he him;

The word for "created" is *bahrah*, as used in chapter 1, to denote man's having been spoken into existence. But the genealogy is that of Adam, not those spoken into existence. The word used here for Adam is capitalized, while the one used for man is a variation and is not.

The balance of this chapter deals with the genealogy of Adam and his successors. It probably isn't meant to be a complete chronological record and may or may not contain omissions. Moses didn't list Cain or Abel here but started with Seth. He also only mentioned there were other sons and daughters who came after Seth who weren't in a direct line to Abraham. Moses' chief interest was apparently to record the lineage from Seth to Abraham. Some scholars have chosen to date the earth on the basis of simply adding these ages, but that's a theory I believe cannot be supported. As previously discussed, a long gap at the end of chapter 1 is much more logical and is consistent with all modern scientific observations. Such errors help discredit Genesis and facilitate the acceptance of other atheistic theories.

I offer the balance of chapter 5 without comment except to note that with the exception of Enoch, all the histories end with the phrase "and he died." This is the proof of what God had promised in the Garden of Eden, that Adam and all who followed would die as a result of his and Eve's disobeying God's command to not eat the fruit of the Tree of Knowledge of Good and Evil.

Enoch is apparently one of two people, the other being the prophet Elijah, whom God took directly without their having to go through the process of actual death. Also of note is the length of the life of these ancients. These people lived before the flood, when conditions were vastly different.

In verse 3 in the next chapter, we will see that with the flood, God trimmed down humans' life expectancy, eventually reaching the predicted 120 years.

VERSE 2

Male and female created he them; and blessed them, and called their name Adam, in the day when they were created.

The word for created is again *bara,* so the reference is to those spoken into existence, and the use of the plural throughout again refutes the reference to a single person.

VERSE 3

And Adam lived an hundred and thirty years, and begat *a son* in his own likeness, after his own image; and called his name Seth:

VERSE 4

And the days of Adam after he had begotten Seth were eight hundred years: and he begat sons and daughters:

VERSE 5

And all the days that Adam lived were nine hundred and thirty years: and he died.

VERSE 6

And Seth lived an hundred and five years, and begat Enos:

VERSE 7

And Seth lived after he begat Enos eight hundred and seven years, and begat sons and daughters:

VERSE 8

And all the days of Seth were nine hundred and twelve years: and he died.

VERSE 9

And Enos lived ninety years, and begat Cainan:

VERSE 10

And Enos lived after he begat Cainan eight hundred and fifteen years, and begat sons and daughters:

VERSE 11

And all the days of Enos were nine hundred and five years: and he died.

VERSE 12

And Cainan lived seventy years, and begat Mahalaleel:

VERSE 13

And Cainan lived after he begat Mahalaleel eight hundred and forty years, and begat sons and daughters:

VERSE 14

And all the days of Cainan were nine hundred and ten years: and he died.

VERSE 15

And Mahalaleel lived sixty and five years, and begat Jared:

VERSE 16

And Mahalaleel lived after he begat Jared eight hundred and thirty years, and begat sons and daughters:

VERSE 17

And all the days of Mahalaleel were eight hundred ninety and five years: and he died.

VERSE 18

> **And Jared lived an hundred and sixty and two years, and he begat Enoch:**

VERSE 19

> **And Jared lived after he begat Enoch eight hundred years, and he begat sons and daughters:**

VERSE 20

> **And all the days of Jared were nine hundred sixty and two years: and he died.**

VERSE 21

> **And Enoch lived sixty and five years, and begat Methuselah:**

VERSE 22

> **And Enoch walked with God after he begat Methuselah three hundred years, and begat sons and daughters:**

VERSE 23

> **And all the days of Enoch were three hundred sixty and five years:**

VERSE 24

> **And Enoch walked with God: and he *was* not; for God took him.**

VERSE 25

> **And Methuselah lived an hundred eighty and seven years, and begat Lamech:**

VERSE 26

> **And Methuselah lived after he begat Lamech seven hundred eighty and two years, and begat sons and daughters:**

VERSE 27

And all the days of Methuselah were nine hundred sixty and nine years: and he died.

It has been computed that Methuselah died in the year of the flood.

VERSE 28

And Lamech lived an hundred eighty and two years, and begat a son:

VERSE 29

And he called his name Noah, saying, This *same* **shall comfort us concerning our work and toil of our hands, because of the ground which the Lord hath cursed.**

VERSE 30

And Lamech lived after he begat Noah five hundred ninety and five years, and begat sons and daughters:

VERSE 31

And all the days of Lamech were seven hundred seventy and seven years: and he died.

VERSE 32

And Noah was five hundred years old: and Noah begat Shem, Ham, and Japeth.

CHAPTER SIX

VERSE 1

And it came to pass, when men began to multiply on the face of the earth, and daughters were born unto them,

VERSE 2

That the sons of God saw the daughters of men that they *were* fair; and they took them wives of all which they chose.

We must really stretch for a translation here if we continue to support the theory that Adam and Eve were the first and only people God created. The interpretation that biblical scholars offer is that the "sons of God" refers to angels and that the "daughters of men" refers to the descendants of Adam. But the phrase "sons of God" (Hebrew *bǝnê hā'ĕlōhîm*) is used elsewhere in the Bible and the Apocrypha to refer to men who were righteous in God's sight. Therefore, the translation here is much more logical if "the sons of God" referred to men who were descendants of Adam and "the daughters of men" were those who descended from of the people created in chapter 1.

Second, the passage reads, "they took them wives." It doesn't say they just came down and slept with them, which is the interpretation in the argument for the sons of God being angels. It's more logical to believe the genes of the widespread population created in chapter 1 would contain sufficient DNA to produce the giants of verse 4.

Furthermore, the word for "sons" is *bên* or *benê*, which denotes a blood relationship or descendant—a son or grandson—more logically refers to living people rather than to angels.

Other interpretations of this passage suggest that the reference is to intermarriage between the descendants of Cain and the descendants of Adam. This is not as accurate a translation, and it ignores the fact of Cain's total banishment; plus, it doesn't answer the question of the DNA for the giants of verse 4, nor is there anything in that interpretation that would account for the origin of the races.

VERSE 3

And the Lord said, My spirit shall not always strive with man, for that he also *is* **flesh; yet his days shall be an hundred and twenty years.**

The actual point of strife is not mentioned, but it can be assumed that it was because of the intermarriages and departure from God's instructions to Adam.

The word for "man" here is âhdâhm, the same as used in chapters 1 and 2, with the context here clearly being that of mankind.

VERSE 4

There were giants in the earth in those days; and also after that, when the sons of God came in unto the daughters of men, and they bare *children* **to them, the same** *became* **mighty men which** *were* **of old, men of renown.**

Some have suggested that the giants here were perhaps not physical giants but merely men of daring or recklessness or perhaps great hunters. The word used is *nephîyl* or *nephil*, which comes from the root meaning "tyrant" or "bully." But the word is used only twice in the Old Testament, and the other time it appears (Numbers 13:33), it clearly indicates a superior physical size. The giants who came later (the Rephaim and Anakim) were also distinguished by their size.

VERSE 5

And God saw that the wickedness of man *was* **great in the earth, and** *that* **every imagination of the thoughts of his heart** *was* **only evil continually.**

This then is the reason God sent the flood. It's probably a good thing we weren't told exactly what the wickedness of man was or what the imaginings were. It's unlikely, however, that it differed a great deal from what is in the world today.

VERSE 6

And it repented the Lord that he had made man on the earth, and it grieved him at his heart.

I have always had trouble with this passage because I know that God doesn't change, that He is all knowing and so knew from the beginning what was going to happen, and that He could have predetermined a different outcome if He had chosen. Therefore, I'm left with the only logical translation to be that He regretted that what He was about to do was necessary. The word used for repented is *nâcham*, which is from a root denoting "a sigh" or "pity," and in that context, the passage is easier to understand.

VERSE 7

And the Lord said, I will destroy man whom I have created from the face of the earth; both man, and beast, and the creeping thing, and the fowls of the air; for it repenteth me that I have made them.

Nâcham is again used here for "repenteth," and this time it can mean pity or something akin to rue, regret, or sorrow. The word for "created" is again *bâhrâh*, as used in chapter 1.

VERSE 8

But Noah found grace in the eyes of the Lord.

VERSE 9

These *are* the generations of Noah: Noah was a just man *and* perfect in his generations, *and* Noah walked with God.

We can conclude from these two verses that Noah did not intermarry with an outsider (the daughters of men in the original creation) and that he remained faithful to God and worshipful. Nothing is said, however, about his sons, who were recorded in the next verse.

I offer the hypothesis that all three sons chose wives from the aboriginal group created in chapter 1. These would have each been of a different background, and each would contain the DNA that would later continue her specific race.

We know that the entire population of the earth descended from this family. This is the only logical explanation for the origin of the basic racial groups, Caucasoid (which is divided into three subdivisions—Nordic, Mediterranean, and Alpine), Mongoloid (which includes Siberians, Eskimos, North American Indians, Japanese, Koreans, Chinese, and Indonesians and Malays), and Negroid (encompassing all Africans from south of the Sahara and Melanesians of the South Pacific). Also somewhere in there has to be included the central African Pygmies, the Bushmen, and the Australoids, all of which were probably the result of overlapping and genetic drift.

I don't believe it's a coincidence that there are three basic racial groups and that humanity was created in the image of God, who is three persons in one. Neither do I believe it coincidental that there are three sons of Noah, from whom the world's entire population of these three basic groups descended. We know these races have been with us as far back as we can determine; Negroes and Caucasians are as distinct in Egyptian mummified remains dating to 3000 BC as they are today. The same is true in ancient Chinese archaeological discoveries.

There has never been an acceptable theory advanced to explain the different races on the basis of development, evolution, or geography. However, we know that the races can generally be identified according to geography, and this certainly fits with the separation of the families after the Tower of Babel, as we will see in chapter 11 (verse 9.).

The only logical conclusion is that the races were all created at the same time by the same Creator. They were spoken into existence and have maintained their individual characteristics from the beginning to the present. Different cultures develop in different places and at different rates, but there is no evidence to suggest that genetic divergence does likewise. This is not to say, however, that no changes have occurred due to such causes as intermarriage, which would cause some genes to become altered or diffused.

Jean Louis Rodolphe Agassiz (1807–1873), a renowned Swiss-American scientist who was a creationist, proposed basically this theory of polygenism at about the same time Darwin was proposing his theory of evolution. Agassiz believed the races came from separate creations, were endowed with unequal attributes, and could be classified into specific climatic zones.

His work has largely been discredited in recent times because it is felt that his views were racist. I refute that by saying that history is not racist. The Bible certainly cannot be called racist—it treats all people as equal—and the suggestion that an analysis of chapter 10, known as the Table of Nations—is an example of racism is unfounded. Chapter 10 lists the migrations of the three families of Noah after God confused and scattered them. How could that be considered racist? Here again, the acceptance of the interpretation of Adam and Eve as the first and only people cloud all succeeding translations of Scripture. There is no racist agenda in the theory proposed here. Racism can be used as an excuse only for disavowing the actual events of history.

Darwin's theory of evolution, as put forth in his second book, *The Descent of Man*, extensively argues against Agassiz's polygenetic views, and Darwin's theories have largely been accepted today even though problems with his single origin of the races and with his model genealogical tree continue to arise. Discounting totally the charge of racism, I believe Agassiz's model better fits both the biblical account of Creation and the genetic fact of divided races.

Is this more difficult to accept than Darwin's "out of Africa," single-origin hypothesis that completely ignored the biblical account of Creation and has us all descending from monkeys, and the monkeys from some other animal, and so on back to tadpoles or something squiggling in the mud? Not for me! When problems arise with evolutionary theory, too often the facts are shaped to fit the theory instead of the other way around. We still do not have a detailed pedigree of where we came from except as is offered in Genesis.

VERSE 10

And Noah begat three sons, Shem, Ham, and Japeth.

VERSE 11

The earth also was corrupt before God, and the earth *was* filled with violence.

The word *'erets* is the most commonly used word translated "earth." A better translation would probably be "world" to distinguish it from the physical land. The meaning is clear enough, however, as it refers to all living things, including humanity.

VERSE 12

And God looked upon the earth, and, behold, it was corrupt; for all flesh had corrupted his way upon the earth.

It is interesting to note that God was displeased with all flesh, not just humanity. In the case of the animals, we weren't told the cause of His displeasure. The next verse, though, hinted at a world filled with violence, so perhaps that is the explanation. Had the dinosaurs and other prehistoric animals all disappeared by then, or were they to go with the flood? There were many major climatic changes over the eons of time, and any one of them could probably account for their disappearance, so it is highly unlikely any of them were still around.

There are several books by Henry M. Morris, *The Genesis Flood* and the *Troubled Waters of Evolution* to name two, that deal with the physical aspects of the earth at the time of the flood and the period immediately thereafter. Dr. Morris's background in civil and hydraulic engineering provides him with the perfect basis for these studies, and they make fascinating reading for the student. Additionally, *The Flood—In Light of the Bible, Geology, and Archaeology* by Alfred M. Rehwinkel (Concordia Publishing House, St. Louis), provides excellent insight into what the world may have been like before, during, and immediately after the flood.

For many years, evolutionists argued that there could not have been a flood such as is described in Genesis because it would interrupt the evolutionary process that depends on uniform progression over eons. Now, however, some are advancing the theory that some catastrophic event such as an asteroid collision could have caused climate change and wiped out the dinosaurs. Isn't it strange that they can't accept one form of interruption but offer another when stumped for a solution to a problem for which they have no answer? It's simply another instance of skewing the facts to fit the theory.

VERSE 13

> **And God said unto Noah, The end of all flesh is come before me; for the earth is filled with violence through them; and, behold, I will destroy them with the earth.**

This could be the key as to what displeased God with the animals. The violence of the prehistoric animal world may well have been intolerable for the advance of civilization.

VERSE 14

> **Make thee an ark of gopher wood; rooms shalt thou make in the ark, and shalt pitch it within and without with pitch.**

This is the only mention of gopher wood in the Bible, and the actual tree is not known today. There are many theories as to the actual definition of gopher wood. Some of them relate to the type of wood, while others suggest that the term *gopher* refers to the wood's treatment, suggesting interpretations such as squared wood, planed wood, or even laminated wood. Some have suggested that it was teakwood, others cypress, or even reeds. Another suggests that the word gopher was really *kopher*, a bitumen substance, thus translating the passage as "pitched wood." But since there is also the instruction to "pitch it within and without," that would seem redundant. Since the wood was grown in the antediluvian world, it is also possible that it simply refers to a type of wood that is no longer in existence.

At the time of this writing, the *Encyclopedia Britannica* had no entry for gopher wood. The *Britannica* entry for Noah's ark considers Noah and the biblical account of the flood to be a myth and groups it with the Babylonian story of Utnapishtim, which has some similarities.

Britannica does say, however, that Noah was mentioned in the genealogy in Luke 3:36 that delineates Jesus' descent from Adam.

In fact, it is not too far a stretch to say the flood of Noah was the basis of the Gilgamesh story of Utnapishtim. The reign of Gilgamesh was approximately 2700 BC, and the earliest writings date from the Third Dynasty of Ur, about 2100–2000 BC, but they are copies of earlier cuneiform tablets. They are highly fragmented and do not contain many details. The same is true of later Akkadian versions, which are dated to about 2000–1500 BC, and still later Babylonian and Assyrian accounts. The full story is not known to exist until tablets dating from c. 1300–1000 BC. There are many similarities between the two accounts, but there are also many differences. Since the Gilgamesh poem was written by idol-worshiping people with polytheistic beliefs, it is understandable that there would be variations and that, over time, their own heroes and thinking would be injected into the story. But the fact that both stories contain such similarities as all the people of earth descending from the survivors of a universal flood who were floating on one boat is, in my opinion, much too coincidental to be ignored.

VERSE 15

And this *is the fashion* **which thou shalt make it** *of:* **The length of the ark** *shall be* **three hundred cubits, the breadth of it fifty cubits, and the height of it thirty cubits.**

Unfortunately, we do not know the exact length of a cubit. It is believed to be the approximate length of a man's forearm, about eighteen to twenty inches. This would make the ark roughly 450 feet long by 75 feet wide and 45 feet high, or probably a little larger. That's a large ship, half again the size of a football field and three stories tall. It was probably the largest ship built until the supertankers and battleships of the twentieth century.

Interestingly, the proportions are the same or nearly the same as many of the largest modern ships. There are lists of the longest wooden ships ever built, and they include the Greek trireme *Tessarakonteres*—420 long by 58 feet wide. It reportedly carried a crew of 400, was powered by 4,000 oarsmen, and transported 2,850 soldiers, according to Athenaeus and Plutarch ("Life of Demetrios"), but there is no solid evidence this ship existed save for those two ancient references. If it did exist, it would rank as the second largest wooden ship ever built. Noah's ark is described in Genesis and in the Qur'an, and at approximately 450 feet by 75 feet, it ranks as the largest.

VERSE 16

A window shalt thou make to the ark, and in a cubit shalt thou finish it above; and the door of the ark shalt thou set in the side thereof; *with* **lower, second, and third** *stories* **shalt thou make it.**

The story of the flood is today classified as myth along with similar flood stories from many other peoples and religions around the world.[4] But to discount the flood or the account of Creation, is also to discount the testimony of Jesus Himself, who mentioned both on more than one occasion (Luke 17:27; Matthew 24:38–39 to name two) and so would, in my opinion, invalidate Christianity. I have no quarrel with those who choose to deny Christianity; that's their choice, and I have no ill feelings toward them. But I do have a bone to pick with people who claim the Bible, or parts of it, are just mythical stories and yet claim to be Christians. If you are a disciple of Christ, you should believe what He believed.

Believers in the historicity of Genesis feel that finding the ark would validate their views on a whole range of matters, from geology to evolution.

If the flood of Noah indeed wiped out the entire human race and its civilization, as the Bible teaches, then the Ark constitutes the one remaining major link to the pre-flood world. No significant artifact could ever be of greater antiquity or importance ... [with] tremendous potential impact on the creation-evolution controversy (including theistic evolution).[5]

I wholeheartedly agree, but unfortunately, I don't believe the ark will ever be found or positively identified, because if it were, it would go too far in offering solid proof of the Bible and therefore Christianity and would remove the factor of faith, which is the necessary ingredient for salvation. But I also believe that if it were discovered, there would still be doubters and skeptics just as there were in the days of Thomas. And there would still be naysayers who for their own purposes and profit would discount or discredit the finding and claim it was a fake or a fraud. There are too many people making a living from preaching the gospel of evolution in our schools today. They are the ones who are "willingly ignorant" of whom Peter writes in 2 Peter 3:5–7.

VERSE 17

> **And, behold, I, even I, do bring a flood of waters upon the earth, to destroy all flesh, wherein *is* the breath of life, from under heaven; *and* every thing that *is* in the earth shall die.**

VERSE 18

> **But with thee will I establish my covenant; and thou shalt come into the ark, thou, and thy sons, and thy wife, and thy sons' wives with thee.**

In verse 8, we learn, "Noah found grace in the eyes of the Lord." Nothing is said about the rest of his family, but as was the case with Lot, his family was to be spared along with him.

VERSE 19

> **And of every living thing of all flesh, two of every *sort* shalt thou bring into the ark, to keep *them* alive with thee; they shall be male and female.**

In the case of the larger animals, is it possible that small or young ones were taken instead of fully grown adults? There may have been some species that didn't survive in the conditions after the flood or became extinct due to natural causes just as many species continue to become extinct today. Note that while at least two of every animal were taken into the ark, it is not stated that they were necessarily adult animals. They could easily have been very young and fairly small.

Had the dinosaurs all died off? One of the latest theories on the disappearance of the dinosaurs is that a long-term climate change killed them off rather than a rogue asteroid such as the one that struck at what is now Chicxulub, Mexico (as was first theorized.)

The climate certainly changed drastically after the flood. But the fact is that the debate continues over what killed them off, and as in the argument for evolution itself, the scientists who proclaim it as fact cannot agree on what exactly the facts are.

VERSE 20

> **Of fowls after their kind, and of cattle after their kind, of every creeping thing of the earth after his kind, two of every** *sort* **shall come unto thee, to keep** *them* **alive.**

Can there still be any doubt that God was fully aware that someday evolution would be taught and that this repetition of "after his kind" was a warning not to heed those teachings?

VERSE 21

> **And take thou unto thee of all food that is eaten, and thou shalt gather** *it* **to thee; and it shall be for food for thee, and for them.**

"All food that is eaten" would include the feed for all the animals as well as for the humans. The majority of animals would have been herbivores and so would be relatively easy to provide for, but what about the carnivores? There had to be food provided for them as well, and so it may be that even more animals were taken onboard than is commonly believed. If the seven clean and two unclean were to be used for repopulating the earth, there may have also been some taken to serve as food for others. And the time spent in the ark, as we shall see, was a little over a year. However, if the carnivores taken were very young, it would perhaps not be so overwhelming.

VERSE 22

> **Thus did Noah; according to all that God commanded him, so did he.**

CHAPTER SEVEN

And the Lord said unto Noah, Come thou and all thy house into the ark; for thee have I seen righteous before me in this generation.

Again, only Noah was seen as righteous, but all his family was to be saved.

VERSE 2

Of every clean beast thou shalt take to thee by sevens, the male and his female: and of beasts that *are* **not clean by two, the male and his female.**

The instructions regarding the number of animals appear to be different from those of 6:19–20. It has been suggested that this was due to different writers, but I'm not satisfied with that explanation since I believe in the overall guidance of God in all the writing and therefore trust that even if there were different writers, they would have all been in agreement.

I offer no logical explanation for the apparent discrepancy except to note that the word used for "bring" in 6:19, *bôw*, is different from the word used here for "take," *lâqach*, and very possibly had a connotation that would have explained the difference. We know the result was that seven of each clean beast and seven of each fowl were taken aboard, as were two of each of the animals considered to be unclean.

The reason for seven, of course, was to have one for sacrifice and three pairs of animals with which to repopulate the earth along with the three pairs of humans for the same purpose. It is not stated here which animals were clean and which weren't, but God must have informed Noah or brought the animals to Noah Himself so Noah didn't have to make the distinction.

It's not until Leviticus 11 that God specified which was which and then perhaps chiefly because of health reasons associated with the conditions of that time.

VERSE 3

Of fowls also of the air by sevens, the male and the female; to keep seed alive upon the face of all the earth.

It is interesting to note that while beasts were either clean or unclean, the fowl were apparently all considered clean. There were, of course, no fish or other denizens of the deep taken aboard as they would not perish in a flood, and that easily explains why there are fish fossils in mountainous regions all over the world. And those fossils confirm the veracity of the biblical account in that the waters covered the entire earth and affirm the fact that the flood was not just local.

Wouldn't it have been silly for God to have Noah go to all the trouble to build a huge ark, which took over a year to construct, and fill it with animals and feed when they could just have moved to an adjacent valley? And yet there are Christians who teach that the flood was just a local occurrence and did not encompass the whole earth.

Furthermore, it's probable that there were inhabitants in virtually every corner of the world. The earth's population as of 2014 is estimated at over 7 billion, this from six people in a matter of possibly 10,000 or 12,000 years. The length of time of man on earth before the flood, as mentioned before, is estimated anywhere from 700,000 years up to perhaps as much as 2.5 million years. And the aging process was much slower due to the antediluvian conditions. Add in the fact of plural marriages and large families and it is easily conceivable that the total population of the earth could have been numbered in the millions if not a great deal more.

VERSE 4

For yet seven days, and I will cause it to rain upon the earth forty days and forty nights; and every living substance that I have made will I destroy from off the face of the earth.

God held up the start of the flood for seven days. It could be that He wanted to give anyone wishing to repent a chance to reconsider or perhaps just to give Noah and his family time to adjust to their new environment.

VERSE 5

And Noah did according unto all that the Lord commanded him.

VERSE 6

And Noah *was* six hundred years old when the flood of waters was upon the earth.

VERSE 7

And Noah went in, and his sons, and his wife, and his sons' wives with him, into the ark, because of the waters of the flood.

VERSE 8

Of clean beasts, and of beasts that *are* not clean, and of fowls, and of every thing that creepeth upon the earth,

VERSE 9

There went in two and two unto Noah into the ark, the male and the female, as God had commanded Noah.

VERSE 10

And it came to pass after seven days, that the waters of the flood were upon the earth.

VERSE 11

In the six hundredth year of Noah's life, in the second month, the seventeenth day of the month, the same day were all the fountains of the great

deep broken up, and the windows of heaven were opened.

Notice the specificity of this account and that of verse 13 in the next chapter; this is no vague remembrance recounted years later but an exact timetable such as one would find in a diary or other firsthand writing. If Moses was the author of this book, his information had been preserved for him in remarkably accurate and precise detail.

And here's a question for the proponents of the big bang theory: if the earth was created as a result of a big bang, where did the water come from that was then and still is deep inside the earth? For that matter, how is it that there was any water in, on, or above the earth at all? No logical or even remotely believable explanation has ever been given for the surface water let alone the underground seas. The theories that have been advanced (such as ice-bearing comets) are laughable to put it charitably.

VERSE 12

And the rain was upon the earth forty days and forty nights.

VERSE 13

In the selfsame day entered Noah, and Shem, and Ham, and Japeth, the sons of Noah, and Noah's wife, and the three wives of his sons with them, into the ark;

VERSE 14

They, and every beast after his kind, and all the cattle after their kind, and every creeping thing that creepeth upon the earth after his kind, and every fowl after his kind, every bird of every sort.

More repetition of the phrase "after his kind."

VERSE 15

And they went in unto Noah into the ark, two and two of all flesh, wherein *is* the breath of life.

VERSE 16

And they that went in, went in male and female of all flesh, as God had commanded him: and the Lord shut him in.

We have no way of knowing exactly how many animals there were in the ark, but it probably wasn't nearly as many as you might expect. Some hold that there were only about three hundred distinct species or "kinds" of beasts and birds at the time and that the number that exists today is the result of microevolution, that is, the influences of climate, crossbreeding, and other factors. That all the varieties of dog could have developed from the three pairs onboard the ark is not an unacceptable idea, and the same is true for cats; they would still have reproduced "after their kind."

Is it possible that all the horse-type animals came from the three original pairs, including the horse, donkey, and zebra? Or as is equally logical, the three pairs were diverse enough to contain the DNA for the various kinds? What is unacceptable is the concept that all the different species, all the kinds, are descended from a common, single ancestor. This is evolution as it is taught today, and is simply refuted here and throughout Genesis. So as the fellow said, "You pays your money and you takes your choice." You either accept the Genesis account or you reject it, but you cannot have both, and you cannot alter or change one in any way to fit a preconceived idea or theory.

These next verses describe the actual conditions of the flood. As the depth of the water increased, the ark gradually lifted. The water eventually reached a depth that was approximately twenty-two feet (fifteen cubits) above the highest hills. Of course, we don't know how high those hills were, but it is safe to say they were probably not the mountains of today, which were formed mainly because of the flood and its effect on the pressures of the land.

It is also safe to say that the wording here precludes any suggestion that the flood was only a local event. As mentioned before, the whole idea of building a huge boat and loading it with all the species of animals and the food necessary to sustain them simply doesn't make any sense if instead Noah's family could just have migrated to another location. And of course, the new location would contain animals, so they wouldn't have had to be considered at all.

By the time of the flood, God's original commands to multiply and fill the earth (1:22, 28) had been fulfilled. There were people and animals throughout the world, so a local flood would have accomplished nothing. Estimates for the actual number of people involved vary of course and are largely speculation. There is some evidence that the population of the earth has reached a bottleneck of sorts at several times and may not have been much more than 1 or 2 million at the time of the flood.

It is interesting to note, however, that the cause for some of these bottlenecks—the Toba catastrophe theory for instance—are put forth as possible explanations but never is a universal flood considered. A climate-changing volcanic eruption can occur that decimates the population of humans and animals, or an asteroid can strike the earth and do the same, but a flood isn't possible? If the Bible had stated that God sent an asteroid to destroy life on earth as we know it, I'd bet some people would then be advocating a universal flood.

It isn't that science and the Bible are incompatible; it's that evolutionists can't accept the Word of God (and in many cases won't accept that God even exists) and either twist the facts to accommodate the theories or create new theories when they have no other answer.

VERSE 17

And the flood was forty days upon the earth; and the waters increased, and bare up the ark, and it was lift up above the earth.

VERSE 18

And the waters prevailed, and were increased greatly upon the earth; and the ark went upon the face of the waters.

VERSE 19

And the waters prevailed exceedingly upon the earth; and all the high hills, that *were* under the whole heaven, were covered.

The repetition here supports the gradual buildup of the water as opposed to a tidal wave or tsunami-type deluge. The water came from rain over the entire earth plus the waters from the fountains of the deep. As mentioned previously, there was obviously a great deal of underground water in the days before the flood, and the atmosphere contained water from the beginning. But the fact that the entire earth was covered is again made clear.

Interestingly, it has recently been stated (*Science*, June 13, 2014) that there is still a vast ocean somewhere near the core of the earth. Evidence is still being examined, but the hidden reservoir is said to contain perhaps as much as three times the water in all the world's surface oceans. Another such underground reservoir beneath Asia, the so-called Beijing Anomaly, said to contain at least as much water as the Arctic Ocean, has also been identified.

Scientists seem to agree that the water contained deep inside the earth was there from the beginning and not brought here by icy comets or other means as was originally theorized. Of course, there is still no mention of the biblical account of Creation or how this would seem to corroborate the facts in the account of the flood as related here.

VERSE 20

Fifteen cubits upward did the waters prevail; and the mountains were covered.

VERSE 21

And all flesh died that moved upon the earth, both of fowl, and of cattle, and of beast, and of every creeping thing that creepeth upon the earth, and every man:

VERSE 22

All in whose nostril *was* the breath of life, of all that *was* in the dry *land*, died.

Do I still hear an argument that this was a local event?

VERSE 23

> **And every living substance was destroyed which was upon the face of the ground, both man, and cattle, and the creeping things, and the fowl of the heaven; and they were destroyed from the earth: and Noah only remained** *alive*, **and they that** *were* **with him in the ark.**

It's impossible to argue logically that this was anything but a universal event in light of the repeated references here that everything on the face of the earth was destroyed. While we aren't told of the cause of God's displeasure with the animals, the animals couldn't have survived a universal flood. If some other form of punishment had been chosen that would have allowed the animals to survive, they would undoubtedly have overwhelmed the few humans who escaped. There were, after all, only eight people left to repopulate the world.

From the beginning, God had given man the power to rule over animals and vegetation, and preserving the animals and for that matter, all vegetation extant in the antediluvian world would have created an intolerable imbalance.

For those Christians who would relegate this and other stories of the Old Testament to the status of myth or hearsay, I point out that the writers of the New Testament were not only aware of the specifics of these accounts but also accepted them at face value. A clear reference to this passage is in 1 Peter 3:20: "When once the long suffering of God waited in the days of Noah, while the ark was a-preparing, wherein few, that is, eight souls were saved by water."

There are stories and traditions of an all-encompassing flood with only a few survivors from which the world was repopulated in nearly every culture. The stories differ in detail but contain enough similarities to ensure they all refer to the same event. It would be a monumental coincidence if the same story had been perpetrated by so many different peoples in so many locations without any basis in fact.

VERSE 24

And the waters prevailed upon the earth an hundred and fifty days.

Why did the flood last for nearly five months? We aren't told, but it probably had to do with a number of things such as the required time for the antediluvian vegetation to die out and the physical changes that were taking place within the earth itself.

Some theorize that the earth actually shifted some 23½ degrees on its axis during this time, thus changing the relation of the earth to the sun and in so doing creating today's climate zones. It is thought that the conditions described in 2:5, "For the Lord God had not caused it to rain upon the earth," indicate a natural greenhouse effect or canopy that would have disseminated the sun's light and heat evenly over all the world and would have made all parts of the world equal in climate and temperature. This was, of course, all to change with the flood and its aftereffects.

CHAPTER EIGHT

VERSE 1

> And God remembered Noah, and every living thing, and all the cattle that *was* with him in the ark: and God made a wind to pass over the earth, and the waters assuaged;

VERSE 2

> The fountains also of the deep and the windows of heaven were stopped, and the rain from heaven was restrained;

VERSE 3

> And the waters returned from off the earth continually; and after the end of the hundred and fifty days the waters were abated.

It's difficult to imagine the amount of water that was necessary to flood the whole world. Where did all this water come from? Where did it all go? Perhaps some of the answer is in 7:1: "And God made the firmament, and divided the waters which *were* under the firmament from the waters which *were* above the firmament, and it was so." This clearly indicated that there was water in the atmosphere, and we just don't know how much was there. The canopy that encompassed the world could easily have contained a vast amount of water.

The fountains of the deep would have to be explained in light of the world before the flood, when in all probability it was flatter and perhaps even contained underground the waters that are now in the oceans. And of course, if the globe was relatively smooth before, the departing waters that were contained underground would have caused the huge depressions that are now the ocean floors. The average depth of the Atlantic Ocean, for instance, is nearly 12,000 feet, with the deepest point being over 28,000 feet. The water would have filled these depressions (oceans) when it ran off after the flood. Evaporation would have refilled the atmosphere in part as well.

As noted earlier, Dr. Henry Morris, the author of the *Genesis Flood* and at least ten other books (with his collaborator Dr. John C. Whitcomb, Jr.) was trained as a hydraulic engineer and taught at several universities before founding the Christian Research Institute. His early training in hydraulics enabled him to explain in fine detail what the runoff process would entail. His work is scholarly and yet easy to understand and highly interesting.

VERSE 4

And the ark rested in the seventh month, on the seventeenth day of the month, upon the mountains of Ararat.

That is, in July (or the seventh month of the calendar in use at the time) and not the seventh month of the flood. How high Mount Ararat was at the time is another matter for conjecture. That the flood caused tremendous upheavals and change is not in doubt, but these changes didn't all occur at once during or immediately after the flood. Some may have occurred at the time the earth was covered with water, but others occurred later and are still taking place today. We know only that all the earth was covered to a depth of twenty or more feet above the highest mountaintop that existed at that time.

VERSE 5

And the waters decreased continually until the tenth month: in the tenth *month*, on the first *day* of the month, were the tops of the mountains seen.

This brought the total time that Noah spent in the ark up to that point to nearly eight months.

VERSE 6

And it came to pass at the end of forty days, that Noah opened the window of the ark which he had made:

Add these forty days to the seven-plus months above, and we're at nearly nine months. And as we shall see in the next few verses, they still had two weeks to go.

Wouldn't it be nice if we had a little more detail about what took place onboard during those nearly ten months? I can imagine births of many animals taking place as well as a tremendous job of feeding and cleaning up by the eight people responsible for those chores. Of one thing I'm certain: as tempting as it would have been with two tables available, they wouldn't have had much time to play any bridge or canasta.

VERSE 7

And he sent forth a raven, which went forth to and fro, until the waters were dried up from off the earth.

VERSE 8

Also he sent forth a dove from him, to see if the waters were abated from off the face of the ground;

VERSE 9

But the dove found no rest for the sole of her foot, and she returned unto him into the ark, for the waters _were_ on the face of the whole earth: then he put forth his hand, and took her, and pulled her in unto him into the ark.

VERSE 10

And he stayed yet other seven days; and again he sent forth the dove out of the ark;

VERSE 11

And the dove came in to him in the evening; and lo, in her mouth _was_ an olive leaf plucked off: so Noah knew that the waters were abated from off the earth.

We are not told whether the olive leaf was from a living olive tree, but if it was, it would indicate that some at least of the vegetation had survived the flood. It is logical to assume that not all vegetation would die out, as some would be needed to feed the animals that would come forth from the ark.

VERSE 12

And he stayed yet other seven days; and sent forth the dove; which returned not again unto him any more.

VERSE 13

And it came to pass in the six hundredth and first year, in the first *month***, the first** *day* **of the month, the waters were dried up from the earth: and Noah removed the covering of the ark, and looked, and, behold, the face of the ground was dry.**

By that time, Noah and his family must have longed to get out and stretch their sea legs. But even though the water had gone, there must have been a great deal of mud—a literal quagmire—for even though they could remove the cover of the ark, they still had to wait nearly two more months to disembark.

VERSE 14

And in the second month, on the seven and twentieth day of the month, was the earth dried.

That is one year and ten days since the start of the flood.

VERSE 15

And God spoke unto Noah saying,

VERSE 16

Go forth of the ark, thou, and thy wife, and thy sons, and thy sons' wives with thee.

VERSE 17

> Bring forth with thee every living thing that *is* with thee, of all flesh, *both* of fowl, and of cattle, and of every creeping thing that creepeth upon the earth; that they may breed abundantly in the earth, and be fruitful, and multiply upon the earth.

VERSE 18

> And Noah went forth, and his sons, and his wife, and his sons' wives with him:

VERSE 19

> Every beast, every creeping thing, and every fowl, *and* whatsoever creepeth upon the earth, after their kinds, went forth out of the ark.

Note the orderliness of the disembarkation and the fact that the author took one more opportunity to repeat the phrase "after their kinds." The phrase as used here is actually "after their families," which also supports the theory that there may have been animals born during the voyage of the ark.

VERSE 20

> And Noah builded an altar unto the Lord; and took of every clean beast, and of every clean fowl, and offered burnt offerings on the altar.

Noah's first act was to worship and give thanks to the Lord for seeing him through the flood. He apparently did this even before seeing to his own needs for shelter and food. Of course, it was this righteousness that had saved him and his family in the first place.

VERSE 21

> And the Lord smelled a sweet savour; and the Lord said in his heart, I will not again curse the ground any more for man's sake; for the imagination of man's heart *is* evil from his youth; neither will I smite any more every living thing, as I have done.

Isaiah 54:9 states, "for as the waters of Noah should no more go over the earth." Here is another example of the agreement of the writers of the Old Testament and of succeeding writers' acceptance of the Genesis account as factual.

VERSE 22

While the earth remaineth, seedtime and harvest, and cold and heat, and summer and winter, and day and night shall not cease.

This is an interesting verse, containing as it does the first hint perhaps of the earth as we know it eventually ceasing to exist. Jesus stated in Matthew 24:35 and again in Luke 21:3, "Heaven and earth shall pass away but my words will not pass away." And Revelation 21:1 states, "I saw a new heaven and a new earth: for the first heaven and the first earth were passed away; and there was no more sea."

CHAPTER NINE

VERSE 1

And God blessed Noah and his sons, and said unto them, Be fruitful, and multiply, and replenish the earth.

The same command given to the wildlife created on the fifth day and the people created on the sixth day (1:22, 28) was repeated to Noah. However, as we learn in the next few verses, there were some differences.

VERSE 2

And the fear of you and the dread of you shall be upon every beast of the earth, and upon every fowl of the air, upon all that moveth *upon* the earth, and upon all the fishes of the sea; into your hands are they delivered.

VERSE 3

Every moving thing that liveth shall be meat for you; even as the green herb have I given you all things.

The dominion of man over the animals is reaffirmed, but this time, the animals would fear all humanity. Whereas in chapter 1, men and animals were given the herbs and fruits of the trees for food, hereinafter, the animals also were to be food for humanity.

VERSE 4

But flesh with the life thereof, which is the blood thereof, shall ye not eat.

The reservations here were that no animal could be eaten alive and no animal blood was to be consumed. As in the restrictions on food later in the Bible, there were very good and logical reasons behind the restrictions. Some of them perhaps can be lifted now with modern preparation such as freezing and canning and cleaning, but they were all valid for the ancients to whom they were given.

Some convincing books propound the health values of adhering to these restrictions even today. On the other side, Jesus seemed to have countermanded these laws when He said in Mark 7:15, "There is nothing from without a man, that entering into him can defile him: but the things which come out of him, those are they that defile the man."

VERSE 5

And surely your blood of your lives will I require; at the hand of every beast will I require it, and at the hand of man; at the hand of every man's brother will I require the life of man.

This is a difficult verse for me to understand. The word used for "require" is *dârash*, a root that means among other things "to follow" or "to worship." It can also mean "to care for." So this passage may be a commission for both men and animals to care for each other, or it may be a command for all to worship the Lord, or possibly even ordaining men to judge each other in matters of law. The next verse seems to point to the latter.

VERSE 6

Whoso sheddeth man's blood, by man shall his blood be shed; for in the image of God made he man.

VERSE 7

And you, be ye fruitful, and multiply; bring forth abundantly in the earth, and multiply therein.

Here is another repetition of the command to repopulate the earth, underlining the importance of the command.

VERSE 8

And God spake unto Noah, and to his sons with him, saying,

VERSE 9

> And I, behold, I establish my covenant with you, and with your seed after you;

VERSE 10

> And with every living creature that *is* with you, of the fowl, of the cattle, and of every beast of the earth with you; from all that go out of the ark, to every beast of the earth.

VERSE 11

> And I will establish my covenant with you; neither shall all flesh be cut off any more by the waters of a flood; neither shall there any more be a flood to destroy the earth.

God didn't promise that the earth would never be destroyed; He promised that it would not again be destroyed by water.

VERSE 12

> And God said, This *is* the token of the covenant which I make between me and you and every living creature that *is* with you, for perpetual generations:

VERSE 13

> I do set my bow in the cloud, and it shall be for a token of a covenant between me and the earth.

VERSE 14

> And it shall come to pass, when I bring a cloud over the earth, that the bow shall be seen in the cloud:

VERSE 15

> And I will remember my covenant, which *is* between me and you and every living creature of all flesh; and the waters shall no more become a flood to destroy all flesh.

VERSE 16

And the bow shall be in the cloud; and I will look upon it, that I may remember the everlasting covenant between God and every living creature of all flesh that *is* upon the earth.

VERSE 17

And God said unto Noah, This *is* the token of the covenant, which I have established between me and all flesh that *is* upon the earth.

A great deal of repetition here between verses 11 and 17 indicates how important the writer considered the covenant to be. Since there had been no rain prior to the flood, the sight of a rainbow was a new experience for Noah and his family. The fact that he and all future generations were promised a rainbow henceforth with every cloud must have been remarkable.

VERSE 18

And the sons of Noah, that went forth of the ark, were Shem, and Ham, and Japeth: and Ham *is* the father of Canaan.

VERSE 19

These *are* the three sons of Noah: and of them was the whole earth overspread.

Note that nothing was said about Noah having any more children. The population of the earth came entirely from his three sons and their wives. This led me to the conclusion that the races already existed and that the three families contained the DNA for their propagation. It is simply illogical to assume that the racial differences could have developed in the time since the flood with nothing more to facilitate their development than different climate and geological locations. And it is yet to be shown that these conditions would result in that development no matter how much time was allowed.

To the contrary, peoples who have migrated from one area to

another have retained their original racial characteristics, and gradual change has occurred only after intermarriage and the mixture of other genes and DNA. The key word here is *mixture*; one race did not develop into another

VERSE 20

And Noah began *to be* an husbandman, and he planted a vineyard:

Many elements in Moses' narration skip over a considerable passage of time because it is not relevant to the main theme of the story. This is an instance where some amount of time would have elapsed, for it takes time to plant and develop a vineyard to the point that it produces wine.

VERSE 21

And he drank of the wine, and was drunken; and he was uncovered within his tent.

This is the first appearance in the Bible of the word for "wine," *yayin*, and it is significant because it's used to refer only to a product that has been fermented and therefore capable of intoxication. This is usually used in reference to grapes because their natural chemical balance is such that they can ferment without the addition of sugars, acids, enzymes, or other nutrients, although it could also refer to a product of other fruits or grains. The interesting note is that the knowledge of how to process the wine existed at that time. In some references, however, Noah is said to have invented the process.

VERSE 22

And Ham, the father of Canaan, saw the nakedness of his father, and told his two brethern without.

VERSE 23

And Shem and Japeth took a garment, and laid *it* upon both their shoulders, and went backward, and covered the nakedness of their father; and

their faces *were* **backward, and they saw not their father's nakedness.**

The word used for "nakedness" is *ervâh*, which implies shame as well as nudity. While just being uncovered doesn't seem so serious to us today, it obviously was at that time and was perhaps exacerbated when coupled with intoxication.

VERSE 24

And Noah awoke from his wine, and knew what his younger son had done unto him.

There are endless debates as to just what Ham actually did, ranging from the somewhat plausible to the far-fetched and ridiculous. Speculation about such matters has no place in this writing. And we are not told how Noah found out it was Ham who had seen him and subsequently therefore Shem and Japeth who had covered him, but of course it is an important distinction because of the curse he foresaw for some of Ham's descendants.

Why the curse should apply to only the descendants of Ham's fourth son, Canaan, we are also not told. It has been suggested that since Ham was Noah's youngest son, the curse was to apply to the descendants of Ham's youngest son, but the connection seems vague at best.

VERSE 25

And he said, Cursed *be* **Canaan; a servant of servants shall he be unto his brethern.**

I do not believe Noah was cursing Canaan but was foretelling what would befall him and his descendants because of Ham's actions. The curse would befall only Canaan and his descendants, not all the descendants of Ham. I have heard the theory advanced that Canaan and his descendants were made black at that time, but I give that no credence at all. In the first place, the curse was a prophecy only; it's illogical to assume that Noah had the power to perform an actual change.

Second, the prophecy applied to only the descendants of Canaan, while virtually all the other descendants of Ham were also black. It seems nothing more than a lame attempt to explain the origin of one of the races without any basis in fact or even biblical reference. If becoming black was to be a part of Canaan's curse, I certainly believe Moses would have at least mentioned it.

It is equally illogical to use this prophecy to justify slavery. However, sadly, that has sometimes been the case. I recommend the article "Negro Slavery and The Myth of Ham's Curse" by Babu G. Ranganathan.

VERSE 26

And he said, Blessed *be* **the Lord God of Shem; and Canaan shall be his servant.**

Note the distinction: it was not Shem or his descendants who were to be blessed but the Lord God of Shem. The descendants of Shem have had very mixed blessings indeed.

The word used here and above for "servant" is *'ebed*, which implies a form of bondage or slavery. It is much more than simply being of service.

VERSE 27

God shall enlarge Japeth, and he shall dwell in the tents of Shem; and Canaan shall be his servant.

The descendants of Japeth have certainly been enlarged in numbers and in geography, including as they do all Europe, most of Asia, and the Western Hemisphere. There are a great many theories about who settled where and who is descended from whom. The original dispersion is not so much in doubt as are the later migration and population by descendants of primarily Shem and Japeth. Scholars are pretty well agreed on the area thought to be populated by the descendants of Ham—Africa and parts of the Middle East, including Egypt.

In the next chapter, we learn that Japeth had seven sons, Shem had five, and Ham four, so the enlargement started immediately. The Greek, Roman, and British Empires among others are good examples of Japeth dwelling in the tents of Shem. And the descendants of Canaan were to be in bondage to the descendants of both Shem and Japeth. It does not state when this condition was to begin, and it does not say that it would last forever but only that it would exist. As we have seen, this prophecy has been fulfilled and is now virtually abolished.

VERSE 28

And Noah lived after the flood three hundred and fifty years.

If Noah and his wife had produced any more children, they would undoubtedly have been mentioned here. So it is a pretty safe assumption that the whole world was repopulated entirely by the descendants of Shem, Ham, and Japeth. Since they all had basically the same DNA as Noah and his wife, it follows that the differences that characterize the three main ethnic groups—Oriental, Negro, and Caucasian—were each passed on through the various wives. And of course these differences began to be blurred from the very beginning due to intermarriage.

VERSE 29

And all the days of Noah were nine hundred and fifty years: and he died.

At 950 years, Noah was the third oldest man listed in the Bible. The longevity of the antediluvian people still held for Noah and his early descendants. It took time for the world's repopulation to begin, and the ageing effects of the atmosphere after the flood (the collapse of the protective canopy among others) apparently had a gradual rather than an immediate impact.

CHAPTER TEN

VERSE 1

Now these *are* the generations of the sons of Noah, Shem, Ham, and Japeth: and unto them were sons born after the flood.

The whole of chapter 10 is a listing of these descendants with only a small amount of commentary by Moses about any particular one. It's apparent that the list of all the descendants after the second generation is incomplete even for the male members, and the list does not mention any of the females, of which by necessity there had to be many.

Moses' main concern for this and other genealogy lists had always been the line that led through Abraham and so to Jesus, and also the lines that had influenced that line. It is a reasonable assumption that, as in the case of the listing of the generations of Adam, there were omissions, and the list is not chronological. It can therefore be argued that Moses has listed the descendants either in the order he considered to be most relevant or in the order they were given to him.

VERSE 2

The sons of Japeth; Gomer, and Magog, and Madai, and Javan, and Tubal, and Meshech, and Tiras.

VERSE 3

And the sons of Gomer; Ashkenaz, and Riphath, and Togarmah.

VERSE 4

And the sons of Javan; Elishah, and Tarshish, Kitim, and Dodanim.

The Hebrew ending *im* on a name is the equivalent of the English "ite"; it refers to the name, founder or member of a tribe or nation.

VERSE 5

By these were the isles of the gentiles divided in their lands; every one after his tongue, after their families, in their nations.

The division came, of course, after the building of the Tower of Babel, covered in the next chapter.

VERSE 6

And the sons of Ham; Cush, and Mizraim, and Phut, and Canaan.

VERSE 7

And the sons of Cush; Seba, and Havilah, and Sabtah, and Raamah, and Sabtechah: and the sons of Raamah; Sheba, and Dedan.

VERSE 8

And Cush begat Nimrod: he began to be a mighty one in the earth.

VERSE 9

He was a mighty hunter before the Lord; wherefore it is said, Even as Nimrod the mighty hunter before the Lord.

Animals must have been plentiful early on, since they too had three sets of parents to start their repopulation, and many would have been able to produce in litters and begin at a much earlier age than humans.

We don't learn if Nimrod gained his reputation from the size of the animals he slew or from their number. At any rate, he was a powerful enough figure that he was able to gain the respect of his peers and thereby start his own kingdom, which in those days probably consisted of several families and a few settlements at first and later developing into what would become a more heavily populated and powerful city-state.

VERSE 10

And the beginning of his kingdom was Babel, and Erech, and Accad, and Calneh, in the land of Shinar.

This is the first mention of a kingdom in the Bible. But the world's first kingdom was undoubtedly small and unimportant when compared to those that would soon follow. They would probably have consisted of mere towns or cities at first. The city of Erech (now Uruk) was a major city of Sumer and later Babylonia. At about 2900 B.C. it reached a population of 50,000-80,000. The site was abandoned shortly after 650 A.D. It was excavated in 1850-1854 by William Kenneth Loftus, a British geologist, explorer and archaeological excavator.

Accad was another city in Shinar. It was located in the mountains, but still near the old bed of the Euphrates River, in northern or upper Babylonia. It was the birthplace of the Accadian Empire. Calneh is said to be the fourth city founded by Nimrod. However it has never been located, and there is some evidence (with which I agree) that the translation of the verse is at fault. The Revised Standard Version of the Bible translates Calneh as meaning 'all of them,' and so reads "And the beginning of his kingdom was Babel, and Erech, and Accad, all of them in the land of Shinar."

VERSE 11

Out of that land went forth Asshur, and builded Nineveh, and the city Rehoboth, and Calah,

Virtually all Noah's descendants became involved in the establishment of a kingdom in the various areas they inhabited. And next of course came expansions—one kingdom would encroach on the territory of its neighbor. Nineveh became the capital of Assyria and the Assyrian Empire when in the seventh century BC, King Sennacherib (705–681 BC) made it his capital.

Jonah described Nineveh as a city of 120,000 people. It was one of the first great cities, along with Asshur and Calah before it, and the Assyrian Empire was one of the first great empires. Its location near the modern city of Mosul was next to the Tigris River in the center of an extremely fertile area. Good articles on Nineveh can be found in Smith's Bible Dictionary, the ISBE Bible Dictionary, Easton's Bible Dictionary, and Fausset's Bible Dictionary. I recommend serious students obtain one or more of these excellent reference works.

VERSE 12

And Resen, between Nineveh and Calah: the same *is* **a great city.**

Resen was across the Tigris from Nineveh. It and the cities of Calah and Asshur were said to have later been combined into the one great city of Nineveh.

VERSE 13

And Mizraim begat Ludim, and Anamim, and Lehabim, and Naphtuhim,

VERSE 14

And Pathrusim, and Casluhim, (out of whom came Philistim,) and Caphtorim.

VERSE 15

And Canaan begat Sidon his firstborn, and Heth,

VERSE 16

And the Jebusite, and the Amorite, and the Girgasite,

VERSE 17

And the Hivite, and the Arkite, and the Sinite,

VERSE 18

And the Arvadite, and the Zemarite, and the Hamathite: and afterward were the families of the Canaanites spread abroad.

VERSE 19

> **And the border of the Canaanites was from Sidon, as thou comest to Gerar, unto Gaza; as thou goest, unto Sodom, and Gomorah, and Amah, and Zeboim, even unto Lasha.**

VERSE 20

> **These** *are* **the sons of Ham, after their families, after their tongues, in their countries,** *and* **in their nations.**

VERSE 21

> **Unto Shem also, the father of all the children of Eber, the brother of Japeth the elder, even to him were** *children* **born.**

The children of Eber are the Hebrews. According to Jewish tradition, Eber refused to help with the building of the Tower of Babel, and for that reason his language was not confused by God. Eber retained his original language, the *lingua humana* in Latin. The name was later changed to Hebrew, named after Eber.

The second part of this sentence indicates that Shem was the middle brother and Japeth the eldest, although as translated it could be the other way around. We know for sure that Ham was the youngest of the three.

VERSE 22

> **The children of Shem; Elam, and Asshur, and Arphaxad, and Lud, and Aram.**

VERSE 23

> **And the children of Aram; Uz, and Hul, and Gether, and Mash.**

VERSE 24

> **And Arphaxad begat Salah, and Salah begat Eber.**

VERSE 25

And unto Eber were born two sons: the name of one *was* **Peleg; for in his days was the earth divided; and his brother's name** *was* **Joktan.**

In verse 5 of this chapter, the word used for "divided" was *pârad* when it was stated that the lands of the Gentiles were divided according to every family, after their tongue, in their nations. The word used here for divided is *pâlag*, a root meaning to physically split or divide. It appears here and in 1 Chronicles 1:19, where it was again stated that in the days of Peleg, the earth was divided. The only other time this word was used was in Job 38:25. The usage in each of these cases clearly indicates a physical division. The accepted translation of this verse, however, is that the families were divided into nations or that the land was divided into separate areas for each family.

But *pâlag* is entirely different from *châlaq*, the word used to indicate apportionment or separation. Châlaq is the word used in Deuteronomy 32:8, which is almost exactly what this usage would have been if it were to have meant an allotment of land for the families. Châlaq is the word used in Joshua 14:5, when the meaning was to divide the land among the children of Israel, and it was the word of choice in most other instances in which the separation was a division that didn't indicate a physical rendering.

It is therefore my hypothesis that this verse means that the continents began to drift apart in the days of Peleg. Since we know that this phenomenon did in fact take place at some time, it's not unreasonable to believe it happened at this time, most probably because of the physical changes and pressures brought about by the flood.

There is evidence that the rendering and drifting is still going on today. In some places, it's going on very gradually, as in the case of continental drift, and in others more pronounced with various tectonic plates clashing with each other as in the cases for example of the Ethiopia Dome and the Kenya Dome. Earthquakes and volcanos around the world are evidence of change still taking place although perhaps not as violently as in the days of Peleg.

VERSE 26

And Joktan begat Almodad, and Sheleph, and Hazarmaveth, and Jerah,

VERSE 27

And Hadoram, and Uzal, and Diklah,

VERSE 28

And Obal, and Abimael, and Sheba,

VERSE 29

And Ophir, and Havilah, and Jobab: all these *were* **the sons of Joktan.**

Thirteen sons were mentioned, and who knows how many daughters? Joktan certainly did his part to "be fruitful and multiply."

VERSE 30

And their dwelling was from Mesha, as thou goes unto Sephar a mount of the east.

These are the boundaries of the sons of Joktan. This is the only mention of Sephar in the Bible, so it is difficult to pinpoint. There is, however, an ancient seaport town of Zafar (Zaphar or Shaphar) on the shore of the Indian Ocean between the Persian Gulf and the Red Sea that most probably took its name from Mount Sephar.

Mesha is said to have been near Mecca and Medina in the southwestern part of the Arabian Peninsula. Here, as in all other places to which the descendants of Noah traveled, people had lived long before the flood. It is said that the inhabitants of the Arabian Peninsula dated back at least as far as 60,000 BC, in the old Stone Age. And they are described as hunters and gatherers. But by 2000 BC, the northern end of the peninsula was inhabited by a Semitic-speaking people who were primarily herders of sheep and goats. In the southern part, however, the people were farmers, and how they got there is unknown except as described in the Bible. The queen of Sheba was likely one of these later inhabitants. Here is another example of the Bible's proven historicity.

VERSE 31

> These *are* the sons of Shem, after their families, after their tongues, in their lands, after their nations.

VERSE 32

> These *are* the families of the sons of Noah, after their generations, in their nations; and by these were the nations divided in the earth after the flood.

The word used here for "divided" is not at all the same as either the one used in verse 25 or the one used in verse 5. The choice here is *çachar*, a word associated with commerce or commercial travel and indicating the place where the nations resided and made their living.

The time period represented by chapter 10 is approximately three generations. However, as noted before, the immediate descendants of Noah still lived to a ripe old age, so those three generations could well encompass several centuries.

CHAPTER ELEVEN

VERSE 1

And the whole earth was of one language, and of one speech.

Chapter 11 goes back to the days immediately after the flood. The narration picks up with all of Noah's descendants still living in one group. Most of the people listed in chapter 10 lived after the events of chapter 11, which is to say after the building of the Tower of Babel and the scattering of the families. We aren't told at exactly what point the tower was built, and we don't know exactly who or how many were involved. It would seem logical that Nimrod and his family were actively involved since Babel was the beginning of his kingdom. And we know that Eber did not help with the building of the tower.

VERSE 2

And it came to pass, as they journeyed from the east, that they found a plain in the land of Shinar; and they dwelt there.

The valley of Shinar is a very fertile valley indeed; it lies between the Tigris and Euphrates rivers. It is the area generally designated as Mesopotamia, also called the Fertile Crescent, often called the cradle of civilization. It's a large area comprising most of Iraq, northeastern Syria, southeastern Turkey, and some of southeastern Iran. From the eighteenth to the sixth centuries BC, it was home to the Babylonian Empire and was then known as Babylonia. The Mesopotamian region was also the home of the early Assyrian, Sumerian, and Akkadian Empires.

The families migrated together. When they came to a fertile valley, they stopped there and established their home. Although the words to "multiply and replenish [refill] the earth" didn't specifically state that the families should separate to comply with this command, the word used for "replenish" is *mâlê* or *mâlâ* and means "to fill" and sometimes with a wide application "to fill completely." This supports the theory that God wanted the families separated and the whole world populated. By remaining together, they obviously fell into habits and practices that were displeasing to God.

VERSE 3

And they said one to another, Go to, let us make brick, and burn them thoroughly. And they had brick for stone, and slime had they for mortar.

The valley contained such good soil that there was apparently no stone or rock or at least not enough to use for building. The word used for "slime," *chêmâr*, refers to bitumen, a mineral that is a pitch or asphalt-like substance found naturally bubbling up from the ground that becomes hard when smeared between bricks and dried. The only other times the word was used were in Exodus 2:3, where it was used along with *zepteth*, from a root meaning "asphalt," and in Genesis 14:10, where it is translated as "slime pits." When I see the words *slime pit*, I think of the La Brea Tar Pits and wonder if they are similar.

VERSE 4

And they said, Go to, let us build us a city and a tower, whose top *may reach* unto heaven; and let us make us a name, lest we be scattered abroad upon the face of the whole earth.

Apparently, the command to replenish the earth was interpreted as involving a separation and scattering of the families. That they would rather stay together for protection and provision was a natural reaction but one God knew would lead to a return to the ways of unrighteousness as seen in verse 6.

VERSE 5

And the Lord came down to see the city and the tower, which the children of men builded.

Here again the word for "children" is *bên* and means simply all the descendants so far. And the word for "men" is *'ādãm*, which could have been translated as "the children of Adam" but was understood to be intended as the men of that day, that is, the descendants of Noah.

VERSE 6

And the Lord said, Behold, the people *is* one, and they have all one language; and this they begin to do: and now nothing will be restrained from them, which they have imagined to do.

The wickedness and imagination of men were basically what caused God to send the flood in the first place (Genesis 6:5). Noah was saved because of his righteousness; his family was saved for Noah's sake, not its own. In 8:21, we saw that God still considered the imagination of man's heart to be evil from his youth. And then, as He had foreseen, they had begun again to do as they pleased.

VERSE 7

Go to, let us go down, and there confound their language, that they may not understand one another's speech.

What an interesting way God chose to ensure that the families would strike out on their own and disperse throughout the world. He chose nothing violent or drastic such as a force of nature but a simple device whereby the people would be forced to go their separate ways because they wouldn't be able to communicate with each other. Eber and his family were the only ones whose language remained unaffected.

Also significant is the use of the plural in "Let us go down."

VERSE 8

So the Lord scattered them abroad from thence upon the face of all the earth: and they left off to build the city.

VERSE 9

Therefore is the name of it called Babel; because the Lord did there confound the language of all the

earth: and from thence did the Lord scatter them abroad upon the face of all the earth.

While most of the families left the area, one—the family of Nimrod—stayed and founded the city that became Babel, the Hebrew equivalent of Akkadian Babilu (Greek Babylon). Nimrod continued to build the city and the famous Tower of Babel, later a temple to the god Marduk, that seemed to reach to the heavens. Marduk is sometimes called Bel, the Akkadian word for "Lord."

The hanging gardens of Babylon, one of the original Seven Wonders of the World, were said to have been built by Nebuchadnezzar II around 600 BC. Some recent researchers have suggested, however, that the hanging gardens were built by Sennacherib about a hundred years earlier.

VERSE 10

These *are* the generations of Shem: Shem *was* an hundred years old, and begat Arphaxad two years after the flood:

VERSE 11

And Shem lived after he begat Arphaxad five hundred years, and he begat sons and daughters.

In 10:22 are listed five sons of Shem, of which Arphaxad is named third. Moses' chief concern, as we have seen in prior listings, in the genealogy beginning here was the line descending from Arphaxad, which led directly to Abraham, the Jewish nation, and Jesus.

VERSE 12

And Arphaxad lived five and thirty years, and begat Salah;

VERSE 13

And Arphaxad lived after he begat Salah four hundred and three years, and begat sons and daughters.

VERSE 14

And Salah lived thirty years, and begat Eber:

VERSE 15

And Salah lived after he begat Eber four hundred and three years, and begat sons and daughters.

VERSE 16

And Eber lived four and thirty years, and begat Peleg:

VERSE 17

And Eber lived after he begat Peleg four hundred and thirty years, and he begat sons and daughters.

VERSE 18

And Peleg lived thirty years, and begat Reu:

VERSE 19

And Peleg lived after he begat Reu two hundred and nine years, and begat sons and daughters.

VERSE 20

And Reu lived two and thirty years, and begat Serug:

VERSE 21

And Reu lived after he begat Serug two hundred and seven years, and begat sons and daughters.

VERSE 22

And Serug lived thirty years, and begat Nahor:

VERSE 23

And Serug lived after he begat Nahor two hundred years, and begat sons and daughters.

VERSE 24

And Nahor lived nine and twenty years, and begat Terah:

VERSE 25

And Nahor lived after he begat Terah an hundred and nineteen years, and begat sons and daughters.

We can see that the life span shortened rather drastically in these nine generations. Noah, born before the flood, lived to be 950. The next generation dropped by about 33 percent as Shem lived to be 600 years. Then there was another drop of nearly a third for Shem's son Arphaxad, who lived to be 438. It stayed fairly even for three generations—433 for Salah and 464 for Salah's son Eber. Then another drop, this time of nearly 50 percent for the next three generations, to 239 years for Peleg, 237 for Peleg's son Reu, and 230 years for Reu's son Serug. The next generation is Serug's son Nahor, who lived only 148 years.

VERSE 26

And Terah lived seventy years, and begat Abram, Nahor, and Haran.

Note that Terah's middle son was named after his grandfather, a practice still common today.

VERSE 27

Now these *are* the generations of Terah: Terah begat Abram, Nahor, and Haran; and Haran begat Lot.

VERSE 28

And Haran died before his father Terah in the land of his nativity, in Ur of the Chaldees.

The city of Ur dates to sometime in the fourth millennium BC. The early founders were thought to have been from Mesopotamia, and they were early farmers. There is evidence that they were destroyed by a flood. I believe it is possible that this area was the same as the one called Nod (4:16), to which Cain fled when he was banished. We know that Nod was very fertile, and we know that Cain's descendants were involved in the sort of arts and crafts that have been found in the area's excavations.

VERSE 29

And Abram and Nahor took them wives: the name of Abram's wife *was* **Sarai; and the names of Nahor's wife, Milcah, the daughter of Haran, the father of Milcah, and the father of Iscah.**

It was inevitable that the repopulation of the earth from only three families, the male members of which were all related, would of necessity mean that the marriages would be between people who were related. Some were no doubt distant cousins, but others, as here, would have been as close as uncle and niece. Leviticus would later outlaw marriages between aunt and nephew (Leviticus 18:14, 20:19), but it didn't rule out marriage between uncle and niece. The Talmud approved of a man who married his sister's daughter. At least the diverse genes from the three wives of Noah's sons would help serve as a buffer to inbreeding.

VERSE 30

But Sarai was barren; she *had* **no child.**

VERSE 31

And Terah took Abram his son, and Lot the son of Haran his son's son, and Sarai his daughter in law, his son Abram's wife; and they went forth with them from Ur of the Chaldees, to go into the land of Canaan; and they came unto Haran, and dwelt there.

Haran is the name of a man and a city. Sometimes the city is spelled Harran, and sometimes they are spelled the same.

VERSE 32

And the days of Terah were two hundred and five years: and Terah died in Haran.

Terah regained a little of the elder status of his ancestors, but the time when lives spanned several hundred years was by then pretty much over. The age of men was slowly coming down to the 120 years God had declared to be their limit. By that time, there would have been many thousands of people in the world (perhaps many millions), and the need for individual longevity would not have been as great.

It's impossible to find population models that agree or population estimates for early civilization that are based on any common denominators. The estimates for the population of the earth before the flood go as high as many millions, and the same is true for the period indicated here.

CHAPTER TWELVE

VERSE 1

> **Now the Lord had said unto Abram, Get thee out of thy country, and from thy kindred, and from thy father's house, unto a land that I will shew thee:**

VERSE 2

> **And I will make of thee a great nation, and I will bless thee, and make thy name great; and thou shalt be a blessing:**

Abram was called by God with the promise of both immediate prosperity and lasting fame. At that time, he had no child to carry on his name.

VERSE 3

> **And I will bless them that bless thee, and curse thee that curseth thee: and in thee shall all families of the earth be blessed.**

Abram accepted the call on faith with no other guarantee than God's word. His faith was strong enough for him to pull up stakes and move his family and all his belongings.

VERSE 4

> **So Abram departed, as the Lord had spoken unto him: and Lot went with him: and Abram was seventy and five years old when he departed out of Haran.**

VERSE 5

> **And Abram took Sarai his wife, and Lot his brother's son, and all their substance that they had gathered, and the souls that they had gotten**

**in Haran; and they went forth to go into the land
of Canaan; and into the land of Canaan they came.**

The land of Canaan comprised roughly what is now Syria, Jordan, Lebanon, and Israel. It was also later known as Phoenicia, from a Greek word meaning "purple people" because of the use of purple dyes there. It was a rich and fertile land.

Students today have a tremendous advantage in that they can read the Bible with a computer at hand. I highly recommend googling the names of people and places as they are encountered. The wealth of maps and archeological information available online would take a lifetime to duplicate.

VERSE 6

**And Abram passed through the land unto the
place of Sichem, unto the plain of Moreh. And the
Canaanite was then in the land.**

The Canaanites descended from Canaan, a son of Ham and grandson of Noah, while Abram came from the line of Shem. The time between the families being separated and their language being confused was at least 365 years at that point and probably somewhat longer; plenty of time for nations to develop.

Later descendants of the Canaanites were the Phoenicians, who reached the height of their development from c.1500 BC to c.300 BC. In fact, the Septuagint translates "Canaanites" as "Phoenicians." The main Phoenician cities were Tyre, Sidon, Byblos, and Arwad. They were all independent city-states and sometimes fierce rivals. The Phoenician Empire or Kingdom is another fascinating early civilization that made many lasting contributions.

VERSE 7

**And the Lord appeared unto Abram, and said, Unto
thy seed will I give this land: and there builded he
an altar unto the Lord, who appeared unto him.**

We aren't told exactly how God appeared to Abram. His appearances are usually called theophanies, which are manifestations of God that were tangible to the human senses. It is not specific as to exactly what form He took. It may have been a dream as with Joseph, a burning bush as with Moses, a human being as with Jacob, or some other form. In Exodus 33:20, God told Moses, "Thou canst not see my face: for there shall no man see me, and live."

VERSE 8

> **And he removed from thence unto a mountain on the east of Bethel, and pitched his tent,** *having* **Bethel on the west, and Hai on the east: and there he builded an altar unto the Lord, and called upon the name of the Lord.**

God reaffirmed his promise to Abram, and Abram built an altar of worship, reaffirming his faith in the promise.

VERSE 9

> **And Abram journeyed, going on still toward the south.**

VERSE 10

> **And there was a famine in the land: and Abram went down into Egypt to sojourn there; for the famine** *was* **grievous in the land.**

We aren't told how much time elapsed since Abram left home or how long he had been in his new land. The journey must have taken a good while, moving with his animals and possessions and all, so it was probably several years later that the famine took place.

A man of lesser faith might well have gone back home to Haran. But Abram's faith was such that he didn't question God or his decision to follow God's call. We are also not told what prompted Abram to go to Egypt other than to seek relief from the famine, but archeology shows that Egypt had been a flourishing monarchy for several centuries and was probably the most civilized and developed kingdom available. And with the Nile River providing irrigation, it was the most reliable source of food in a drought.

VERSE 11

> **And it came to pass, when he was come near to enter into Egypt, that he said unto Sarai his wife, Behold now, I know that thou art a fair woman to look upon:**

The word used here for "fair" is *yâpheh*, meaning "beautiful" or "fair to look upon." It was most often used to denote a light or fair skin, as was used in 1 Samuel 17:42, in which David was described: "And when the Philistine [Goliath] looked about, and saw David, he disdained him: for he was but a youth, and ruddy, and of a fair countenance."

The word was clearly meant to convey the idea that the person described had light skin. Remember that the descendants of Ham founded Egypt and therefore the Egyptians were a dark-skinned people. This fact makes these passages more logical and supports the hypothesis that the races had all existed from the beginning with their various genes passed down from their origin at Creation.

VERSE 12

> **Therefore it shall come to pass, when the Egyptians shall see thee, that they shall say, This *is* his wife: and they will kill me, but they will save thee alive.**

VERSE 13

> **Say, I pray thee, thou *art* my sister: that it may be well with me for thy sake; and my soul shall live because of thee.**

Was he deceiving Sarai or himself? At any rate, Abram was afraid for his safety, and his faith in God's promise at last seemed to waver.

VERSE 14

> **And it came to pass, that, when Abram was come into Egypt, the Egyptians beheld the woman that she *was* very fair.**

VERSE 15

The princes also of Pharaoh saw her, and commended her before Pharaoh: and the woman was taken into Pharaoh's house.

VERSE 16

And he entreated Abram well for her sake; and he had sheep, and oxen, and he asses, and menservants, and maidservants, and she asses, and camels.

Abram was living well indeed because of his deception. It's interesting to note the order in which Abram's possessions were listed. I assume that was not necessarily the order of their importance or value.

VERSE 17

And the Lord plagued Pharaoh and his house with great plagues because of Serai Abram's wife.

VERSE 18

And Pharaoh called Abram, and said, What *is* this *that* thou hast done unto me? Why didst thou not tell me she *was* thy wife?

We don't know how Pharaoh discovered Serai was Abram's wife. I think Serai confessed the truth during a discussion of the plagues or sent word to Pharaoh to advise him of the truth because of the severity of the plagues.

VERSE 19

Why saidist thou, She *is* my sister? So I might have taken her to me to wife: now therefore behold thy wife, take *her*, and go thy way.

VERSE 20

And Pharaoh commanded *his men* **concerning him; and sent him away, and his wife, and all that he had.**

This certainly was a fairer treatment than Abram deserved or could have imagined. It was nothing like the reception he originally envisioned in which he would be killed and Serai taken captive.

CHAPTER THIRTEEN

VERSE 1

> **And Abram went up out of Egypt, he, and his wife, and all that he had, and Lot with him, into the south.**

Again, we aren't told the length of the sojourn in Egypt. However, based on the age listed for Abram before his journey (seventy-five) and his age when Hagar bore his son Ishmael (eighty-six) and all that transpired in between, he couldn't have been in Egypt for very long.

While that would explain why Pharaoh hadn't gotten around to taking Serai as his wife, it wouldn't explain the large increase in Abram's and Lot's wealth and herds. The only logical explanation is that Pharaoh had been very generous indeed and that Abram was a shrewd businessman in the handling of his goods and livestock while he was there.

VERSE 2

> **And Abram *was* very rich in cattle, in silver, and in gold.**

VERSE 3

> **And he went on his journeys from the south even to Bethel, unto the place where his tent had been at the beginning, between Bethel and Hai;**

Bethel is also written as Beth El or Beth-El, "House of God." It was a town in ancient Israel about ten miles north of Jerusalem. It is the modern city of Baytin on the West Bank.

The word translated as Hai here and in the preceding chapter is variously translated as Ai, Aiath and Aija, all the same town just east of Bethel. This would correspond to the large early Bronze Age site now called At-Tall.

VERSE 4

Unto the place of the altar, which he had made there at the first: and there Abram called on the name of the Lord.

VERSE 5

And Lot also, which went with Abram, had flocks, and herds, and tents.

VERSE 6

And the land was not able to bear them, that they might dwell together; for their substance was great, so that they could not dwell together.

VERSE 7

And there was strife between the herdmen of Abram's cattle and the herdmen of Lot's cattle: and the Canaanite and the Perizzite dwelled then in the land.

This is a bit of a non sequitur, as the two halves of this verse don't seem complementary to each other. This could be due to the later assignment of chapter and verse headings. There would not otherwise appear to be any relevance between the two.

The word *Perizzite* refers specifically to people who live in villages as opposed to nomads. They are mentioned about sixteen times in the Old Testament as being one of the tribes God ordered expelled from the land He gave to Abraham. They, along with the Amorites, Arkites, Arvadites, Zemarites, Hamathites, Hittites, Jebusites, Girgasites, and Hivites, were descendants from Ham through Canaan. These were all tribes that had been cursed following the incident with Noah when he was drunk after the flood. Their curse was not because of that incident, however, but because they were all a very ungodly, idol-worshiping people who would commit unspeakable acts, sometimes even sacrificing their own children in fire to their gods.

Another tribe descending from Canaan was the Sinites. There is evidence that some at least of the Chinese were descendants of the

Sinites (note the prefix *sino* used in reference to China) as well as perhaps the American Indians, Japanese, Koreans, Vietnamese, and Thai peoples. It is also thought that the first Chinese were black, but I'm unconvinced of that. The "land of Sinim" mentioned in Isaiah 49:12 is thought by some to be China, so called because it was peopled by the descendants of the Sinites.

VERSE 8

> **And Abram said unto Lot, Let there be no strife, I pray thee, between me and thee, and between my herdmen and thy herdmen; for we *be* brethren.**

VERSE 9

> *Is* **not the whole land before thee? Separate thyself, I pray thee, from me; if *thou wilt take* the left hand, then I will go to the right; or if *thou depart* to the right hand, then I will go to the left.**

Abram made a generous and benevolent offer. As we saw in verse 4, Abram had again called on the name of the Lord. Perhaps this offer was a direct result of his regaining some of the righteousness he'd lost in Egypt.

VERSE 10

> **And Lot lifted up his eyes, and beheld all the plain of Jordan, that is *was* well watered every where, before the Lord destroyed Sodom and Gomorrah, *even* as the garden of the Lord, like the land of Egypt, as thou comest unto Zoar.**

Lot, obviously standing on a hill, could see the entire plain on both sides of the Jordan. It was described as an area much like the Garden of Eden, so it must then have been a truly fertile valley. Lot, though sometimes a godly man, was quick to seize on that piece of land for himself without regard to Abram, who was, after all, his uncle and his benefactor.

The fact that everything Lot owned was a direct result of Abram's having taken Lot with him when he left Haran to go into Egypt was also of no consequence to Lot. He was interested only in the worldly possessions and immediate riches he could gain when he should have been thinking of what might come later.

VERSE 11

> Then Lot chose him all the plain of Jordan; and Lot journeyed east; and they separated themselves the one from the other.

VERSE 12

> Abram dwelled in the land of Canaan, and Lot dwelled in the cities of the plain, and pitched *his* tent toward Sodom.

The Land of Canaan as it is used here denotes an extent of land from Lebanon across Gaza and eastward to the Jordan Valley, which includes modern Israel and the Palestinian territories.

Sodom was one of a group of five towns, known as the Pentapolis (Wisdom 10:6): Sodom, Gomorrah, Admah, Zeboim, and Bela, also called Zoar (Genesis 19:22). They are also referred to as the cities of the plain. Lot most likely chose to live in Sodom because of the proximity to good grazing for his flocks.

VERSE 13

> But the men of Sodom *were* wicked and sinners before the Lord exceedingly.

VERSE 14

> And the Lord said unto Abram, after that Lot was separated from him, Lift up now thine eyes, and look from the place where thou art northward, and southward, and eastward, and westward:

VERSE 15

> For all the land which thou seest, to thee will I give it, and to thy seed for ever.

VERSE 16

And I will make thy seed as the dust of the earth: so that if a man can number the dust of the earth, *then* shall thy seed also be numbered.

VERSE 17

Arise, walk through the land in the length of it and in the breadth of it; for I will give it unto thee.

VERSE 18

Then Abram removed *his* tent, and came and dwelt in the plain of Mamre, which *is* in Hebron, and built there an altar unto the Lord.

The Lord renewed his covenant with Abram, and Abram showed his gratitude and reaffirmed his faith by erecting a new altar of worship at the grove of Mamre.

Mamre is sometimes called the "plains of Mamre" and sometimes the "oaks of Mamre," but all refer to a grove where Abraham lived near Hebron. The location of the grove itself is still in question; it's thought to be either about a mile and a half west or two miles north of Hebron.

CHAPTER FOURTEEN

VERSE 1

And it came to pass in the days of Amraphel king of Shinar, Arioch king of Ellasar, Chedorlaomer king of Elam, and Tidal king of nations;

VERSE 2

That these **made war with Bera king of Sodom, and with Birsha king of Gomorrah, Shinab king of Admah, and Shemeber king of Zeboiim, and the king of Bela, which is Zoar.**

Note that each city had a king. While the kings undoubtedly had considerable power over their subjects, they were still just cities and the surrounding farmland. The population may have been in the thousands but was unlikely to have been much higher. While they were called kings, perhaps a better title would have been mayors or at best governors to put them in perspective.

VERSE 3

All these were joined together in the vale of Siddim, which is the salt sea.

Vale of Siddim, or valley of the broad plains "which is the salt sea," is thought by most to be between Engedi and the cities of the plain at the south end of the Dead Sea. There is some evidence that the valley could have been at the north end, but the strongest evidence is for the south.

It's very likely that the geography underwent a dramatic change, probably at the time of the destruction of Sodom and Gomorrah, and that much of the valley, along with the remains of those cities, now lies somewhere under the waters of the Dead Sea. Underwater excavations are ongoing at present.

The Dead Sea, in the Great Rift Valley (the Syro-African Rift), is the lowest point on the earth's surface that isn't covered by water or ice. It is about 1300 feet below sea level. The north end has a depth of over 1,000 feet, while the south end is very shallow. If the remains of the cities are in the south end, they would almost surely be buried in the mud under the bottom of the sea.

VERSE 4

Twelve years they served Chedorlaomer, and in the thirteenth year they rebelled.

This refers to the five kings listed in verse 2. After twelve years of being subservient to Chedorlaomer, the kings of the five cities had rebelled and gained their freedom.

VERSE 5

And in the fourteenth year came Chedorlaomer, and the kings that *were* with him, and smote the Rephaims in Ashteroth Karnaim, and the Zuzims in Ham, and the Emims in Shaveh Kiriathaim,

VERSE 6

And the Horites in their mount Seir, unto Elparan, which *is* by the wilderness.

One year after the rebellion, Chedorlaomer and his three allies were involved in battles with several tribes, many of whose members were generally accepted as giants. In virtually every passage in which these people are mentioned, they are equated with men of great physical stature. The fact that they could be defeated leaves one to wonder at their intelligence and dexterity, but apparently their size was a given. As is often the case, the side that prevailed might have done so because of superior weapons or military strategy rather than individual size or strength.

The time period for these events is variously listed as being sometime during the Bronze Age, either early or late depending on the source, which places it roughly somewhere between 2500 and 1500 BC. It is entirely possible that some of these tribes possessed sophisticated armor and weapons. Most of the material on these tribes attributes their size to the mating of (fallen) angels with humans as interpreted from Genesis 6:2, 4, which as mentioned earlier I believe is a mistaken translation. Even were that translation to be accurate, it would not account for the giants listed here, because those matings all took place before the flood and no mention is made of them having been repeated.

So we're left with the theories that either there were more fallen angels having more liaisons with the women in these times or that the DNA was passed down through Noah's sons' wives along with the DNA for the various races. Again, the logical conclusion is that these giants were a result of the genes from those people, male and female, created by God in His likeness in 1:27 on the sixth day of Creation.

VERSE 7

> **And they returned, and came to Enmishpat, which is Kadesh, and smote all the country of the Amalekites, and also the Amorites, that dwelt in Hazezontamar.**

Hazezontamar (pruning of palm trees) is the ancient name of Engedi.

VERSE 8

> **And there went out the king of Sodom, and the king of Gomorrah, and the king of Admah, and the king of Zeboiim, and the king of Bela (the same *is* Zoar;) and they joined battle with them in the vale of Siddim;**

Chedorlaomer invaded the five cities of the plain to reclaim the territory and the tribute he had lost with the cities' revolt and independence.

VERSE 9

> **With Chedorlaomer the king of Elam, and with Tidal king of nations, and Amraphel king of Shinar, and Arioch king of Ellasar, four kings with five.**

COMMON SENSE AND GENESIS | 103

Most other Bible versions translate this as "Tidal, king of Goiim," which is probably more accurate. The location of Goiim or the people to whom the term refers is not known but was most probably a region in what is now Syria; it may have included a coalition of several tribes.

Actually, four kings against five. We have no way of knowing how many men these kings controlled, so we can't know how many were involved in the battle. It's probably a much smaller number than we would envision today, as the domain of the various kings, that is, their kingdoms, would often be no more than a city. The earlier campaign against the other tribes would also have to have taken a toll on Chedorlaomer's forces.

VERSE 10

And the vale of Siddim *was* *full of* slimepits; and the kings of Sodom and Gomorrah fled, and fell there; and they that remained fled to the mountain.

Apparently, the slime pits, or tar pits, or pits of bitumen as they were variously called, had a direct influence on the battle. Probably, Chedorlaomer and his allies were more familiar with the area and the hazards presented by the pits and were therefore better prepared and probably better equipped, because they did prevail.

Because the Vale of Siddim is now under the Dead Sea, it has so far been impossible to explore and retrieve relics of the battle, but some may well have been preserved in the pits and perhaps someday will be recovered. The improving technology of underwater archaeology will also certainly reveal some of the secrets of the Dead Sea.

VERSE 11

And they took all the goods of Sodom and Gomorrah, and all their victuals, and went their way.

VERSE 12

And they took Lot, Abram's brother's son, who dwelt in Sodom, and his goods, and departed.

VERSE 13

And there came one that had escaped, and told Abram the Hebrew; for he dwelt in the plain of Mamre the Amorite, brother of Eschol, and brother of Aner: and these *were* **confederate with Abram.**

VERSE 14

And when Abram heard that his brother was taken captive, he armed his trained *servants***, born in his own house, three hundred and eighteen, and pursued** *them* **unto Dan.**

This gives a clue to the size of the various armies involved. We are told that Abram had three hundred and eighteen men and that he defeated what was left of Chedorlaomer's forces, which no doubt had been depleted by the earlier battles. Nevertheless, the combined armies of the five kings couldn't have been much over a thousand men if that.

There is also an interpretation, cited for example by Rashi, that Eliezer went alone with Abraham to rescue Lot, with the reference to 318 men being the numerical value of Eliezer's name in Hebrew. It seems unlikely, though, that just two men could have accomplished the defeat of Chedorlaomer's forces. Rabbi Shlomo Yitzhaki, better known by the acronym Rashi (February 22, 1040– July 13, 1105), was a rabbi from France famed as the author of the first comprehensive commentary on the Talmud and comprehensive commentary on the Tanakh, the canon of the Hebrew Bible.

It is generally conceded that Dan was the city of Laish, also called Leshem. It was portrayed as the northernmost town of the Kingdom of Israel and formerly as the main town of the tribe of Dan. The town has been securely identified with the archaeological site known as Tel el-Qadi, which consequently has become known to Israelis as Tel Dan.

VERSE 15

And he divided himself against them, he and his servants, by night, and smote them, and pursued

them unto Hobah, which *is* **on the left hand of Damascus.**

Damascus is now the capital and largest city of Syria. According to Flavius Josephus, it was founded by Us, grandson of Shem. The dates for its founding range from 10,000 BC to the third millennium BC, depending on your source. It is one of the oldest continuously inhabited cities in the world, perhaps the very oldest. Population estimates vary from about 1.71 million to over 2.5 million (2009). Upon visiting the city in 1867, Mark Twain wrote, "To Damascus years are only moments, decades are only flitting trifles of time. She measures time not by days and months and years, but by the empires she has seen rise and prosper and crumble to ruin. She is a type of immortality."

The balance of chapter 14 tells of Abram's return home from the battle and subsequent defeat of Chedorlaomer and the four kings who were his allies. Abram not only recaptured Lot and his people and all the possessions that had been taken; he also gained the spoils of the war—the goods and people—taken from the enemy.

The victory accomplished more than just the return of Lot. In defeating the combined forces of Chedorlaomer, Abram again freed Sodom and the adjoining cities from Chedorlaomer's oppression. He became an instant hero who was welcomed home by the king of Sodom and especially by Melchizedek.

We aren't told much about Melchizedek here except that he was the priest of the most high God. We learn that he offered Abram bread and wine and blessed both Abram and God, who had delivered him. That Melchizedek was of considerable consequence is evidenced by the fact that he was mentioned by David in Psalm 110 and nine times by Paul in the letter to the Hebrews. In nearly every instance, the phrase "after the order of Melchizedek" was used. In Hebrews 7:1, Paul referred to this meeting between Abram and Melchizedek, again testifying to the fact that the authors of the New Testament accepted Genesis as historical fact.

When Abram was greeted by Melchizedek, Abram offered him a tithe, a tenth of all he had won in the battle, confirming that Abram recognized the priest's authority. But when Bera, the king of Sodom, told Abram to keep the rest of the goods that were captured, Abram replied that he had taken an oath that he would not keep a single thread or shoelace so that Bera would not be able to say he had made Abram wealthy.

VERSE 16

> **And he brought back all the goods, and also brought again his brother Lot, and his goods, and the women also, and the people.**

Lot was sometimes called Abram's brother because of the custom of calling all relatives brothers and sisters; it's not a mistake or misprint.

VERSE 17

> **And the king of Sodom went out to meet him after his return from the slaughter of Chedorlaomer, and of the kings that *were* with him, at the valley of Shaveh, which *is* the king's dale.**

Valley of Shaveh means "valley of the plain," the ancient name of the "king's dale," Kidron, on the north side of Jerusalem.

VERSE 18

> **And Melchizedek king of Salem brought forth bread and wine: and he *was* the priest of the most high God.**

Salem was a reference to Jerusalem. Melchizedek was commemorated as one of the holy forefathers in the calendar of saints of the Armenian Apostolic Church on July 30; in the Roman rite, his commemoration is August 26.

VERSE 19

> **And he blessed him, and said, Blessed *be* Abram of the most high God, possessor of heaven and earth:**

VERSE 20

And blessed be the most high God, which hath delivered thine enemies into thy hand. And he gave them tithes of all.

That is, Abram gave the tithes to Melchizedek.

VERSE 21

And the king of Sodom said unto Abram, Give me the persons, and take the goods to thyself.

VERSE 22

And Abram said to the king of Sodom, I have lift up mine hand unto the Lord, the most high God, the possessor of heaven and earth,

"I have lift up my hand" means simply "I have sworn an oath."

VERSE 23

That I will not _take_ from a thread even to a shoelatchet, and that I will not take anything that _is_ thine, lest thou shouldest say, I have made Abram rich:

VERSE 24

Save only that which the young men have eaten, and the portion of the men which went with me, Aner, Eschol, and Mamre; let them take their portion.

These are the three brothers mentioned in chapter 13.

CHAPTER FIFTEEN

VERSE 1

After these things the word of the Lord came unto Abram in a vision, saying, Fear not, Abram: I *am* **thy shield,** *and* **thy exceeding great reward.**

VERSE 2

And Abram said, Lord God, what wilt thou give me, seeing I go childless, and the steward of my house *is* **this Eliezer of Damascus?**

According to the Targum, the Aramaic translation of the Hebrew Bible, Eliezer was the son of Nimrod, who was the son of Cush and the grandson of Ham. There are translations that list Eliezer as Abraham's heir, and that would seem logical up until the time Abraham had sons and daughters of his own. I believe the theory that Eliezer was a son of Abraham by his concubine Mesek cannot be supported in light of the text here stating he was childless.

VERSE 3

And Abram said, Behold, to me thou hast given no seed: and, lo, one born in my house is mine heir.

VERSE 4

And, behold, the word of the Lord *came* **unto him, saying, This shall not be thine heir; but he that shall come forth out of thine own bowels shall be thine heir.**

The word translated as "bowels" here is *mêâh*, a word defined in Strong's Concordance as being "from an unused root probably meaning to be soft; used only in plural., the intestines or the abdomen ... the stomach, the uterus (or of men, the seat of generation), the heart ... belly, bowels, heart, womb." It would correspond to our use of the word "loins," which when used in this connotation would be equally difficult to translate into another language.

VERSE 5

> And he brought him forth abroad, and said, Look now toward heaven, and tell the stars, if thou be able to number them: and he said unto him, So shall thy seed be.

The important part of these two verses was God's promise to Abram, a man of some eighty-plus years, that he would not only have an heir but also that the heir would be the start of a line that would rival the stars in number.

VERSE 6

> And he believed in the Lord; and he counted it to him for righteousness.

VERSE 7

> And he said unto him, I *am* the Lord that brought thee out of Ur of the Chaldees, to give thee this land to inherit it.

VERSE 8

> And he said, Lord God, whereby shall I know that I shall inherit it?

Abram appeared to be asking for a sign to seal this covenant with God.

VERSE 9

> And he said unto him, Take me an heifer of three years old, and a she goat of three years old, and a ram of three years old, and a turtledove, and a young pigeon.

VERSE 10

And he took unto him all these, and divided them in the midst, and laid each piece one against another: but the birds he divided not.

This ritual or something very similar to it in which both parties pass between the elements of the offerings is one of several typical ceremonies among Eastern peoples between two parties entering an agreement. How this evolved into a Western handshake (if it did) is not known, but the handshake was practiced as early as the second century BC. Similarities with this ritual still exist in some Eastern cities today, much as do certain marriage ceremonies.

VERSE 11

And when the fowls came down upon the carcases, Abram drove them away.

We are not told what becomes of the animals, but one would presume that when the ceremony was between two ordinary persons, they were cooked and eaten.

VERSE 12

And when the sun was going down, a deep sleep fell upon Abram; and, lo, an horror of great darkness fell upon him.

The word for horror is *'êymâh* and could probably have been better translated as a "terrible dream" as it had the connotation of a nightmare or bad dream.

VERSE 13

And he said unto Abram, Know of a surety that thy seed shall be a stranger in a land *that is* **not theirs, and shall serve them; and they shall afflict them four hundred years;**

There is some controversy as to whether this foretold the captivity of the Israelites in Egypt leading to the Exodus or some other captivity.

My opinion is that it referred to the Egyptian captivity, but there are good arguments on the other side.

VERSE 14

And also that nation, whom they shall serve, will I judge: and afterward shall they come out with great substance.

This verse leads me to believe the captivity referred to Egypt. Although there were other periods of captivity, it was from Egypt that the Israelites were able to leave with a great abundance of wealth.

VERSE 15

And thou shalt go to thy fathers in peace; thou shalt be buried in a good old age.

VERSE 16

But in the fourth generation they shall come hither again; for the iniquity of the Amorites is not yet full.

The Amorites were conquered along with the other tribes in Canaan (the Hittites, the Canaanites, the Perizzites, the Hivites, and the Jebuzites) according to the command of the Lord in Deuteronomy 20:16–18: "That they teach you not to do after all their abominations, which they have done for their gods; so should ye sin against the Lord your God."

VERSE 17

And it came to pass, that, when the sun went down, and it was dark, behold a smoking furnace, and a burning lamp that passed between those pieces.

VERSE 18

In the same day the Lord made a covenant with Abram, saying, Unto thy seed have I given this land, from the river of Egypt unto the great river, the river Euphrates:

VERSE 19

The Kenites, and the Kenizzites, and the Kadmonites,

We don't know much about any of these tribes. We know that Moses' father was a priest of the Kenites, and we know they were coppersmiths and metalworkers.

The Kenizzites are thought to be descended from Kenaz, son of Eliphaz, son of Esau. Jewish tradition suggests that the Kadmonites were oriental relatives of the Hebrews.

VERSE 20

And the Hittites, and the Perizzites, and the Rephaims,

In attempting to research the history of the Hittites, you will come across an interesting dilemma. It seems that the original Hittites (referenced as biblical Hittites) were purportedly descended from Heth, a son of Canaan, son of Ham, and they were mentioned in Genesis as having sold land to Abraham.

Given the casual tone in which the Hittites were mentioned in most Old Testament references, biblical scholars before the age of archaeology traditionally regarded them as a smaller tribe living in the hills of Canaan during the era of the patriarchs, including Abraham.

This picture was completely changed by the archaeological finds that placed the center of their civilization far to the north, in modern-day Bogazköy (Hattusas), Turkey, relegating the Hittites in Canaan to a periphery.

The question whether the biblical Hittites of the first half of the first millennium BC were identical to the earlier Anatolian Hittites is still disputed in academic biblical and ancient Near Eastern studies. Ongoing excavations and discoveries are continually adding to our knowledge of the Hittite empire(s) of which there may be as many as three (Old, Middle, and New Kingdoms). They are referred to as the forgotten empire by one source, and their origin still remains a mystery. But what is known is that from approximately 1800 to about 1200 BC, they were a powerful and very civilized kingdom with advanced laws and government and skilled at metalworking and even iron smelting—although they were not the first to do so—and accomplished traders from Egypt to Greece.

The Perizzites are mentioned as a specific group of people who lived in the Promised Land for many generations, from the time of Abraham (Genesis 13:7) even to the time of Ezra and Nehemiah (Ezra 9:1–2). However, the time during which they were mostly at odds with the Kingdom of Israel seems to have been the time of Joshua in the early period of the judges. It appears as though a peace between the Israelites and the Perizzites eventually came to pass, with intermarriage as well as religious conversion to idolatry as being part of this peace (Judges 3:5–6; Ezra 9:1–2). Some of these tribes are thought to have been giants in the nature of Goliath and others.

Rephaim is used to describe an ancient race of giants. The word literally means "terrible ones." There is no doubt that the people described as Rephaites were of greater than normal stature. They are called by many different names in the Bible, but they may well have been the same people or at least related. The last of the Rephaim is said to have been Og, king of Bashan (Joshua 12:4, 13:12; Deuteronomy 3:11). But who's to say that the people known as Tutsis (Watusi) in Burundi and Rwanda, who are known to be of Nilotic origin, are not descended from those ancient Rephaim?

Once again, we run headlong into some of the myths that have endured due to earlier interpretations. I refer of course to the myth of angels cohabitating with the daughters of men and producing offspring that were giants. Only one verse has led to this interpretation (6:4.) So if we accept the myth, the DNA of these offspring would have the same characteristics of normal humans and would have been passed on through Noah's family to survive the flood and then reemerge through one or more of the son's lines. Or the angels would again come down and revisit the ladies to produce more of the giant progeny, or as some sources now proclaim, the flood was not a worldwide event and they survived by being out of harm's way.

I have dealt with the absurdity of Noah's building an ark and loading up all the animals when he could just have moved to the next valley or wherever in the discussion of chapter 7. The other two explanations also lack validity; they cannot stand the scrutiny of logic, and they exist solely because some explanation has to be found for the existence of the giants, whose origin was inadvertently identified incorrectly. That of course was necessitated by the assumption that Adam and Eve were the first and only people God created.

VERSE 21

And the Amorites, and the Canaanites, and the Girgashites, and the Jebusites.

Amorite refers to a Semitic people who occupied the country west of the Euphrates from the second half of the third millennium BC. The term *Amurru* also refers to them as well as to their principal deity.

Canaan and the Canaanite people simply indicate the region and people in the area of the present-day Gaza Strip, Israel, the West Bank, and Lebanon. They were known to be very idolatrous people.

Little is known of the Girgashites beyond their name. Nehemiah 9:7–8 cites the fact that they were driven out of Canaan as a fulfillment of the Lord's promise to Abraham.

The Jebusites were a Canaanite tribe who inhabited the city of Jebus prior to its capture by David. The city later became Jerusalem, the single, most-often captured city in the world. It has been pillaged, ravished, burned, and destroyed at least twenty-seven times throughout history.

These ten tribes occupied the land God promised to the descendants of Abraham. Later, we will see that God commanded that all these tribes be completely obliterated, because if they were not, intermarriage would eventually take place and the children of Israel would assume some of the idolatrous practices of the people they conquered. We know that was exactly what happened when God's instructions were not carried out to the letter.

CHAPTER SIXTEEN

VERSE 1

Now Sarai Abram's wife bare him no children: and she had an handmaid, an Egyptian, whose name *was* **Hagar.**

VERSE 2

And Sarai said unto Abram, Behold now, the Lord hath restrained me from bearing: I pray thee, go in unto my maid; it may be that I may obtain children by her. And Abram hearkened to the voice of Sarai.

VERSE 3

And Sarai Abram's wife took Hagar her maid the Egyptian, after Abram had dwelt ten years in the land of Canaan, and gave her to her husband Abram to be his wife.

VERSE 4

And he went in unto Hagar, and she conceived: and when she saw that she had conceived, her mistress was despised in her eyes.

God had made a covenant with Abram that he would have heirs without number. Abram believed God's promise, but apparently, his wife thought it wasn't possible that the heirs would come from her. She doubted God's ability to fulfill the covenant and decided to take matters into her own hands. She convinced Abram to go along with her plan.

I see a similarity here to Eve's convincing Adam to disobey God's admonition to not eat the forbidden fruit. The consequences of Sarai's transgression are still very much in evidence today as the descendants of Ishmael continue to strive with the rest of the world.

One can only wonder what the history of the world would have been like had she accepted God's covenant without doubt. Whether the Islamic faith, founded by Muhammad, a descendant of Ishmael through his son Kedar, would have developed at all is a matter for pure conjecture. But the history of the Western world from the second century on would certainly have been a great deal different without such events as the Holy Wars and all the other strife and confrontations that have taken place between the Muslim and Judeo-Christian worlds.

It's difficult to imagine what the world would be like today if the Israelites had followed God's plan to solely occupy the land of Canaan and banish all the earlier inhabitants from that land and if Sarai had trusted God's word and not involved Hagar. There would probably be Arab nations but perhaps without the animosity some of them now show toward the nations they call "infidel."

VERSE 5

> **And Sarai said unto Abram, My wrong** *be* **upon thee: I have given my maid into thy bosom; and when she saw that she had conceived, I was despised in her eyes: the Lord judge between me and thee.**

VERSE 6

> **But Abram said unto Sarai, Behold, thy maid** *is* **in thy hand; do to her as it pleaseth thee. And when Sarai dealt hardly with her, she fled from her face.**

Hagar was the property of Sarai, either a bondservant or slave, as was the custom of that time. It would not have been proper for Abram to punish her, and he did not. Instead, he left the discipline to Sarai, who apparently meted out a harsh punishment for Hagar's insubordination. As a result, Hagar ran away.

VERSE 7

> **And the angel of the Lord found her by a fountain of water in the wilderness, by the fountain in the way to Shur.**

Shur is the name of a desert east of the Gulf of Suez. Hagar was pregnant; she was apparently trying to return to her home when she became lost or just stopped for rest and water. The location of the well is pretty well pinpointed on the east of the Red Sea between Palestine and Egypt and east of the Bitter Lakes. The two Bitter Lakes (Greater and Little) are now part of the Suez Canal.

VERSE 8

And he said, Hagar, Sarai's maid, whence camest thou? and whither wilt thou go? And she said, I flee from the face of my mistress Sarai.

VERSE 9

And the angel of the Lord said unto her, Return to thy mistress, and submit thyself under her hands.

VERSE 10

And the angel of the Lord said unto her, I will multiply thy seed exceedingly, that it shall not be numbered for multitude.

VERSE 11

And the angel of the Lord said unto her, Behold, thou *art* **with child, and shall bear a son, and shalt call his name Ishmael; because the Lord hath heard thy affliction.**

The name Ishmael is derived from two words meaning "God hears."

VERSE 12

And he will be a wild man; his hand *will be* **against every man, and every man's hand against him; and he shall dwell in the presence of all his brethren.**

VERSE 13

And she called the name of the Lord that spake unto her, Thou God seest me; for she said, Have I also here looked after him that seeth me?

VERSE 14

Wherefore the well was called Beerlahairoi; behold it is between Kadesh and Bered.

Kadesh (also spelled Qadesh) was an ancient city of the Levant on or near the Orontes River. It is thought to correspond to the ruins at Tell Nebi Mend, Syria. It was from Kadesh that Moses sent forth the twelve spies to investigate the Promised Land..

This is the only mention of Bered (meaning "hail") as a place in the Bible. The site of the town has never been determined.

VERSE 15

And Hagar bare Abram a son: and Abram called his son's name, which Hagar bare, Ishmael.

VERSE 16

And Abram *was* fourscore and six years old, when Hagar bare Ishmael to Abram.

CHAPTER SEVENTEEN

VERSE 1

> And when Abram was ninety years old and nine, the Lord appeared to Abram, and said unto him, I *am* the Almighty God; walk before me, and be thou perfect.

VERSE 2

> And I will make my covenant between me and thee, and will multiply thee exceedingly.

VERSE 3

> And Abram fell on his face: and God talked with him, saying,

VERSE 4

> As for me, behold, my covenant *is* with thee, and thou shalt be a father of many nations.

VERSE 5

> Neither shall thy name any more be called Abram, but thy name shall be Abraham; for a father of many nations have I made thee.

VERSE 6

> And I will make thee exceedingly fruitful, and I will make nations of thee, and kings shall come out of thee.

VERSE 7

> And I will establish my covenant between me and thee and thy seed after thee in their generations for an everlasting covenant, to be a God unto thee, and to thy seed after thee.

VERSE 8

And I will give unto thee, and to thy seed after thee, the land wherein thou art a stranger, all the land of Canaan, for an everlasting possession; and I will be their God.

VERSE 9

And God said unto Abraham, Thou shall keep my covenant therefore, thou, and thy seed after thee in their generations.

VERSE 10

This *is* my covenant, which ye shall keep, between me and you and thy seed after thee; Every man child among you shall be circumcised.

VERSE 11

And ye shall circumcise the flesh of your foreskin; and it shall be a token of the covenant betwixt me and you.

VERSE 12

And he that is eight days old shall be circumcised among you, every man child in your generations, he that is born in the house, or bought with money of any stranger, which *is* not of thy seed.

VERSE 13

He that is born in thy house, and he that is bought with thy money, must needs be circumcised: and my covenant shall be in your flesh for an everlasting covenant.

VERSE 14

And the uncircumcised man child whose flesh of his foreskin is not circumcised, that soul shall be cut off from his people; he hath broken my covenant.

VERSE 15

And God said unto Abraham, As for Sarai thy wife, thou shalt not call her name Sarai, but Sarah *shall her name be.*

VERSE 16

And I shall bless her, and give thee a son also of her: yea, I will bless her, and she shall be *a mother* of nations; kings of people shall be of her.

VERSE 17

Then Abraham fell upon his face, and laughed, and said in his heart, Shall *a child* be born unto him that is an hundred years old? And shall Sarah, that is ninety years old, bear?

VERSE 18

And Abraham said unto God, O that Ishmael might live before thee!

VERSE 19

And God said, Sarah thy wife shall bear thee a son indeed; and thou shalt call his name Isaac; and I will establish my covenant with him for an everlasting covenant, *and* with his seed after him.

VERSE 20

And as for Ishmael, I have heard thee: Behold, I have blessed him, and will make him fruitful, and will multiply him exceedingly; twenty princes shall he beget, and I will make him a great nation.

VERSE 21

But my covenant will I establish with Isaac, which Sarah shall bear unto thee at this set time in the next year.

VERSE 22

And he left off talking with him, and God went up from Abraham.

The date that this conversation between God and Abraham took place is not known exactly but is estimated by some to be as recent as 2000 BC. This conversation and the covenant it established is recognized as the beginning of the Jewish nation and faith.

Circumcision was probably practiced long before that time, however, as no explanation of the actual procedure was given or deemed necessary, and there are indications it was practiced by early Egyptians. At any rate, it was and is not restricted to Jews. As we see in the next verses, Ishmael, as part of Abraham's household, was also circumcised.

In Islam, though not discussed in the Qur'an, circumcision is widely practiced. Circumcision in various forms and rituals is performed today throughout the world, including some of the most remote and pagan areas.

Circumcision is most prevalent in the Muslim world, parts of Southeast Asia, Africa, the United States, the Philippines, Israel, and South Korea. It is relatively rare in Europe, Latin America, parts of southern Africa, and most of Asia and Oceania.

Its prevalence is near universal in the Middle East and Central Asia. The benefits, effects, and even the legality of the operation are still being argued. There are valid points on both sides of the question, and God didn't explain why He chose this particular method of sealing His covenant. But since He did, I would have to believe that as was the case with His later laws regarding clean and unclean things to eat, there were logical and probably health-related reasons for it. One of the benefits now being listed in favor of circumcision is that it helps prevent the spread of the HIV and the HPV virus.

VERSE 23

> And Abraham took Ishmael his son, and all that were born in his house, and all that were bought with his money, every male among the men of Abraham's house; and circumcised the flesh of their foreskin in the selfsame day, as God had said unto him.

VERSE 24

> And Abraham *was* ninety years old and nine, when he was circumcised in the flesh of his foreskin.

VERSE 25

> And Ishmael his son *was* thirteen years old, when he was circumcised in the flesh of his foreskin.

VERSE 26

> In the selfsame day was Abraham circumcised, and Ishmael his son.

VERSE 27

> And all the men of his house, born in the house, and bought with money of the stranger, were circumcised with him.

CHAPTER EIGHTEEN

VERSE 1

And the Lord appeared unto him in the plains of Mamre: and he sat in the tent door in the heat of the day;

The word used here for "plains" is probably better translated as "oaks" or "oak grove" as it is in the New American Standard Bible, the American Standard Version, the English Revised Version, Young's Literal Translation, and The Darby Bible Translation. The Douay-Rheims Bible translates it as "vale," which is also acceptable.

VERSE 2

And he lift up his eyes and looked, and, lo, three men stood by him: and when he saw *them***, he ran to meet them from the tent door, and bowed himself toward the ground,**

Abraham recognized the importance of his guests right away and hastened to greet them and offer refreshment, as was the custom. Had he recognized them only as regular travelers, he would have merely stood and remained waiting for them to approach the tent.

VERSE 3

And said, My Lord, if now I have found favour in thy sight, pass not away, I pray thee, from thy servant:

VERSE 4

Let a little water, I pray you, be fetched, and wash your feet, and rest yourselves under the tree:

The washing of feet was a courtesy extended to all travelers in the day, especially those in the desert, because of the dust and heat of the roads. Moreover, the footwear was nearly always sandals with no socks or stockings. So a traveler would have hot, dirty feet to add to his discomfort.

VERSE 5

> **And I will fetch a morsel of bread, and comfort ye your hearts; after that ye shall pass on: for therefore are ye come to your servant. And they said, So do, as thou hast said.**

VERSE 6

> **And Abraham hastened into the tent unto Sarah, and said, Make ready quickly three measures of fine meal, knead** *it*, **and make cakes upon the hearth.**

VERSE 7

> **And Abraham ran unto the herd, and fetched a calf tender and good, and gave** *it* **unto a young man; and he hasted to dress it.**

VERSE 8

> **And he took butter, and milk, and the calf which he had dressed, and set** *it* **before them; and he stood by them under the tree, and they did eat.**

This offering followed the custom of the day in treating honored guests. From washing the feet and making cakes to the final bowl of camel's milk to end the meal, the ritual was pretty much the same for greeting distinguished travelers. Even the host's standing while the guests ate was customary. The dressing of a calf instead of a kid or lamb indicated that Abraham deemed his guests worthy of special consideration, although he may not yet have known exactly who they were. He did know, however, that they had come to see him specifically since they walked directly to his tent, which would have been easily distinguishable from all the other tents in his camp.[6]

VERSE 9

And they said unto him, Where *is* Sarah, thy wife? And he said, behold, in the tent.

VERSE 10

And he said, I will certainly return unto thee according to the time of life; and, lo, Sarah thy wife shall have a son. And Sarah heard *it* in the tent door, which *was* behind him.

VERSE 11

Now Abraham and Sarah *were* old *and* well stricken in age; *and* it ceased to be with Sarah after the manner of women.

VERSE 12

Therefore Sarah laughed within herself, saying, After I am waxed old shall I have pleasure, my lord being old also?

VERSE 13

And the Lord said unto Abraham, Wherefore did Sarah laugh, saying, Shall I of a surety bear a child, which am old?

VERSE 14

Is any thing too hard for the Lord? At the time appointed I will return unto thee, according to the time of life, and Sarah shall have a son.

VERSE 15

Then Sarah denied, saying, I laughed not; for she was afraid. And he said, Nay, but thou didst laugh.

At that point, Abraham knew who his visitors were. We can assume he was embarrassed by Sarah's laughter and by her denial and subsequent rebuke. The Lord didn't seem to be overly offended with Sarah's denial, and so as in other instances when He was told an untruth, He offered the rebuke and moved on.

VERSE 16

> **And the men rose up from thence, and looked toward Sodom: and Abraham went with them to bring them on the way.**

VERSE 17

> **And the Lord said, shall I hide from Abraham that thing which I do;**

What the Lord was about to reveal to Abraham was Sodom and Gomorrah's fate.

VERSE 18

> **Seeing that Abraham shall surely become a great and mighty nation, and all the nations of the earth shall be blessed in him?**

VERSE 19

> **For I know him, that he will command his children and his household after him, and they shall keep the way of the Lord, to do justice and judgment; that the Lord may bring upon Abraham that which he hath spoken of him.**

VERSE 20

> **And the Lord said, Because the cry of Sodom and Gomorrah is great, and because their sin is very grievous;**

VERSE 21

> **I will go down now, and see whether they have done altogether according to the cry of it, which is come to me; and if not, I will know.**

VERSE 22

And the men turned their faces from thence, and went toward Sodom; but Abraham stood yet before the Lord.

Abraham was set to make his plea for the safety of Sodom if there were righteous men there. His argument was awkward, but the Lord didn't seem to lose patience.

VERSE 23

And Abraham drew near, and said, Wilt thou also destroy the righteous with the wicked?

VERSE 24

Peradventure there be fifty righteous within the city; wilt thou also destroy and not spare the place for the fifty righteous that *are* therein?

VERSE 25

That be far from thee to do after this manner, to slay the righteous with the wicked: and that the righteous should be as the wicked, that be far from thee: Shall not the Judge of all the earth do right?

VERSE 26

And the Lord said, If I find in Sodom fifty righteous within the city, then I will spare all the place for their sakes.

VERSE 27

And Abraham answered and said, Behold now, I have taken upon me to speak unto the Lord, which *am but* dust and ashes:

VERSE 28

Peradventure there shall lack five of the fifty righteous: wilt thou destroy all the city for *lack of*

five? And he said, If I find there forty and five, I will not destroy *it.*

VERSE 29

And he spake unto him yet again, and said, Peradventure there shall be forty found there. And he said, I will not do *it* **for forty's sake.**

VERSE 30

And he said *unto him,* **Oh let not the Lord be angry, and I will speak: Peradventure there shall thirty be found there. And he said, I will not do** *it,* **if I find thirty there.**

VERSE 31

And he said, Behold now, I have taken upon me to speak unto the Lord: Peradventure there shall be twenty found there. And he said, I will not destroy *it* **for twenty's sake.**

VERSE 32

And he said, Oh let not the Lord be angry, and I will speak yet but this once: Peradventure ten shall be found there. And he said, I will not destroy *it* **for ten's sake.**

VERSE 33

And the Lord went his way, as soon as he had left communing with Abraham: and Abraham returned unto his place.

There were not even ten righteous men in Sodom. In fact, there was only one. He might have been destroyed along with the city if God hadn't intervened and helped him escape, and perhaps that was at least in part because of Abraham's earnest pleas. God destroyed four cities during that earthquake or volcanic eruption.

As mentioned before, Sodom was one of a group of five towns, the Pentapolis (Wisdom 10:6): Sodom, Gomorrah, Admah, Zeboim, and Bela, also called Zoar (Genesis 19:22). Bela was spared due to Lot's plea as we shall see in the next chapter.

There are many stories about the sins and inhospitality of the inhabitants of those cities that caused their destruction. One that I find particularly interesting from Jewish tradition is about a man named Eliezer, Abraham's servant, who went to visit Lot in Sodom and got into a dispute with a Sodomite over a beggar. Eliezer was hit in the forehead with a stone, making him bleed. The Sodomite who hit him demanded Eliezer pay him for the service of bloodletting, and a Sodomite judge sided with the Sodomite. Eliezer then struck the judge in the forehead with a stone and asked the judge to pay the Sodomite.

The location of the five cities is still in doubt. There has been much work done in the area since 1965, and the results of those efforts are still being published. It is believed by some that the cities are near or even under what is now the Dead Sea. With the destruction by earthquake or volcano or similar catastrophic event, the path of the river and the location of the Dead Sea may well have been altered, and the ruins of some of the cities could have been buried. There is even a theory that an asteroid caused the destruction.

My own choice is that an eruption of sulfur and gasses came from beneath the surface, perhaps caused by an earthquake (the area is on a fault line), shooting the material high in the air much like a volcano that then rained down on the whole plain.

Bab edh-Dhra, the site of an early Bronze Age city near the Dead Sea, is touted as a candidate for the location of Sodom. Bitumen and petroleum deposits in the area contain sulfur and natural gas (as such deposits normally do), and one theory suggests that a pocket of natural gas led to the incineration of the city.

Tall el-Hammam is another possibility for the site of Sodom and perhaps better fits the biblical description of Sodom's location. Numeira, an archaeological site near the Dead Sea, has been proposed as the location for the Gomorrah; the site has substantial early Bronze Age remains. Numeira is also the name given to the river and valley adjacent to the archaeological site, and the river is significantly eroding the site.

Scholars have set the date of c. 2070 BC for the destruction of the four cities, although some prefer an earlier date of c. 2300 BC due to the discoveries resulting from excavations made beginning in the late 1970s and early 1980s.

At any rate, scholars agree that the four cities were all destroyed and abandoned about the same time.

CHAPTER NINETEEN

VERSE 1

> **And there came two angels to Sodom at even; and Lot sat in the gate of Sodom: and Lot seeing** *them* **rose up to meet them; and he bowed himself with his face toward the ground;**

VERSE 2

> **And he said, Behold now, my lords, turn in, I pray you, into your servant's house, and tarry all night, and wash your feet, and ye shall rise up early, and go on your ways. And they said, Nay; but we will abide in the street all night.**

VERSE 3

> **And he pressed upon them greatly; and they turned in unto him, and entered into his house; and he made them a feast, and did bake unleavened bread, and they did eat.**

Again, this was the typical greeting for travelers according to the custom of the day. The traveler would be brought into the house and offered water to drink and to wash his feet. His animals if he had any would be looked after, and he would be offered a meal all before any discussion of who he was, where he was going, or why he was there. Any visitor would receive the protection of the host for as long as he remained under his roof. This custom was still in practice through the Middle Ages and beyond and even in some smaller towns today.

VERSE 4

> **But before they lay down, the men of the city,** *even* **the men of Sodom, compassed the house round, both old and young, all the people from every quarter;**

VERSE 5

And they called unto Lot, and said unto him, Where *are* **the men which came in to thee this night? Bring them out unto us, that we may know them.**

VERSE 6

And Lot went out at the door unto them, and shut the door after him,

VERSE 7

And said, I pray you, brethren, do not so wickedly.

VERSE 8

Behold now, I have two daughters which have not known man; let me, I pray you, bring them out unto you, and do ye to them as *is* **good in your eyes: only unto these men do nothing; for therefore came they under the shadow of my roof.**

Lot so stringently observed the law concerning the protection of a guest while under a host's roof that he made what would seem today to be an unbelievable offer. He offered his own two virgin daughters in place of the two visitors. And remember: Lot at that time still didn't know the identity of the men; to him, they were simply two travelers he had met at the city gate. They hadn't even sought sanctuary from him; rather, Lot had invited them to his house and insisted they accept his hospitality when they at first refused.

VERSE 9

And they said, Stand back. And they said *again,* **This one** *fellow* **came in to sojourn, and he will be a judge: now will we deal worse with thee, than with them. And they pressed sore upon the man,** *even* **Lot, and came near to break the door.**

This was typical crowd mentality; they threatened Lot, whom they knew, because of their lust for the strangers.

VERSE 10

But the men put forth their hand, and pulled Lot into the house to them, and shut the door.

VERSE 11

And they smote the men that *were* **at the door with blindness, both small and great: so that they wearied themselves to find the door.**

Prior to that, Lot would have considered the two men simply ordinary travelers. At that point, he would have known there was something very special about his visitors.

VERSE 12

And the men said unto Lot, Hast thou here any besides? Son in law, and thy sons, and thy daughters, and whatsoever thou hast in the city, bring *them* **out of this place:**

VERSE 13

For we will destroy this place, because the cry of them is waxen great before the face of the Lord; and the Lord hath sent us to destroy it.

VERSE 14

And Lot went out, and spake unto his sons in law, which married his daughters, and said, Up, get you out of this place; for the Lord will destroy this city. But he seemed as one mocked unto his sons in law.

We don't learn the size of Lot's family. We don't know the number of married daughters he had or if he had grandchildren. Though the angels mentioned the possibility that he had sons, we are told nothing of them. We can assume there were at least several and perhaps many, according to the custom of the time.

Apparently, his wife and two daughters were all who were left in his immediate household, and they were the only ones who had listened to his warning. Everyone else laughed at him much as the people laughed at the warnings of Noah in the days before the flood.

VERSE 15

And when the morning arose, then the angels hastened Lot, saying, Arise, take thy wife, and thy two daughters, which are here; lest thou be consumed in the iniquity of the city.

VERSE 16

And while he lingered, the men laid hold upon his hand, and upon the hand of his wife, and upon the hand of his two daughters; the Lord being merciful unto him: and they brought him forth, and set him without the city.

Lot was a wealthy man; he no doubt lingered because he was reluctant to leave all his possessions and other relatives, even those who had mocked him.

VERSE 17

And it came to pass, when they had brought them abroad, that he said, Escape for thy life; look not behind thee, neither stay thou in all the plain; escape to the mountain, lest thou be consumed.

VERSE 18

And Lot said unto them, Oh, not so, my Lord:

VERSE 19

Behold now, thy servant hath found grace in thy sight, and thou hast magnified thy mercy, which thou hast shewed unto me in saving my life; and I cannot escape to the mountain, lest some evil take me, and I die;

Lot was righteous but also somewhat dense. He acknowledged

that he'd been saved from a city about to be destroyed but didn't think he could be saved in the mountains.

VERSE 20

> **Behold now, this city *is* near to flee unto, and it *is* a little one: Oh, let me escape thither, (*is* it not a little one?) and my soul shall live.**

VERSE 21

> **And he said unto him, See, I have accepted thee concerning this thing also, that I will not overthrow this city, for the which thou hast spoken.**

VERSE 22

> **Haste thee, escape thither; for I cannot do any thing till thou be come thither. Therefore the name of the city was called Zoar.**

The name Zoar comes from the root *tsôar*, "small" or "little." Prior references to this city in 14:2 and 8 used the name Bela, with the qualifying "which is Zoar" and "the same is Zoar." From here on, the city was called only Zoar, so it's logical to assume the name was changed then due to the plea and description of Lot.

As with the other of the five cities of the plain, its exact location is still in dispute. Opinions vary from a location at the modern Tell esh-Shaghur to a site buried under the southern end of the Dead Sea, while other scholars argue that all the cities should be located toward the northern end of the sea whether submerged or not.

The Dead Sea at present is about forty-two miles long and could have been even larger then, with the plain occupying many square miles. Some of the difficulty in attempting to pinpoint the cities of the plain is a disagreement as to whether they were at the northern or the southern end of the sea. If Bab al-Dhra' and Numeira are good candidates for Sodom and Gomorrah, such cities as Feifa, Safi, and Khneizirah could well be the sites for Admah, Zeboim, and Zoar. I'm confident much will be learned through discoveries made in the next few years.[7]

VERSE 23

The sun was risen upon the earth when Lot entered into Zoar.

VERSE 24

Then the Lord rained upon Sodom and upon Gomorrah brimstone and fire from the Lord out of heaven;

The method of destruction is still being debated. The most logical explanation is that it was an explosion of natural gas and the bitumen indigenous to the area either with or without an earthquake. There is also a theory that it was an asteroid strike. The basis for that theory is the discovery of a tablet some 150 years ago whose code has finally been cracked. It described the sighting of an asteroid strike by a Sumerian astronomer. Using computers to recreate the night sky, scientists have pinpointed his sighting to the night of June 29, 3123 BC. But that date is really too early, as the cities in question had not yet been fully developed. Common sense dictates that something natural happened, and because it had been foretold, it was a result of God's will.

VERSE 25

And he overthrew those cities; and all the plain, and all the inhabitants of the cities, and that which grew upon the ground.

VERSE 26

But his wife looked back from behind him, and she became a pillar of salt.

VERSE 27

And Abraham gat up early in the morning to the place where he stood before the Lord:

VERSE 28

And he looked toward Sodom and Gomorrah, and toward all the land of the plain, and beheld, and, lo, the smoke of the country went up as the smoke of a furnace.

This passage strongly suggests a volcanic event or the explosion of underground gasses.

VERSE 29

And it came to pass, when God destroyed the cities of the plain, that God remembered Abraham, and sent Lot out of the midst of the overthrow, when he overthrew the cities in which Lot dwelt.

VERSE 30

And Lot went up out of Zoar, and dwelt in the mountain, and his two daughters with him; for he feared to dwell in Zoar: and he dwelt in a cave, he and his two daughters.

No reason is given for Lot's change of heart. He had begged to be allowed to find sanctuary in Zoar when he was fleeing from Sodom, and he had not only been granted his plea, but also, the whole city was spared because of it, and then immediately he feared to remain there and left for the mountain he had been directed to in the first place. An interesting case of man telling God what's best and then finding out God knew what was best after all.

VERSE 31

And the firstborn said unto the younger, Our father *is* old, and *there is* not a man in the earth to come in unto us after the manner of all the earth:

VERSE 32

Come, let us make our father drink wine, and we will lie with him, that we may preserve seed of our father.

VERSE 33

> And they made their father drink wine that night: and the firstborn went in, and lay with her father; and he perceived not when she lay down, nor when she arose.

VERSE 34

> And it came to pass on the morrow, that the firstborn said unto the younger, Behold, I lay yesternight with my father: let us make him drink wine this night also; and go thou in, *and* lie with him, that we may preserve seed of our father.

VERSE 35

> And they made their father drink wine that night also: and the younger arose, and lay with him; and he perceived not when she lay down, nor when she arose.

VERSE 36

> Thus were both the daughters of Lot with child by their father.

VERSE 37

> And the firstborn bare a son, and called his name Moab: the same *is* the father of the Moabites unto this day.

VERSE 38

> And the younger, she also bare a son, and called his name Benammi: the same *is* the father of the children of Ammon unto this day.

The argument that there were no men on the earth for the women was of course a lie. They had just left a town, albeit a small one, where there were men, and they would have had ample reason to believe there were other places where men existed. So they were driven by some other motive, although we're not told exactly what it was.

Perhaps it was only lasciviousness due to the influence of their life in Sodom. Lot's weakness is further demonstrated here by the fact that he allowed it to happen.

In spite of their beginnings, however, the two children who were the result of these unions went on to each found a nation that would bear their names respectively. The nations called Moab and Ammon are nearly always considered together because the founding fathers, Moab and Ammon, were brothers. Both nations became large and powerful, and their history was intertwined with biblical history.

The existence of both nations has been corroborated by archaeological finds such as the Mesha Stele as well as Assyrian records and others. The Moabite Kingdom's capital was Didon, in modern Jordan. The Kingdom of Ammon was in northwestern Arabia.

CHAPTER TWENTY

VERSE 1

And Abraham journeyed from thence toward the south country, and dwelled between Kadesh and Shur, and sojourned in Gerar.

Gerar was an ancient city in Palestine and near the Mediterranean. It was probably the birthplace of Abraham's son Isaac. It is now an archeological site in Israel.

VERSE 2

And Abraham said of Sarah his wife, She *is* my sister: and Abimelech king of Gerar sent, and took Sarah.

This is the second time Abraham used this ruse. The first time (12:13) was in Egypt when Abraham sought relief from a famine and misled Pharaoh with the same lie. That worked out well for him though, since Pharaoh presented him with "sheep, oxen, he asses, menservants, maidservants, she asses and camels" (v. 16) because he thought he was Sarah's brother. He was allowed to keep everything even after Pharaoh discovered the lie and sent them away. So it's no wonder he would try the same subterfuge again even though he was now wealthy and in need of nothing.

VERSE 3

But God came to Abimelech in a dream by night, and said unto him, Behold, thou *art but* a dead man, for the woman which thou hast taken; for she *is* a man's wife.

VERSE 4

But Abimelech had not come near her: and he said, Lord, wilt thou slay a righteous nation?

VERSE 5

Said he not unto me, She *is* my sister? And she, even herself said, He *is* my brother: in the integrity of my heart and innocency of my hands have I done this.

VERSE 6

And God said unto him in a dream, Yea, I know that thou didst this in the integrity of thy heart; for I also withheld thee from sinning against me: therefore suffered I thee not to touch her.

VERSE 7

Now therefore restore the man *his* wife; for he *is* a prophet, and he shall pray for thee, and thou shalt live: and if thou restore *her* not, know thou that thou shalt surely die, thou, and all that *are* thine.

VERSE 8

Therefore Abimelech rose early in the morning, and called all his servants, and told all these things in their ears: and the men were sore afraid.

VERSE 9

Then Abimelech called Abraham, and said unto him, What hast thou done unto us? and what have I offended thee, that thou hast brought on me and on my kingdom a great sin? thou hast done deeds unto me that ought not to be done.

VERSE 10

And Abimelech said unto Abraham, What sawest thou, that thou hast done this thing?

VERSE 11

And Abraham said, Because I thought, Surely the fear of God *is* not in this place; and they will slay me for my wife's sake.

VERSE 12

And yet indeed *she is* my sister; she *is* the daughter of my father, but not the daughter of my mother; and she became my wife.

Actually, Sarai was the niece of Abraham, being the daughter of his brother Haran. But it was customary to refer to relatives or members of the same tribal clan as brothers or sisters, so technically, this wasn't a lie. However, it was clearly a deception to conceal the fact that Sarah was also Abraham's wife just as it had been in the case with Pharaoh. And as was previously the case, Abraham was rebuked for the deception. He was a servant of God and was chastised by someone he considered a heathen for committing such a sin. However, as was also the case with Pharaoh, he wound up much the richer for the experience—not exactly the lesson about truthfulness we would want to pass on.

VERSE 13

And it came to pass, when God caused me to wander from my father's house, that I said unto her, This *is* thy kindness which thou shalt show unto me; at every place whither we shall come, say of me, He *is* my brother.

VERSE 14

And Abimelech took sheep, and oxen, and menservants, and womenservants, and gave *them* unto Abraham, and restored him Sarah his wife.

VERSE 15

And Abimelech said, Behold, my land *is* before thee: dwell in it where it pleaseth thee.

VERSE 16

And unto Sarah he said, Behold, I have given thy brother a thousand *pieces* **of silver: behold, he** *is* **to thee a covering of the eyes, unto all that** *are* **with thee, and with all** *other***: thus she was reproved.**

If you google "a covering of the eyes," you'll get an explanation of this passage with which I disagree. The interpretation given there has something to do with Sarah's wearing a veil to show she was a married woman. Others seem to refer to a veil being worn by those dealing with Sarah, or that Abimelech's 1,000 pieces of silver had bought a vindication for her or of his own actions.

I believe the key to the meaning is the word *reprove*, which doesn't mean "vindication." It's criticism, a scolding. The word in Hebrew is *yâkach*, "to chasten or correct," and I believe the original translation of "reprove" is correct. Therefore, I believe the proper interpretation should be that Abimelech was saying that Abraham had caused Sarah to be blind to what was going on and was scolding her for letting that happen.

VERSE 17

So Abraham prayed unto God: and God healed Abimelech, and his wife, and his maidservants; and they bare *children*.

As stated in verse 7 above, Abraham first prayed for Abimelech and then Abimelech was healed.

VERSE 18

For the Lord had fast closed up all the wombs of the house of Abimelech, because of Sarah Abraham's wife.

CHAPTER TWENTY-ONE

VERSE 1

And the Lord visited Sarah as he had said, and the Lord did unto Sarah as he had spoken.

VERSE 2

For Sarah conceived, and bare Abraham a son in his old age, at the set time of which God had spoken to him.

VERSE 3

And Abraham called the name of his son that was born unto him, whom Sarah bare to him, Isaac.

VERSE 4

And Abraham circumcised his son Isaac being eight days old, as God had commanded him.

VERSE 5

And Abraham was an hundred years old, when his son Isaac was born unto him.

God fulfilled His promise in 17:15–16 to give Abraham a son by Sarah. Abraham followed through with his part of the bargain by naming the boy Isaac and having him circumcised. While he might have doubted God's ability to protect him from Abimelech, his faith had apparently been restored with the birth of his son.

VERSE 6

And Sarah said, God hath made me to laugh, *so that* all that hear will laugh with me.

VERSE 7

And she said, Who would have said unto Abraham, that Sarah should have given children suck? For I have born *him* a son in his old age.

VERSE 8

And the child grew, and was weaned: and Abraham made a great feast the *same* day that Isaac was weaned.

Isaac was weaned probably around age three as children were suckled longer in that day. A feast to celebrate the weaning of Isaac (*Yitchack*, "the one who will laugh"), is probably the origin of the weaning feast still practiced in some parts of the East.

VERSE 9

And Sarah saw the son of Hagar the Egyptian, which she had born unto Abraham, mocking.

The word used here for "mocking" is *tsâchaq*, which comes from a root meaning alternately "laughing out loud," "making sport of," or "playing with." It's unclear exactly what Ishmael was doing, but whatever it was angered Sarah enough to order Abraham to have Ishmael and Hagar banished, which could have easily resulted in their deaths.

VERSE 10

Wherefore she said unto Abraham, Cast out this bondwoman and her son: for the son of this bondwoman shall not be heir with my son, *even* with Isaac.

VERSE 11

And the thing was very grievous in Abraham's sight because of his son.

Abraham obviously had feelings for Ishmael, as he was his firstborn son and natural heir and about fifteen years Isaac's senior.

He gave in to his wife's request only after God told him He would take care of Ishmael since he was also a descendant of Abraham.

Ishmael means "God has hearkened" or "God hears." It is recognized by Jewish and Islamic traditions that Ishmael was the father of the Arabs. The Qur'an views him as an Islamic prophet and the ancestor of Muhammad.

The conflict that exists today between the Arabs and Jews most likely dates back to Ishmael and Isaac or maybe even further back to Sarah and Hagar.

VERSE 12

And God said unto Abraham, Let it not be grievous in thy sight because of the lad, and because of thy bondwoman; in all that Sarah hath said unto thee, hearken unto her voice; for in Isaac shall thy seed be called.

VERSE 13

And also of the son of the bondwoman will I make a nation, because he *is* thy seed.

VERSE 14

And Abraham rose up early in the morning, and took bread, and a bottle of water, and gave *it* unto Hagar, putting *it* on her shoulder, and the child, and sent her away: and she departed, and wandered in the wilderness of Beer-sheba.

The wilderness of Beersheba is probably what is now the Negev Desert in southern Israel, which accounts for over half of Israel's land area.

VERSE 15

And the water was spent in the bottle, and she cast the child under one of the shrubs.

VERSE 16

> **And she went, and sat her down over against** *him*
> **a good way off, as it were a bowshot: For she said,**
> **Let me not see the death of the child. And she sat**
> **over against** *him*, **and lift up her voice, and wept.**

Hagar evidently had forgotten the promise made to her at the well in 16:10–12, or else she no longer believed it.

VERSE 17

> **And God heard the voice of the lad; and the angel**
> **of God called to Hagar out of heaven, and said**
> **unto her, What aileth thee, Hagar? Fear not; for**
> **God hath heard the voice of the lad where he** *is*.

VERSE 18

> **Arise, lift up the lad, and hold him in thine hand;**
> **for I will make him a great nation.**

VERSE 19

> **And God opened her eyes, and she saw a well**
> **of water; and she went, and filled the bottle with**
> **water, and gave the lad drink.**

VERSE 20

> **And God was with the lad; and he grew, and dwelt**
> **in the wilderness, and became an archer.**

VERSE 21

> **And he dwelt in the wilderness of Paran: and his**
> **mother took him a wife out of the land of Egypt.**

The wilderness of Paran was mentioned a number of times in the early books of the Bible. It's the desert in the northeastern portion of the Sinai Peninsula where much of the Israelites' wanderings took place after leaving Egypt.

VERSE 22

And it came to pass at that time, that Abimelech and Phichol the chief captain of his host spake unto Abraham, saying, God *is* with thee in all that thou doest:

VERSE 23

Now therefore swear unto me here by God that thou wilt not deal falsely with me, nor with my son, nor with my son's son: *but* according to the kindness that I have done thee, thou shalt do unto me, and to the land wherin thou hast sojourned.

VERSE 24

And Abraham said, I will swear.

VERSE 25

And Abraham reproved Abimelech because of a well of water, which Abimelech's servants had violently taken away.

VERSE 26

And Abimelech said, I wot not who hath done this thing: neither didst thou tell me, neither yet heard I *of it*, but today.

VERSE 27

And Abraham took sheep and oxen, and gave them unto Abimelech; and both of them made a covenant.

VERSE 28

And Abraham set seven ewe lambs of the flock by themselves.

VERSE 29

And Abimelech said unto Abraham, What *mean* **these seven ewe lambs which thou hast set by themselves?**

VERSE 30

And he said, For *these* **seven ewe lambs shalt thou take of my hand, that they may be a witness unto me, that I have digged this well.**

VERSE 31

Wherefore he called that place Beersheba; because there they sware both of them.

Beersheba was the southernmost city of Israel. The expression "from Dan to Beersheba" (Judges 20) described the whole kingdom as Dan was the northernmost outpost. Beersheba is believed to have been populated since the fourth millennium BC, having been destroyed and rebuilt many times. It is an important city to this day, ranking just below Tel Aviv, Jerusalem, and Haifa in population.

VERSE 32

Thus they made a covenant at Beersheba: then Abimelech rose up, and Phichol the chief captain of his host, and they returned into the land of the Philistines.

VERSE 33

And Abraham planted a grove in Beersheba, and called there on the name of the Lord, the everlasting God.

VERSE 34

And Abraham sojourned in the Philistines' land many days.

CHAPTER TWENTY-TWO

VERSE 1

> **And it came to pass after these things, that God**
> **did tempt Abraham, and said unto him, Abraham:**
> **and he said, Behold,** *here* **I** *am*.

The word translated as "tempt" here is *nâçâh*, a root meaning "to prove or test" rather than "to entice or allure to do something often regarded as unwise, wrong, or immoral," which is *Webster*'s first definition. "Prove" or "test" would be a better translation than "tempt" here.

The same word is used many times in the Old Testament and usually in the reverse of this instance, as in Exodus 17:2, Deuteronomy 6:16, and Isaiah 7:12, all of which are admonitions against tempting the Lord or asking Him to prove Himself.

VERSE 2

> **And he said, Take now thy son, thine only** *son*
> **Isaac, whom thou lovest, and get thee into the land**
> **of Moriah; and offer him there for a burnt offering**
> **upon one of the mountains which I will tell thee of.**

Although Isaac was specifically mentioned here, many Muslims today believe it was Ishmael who had been slated for sacrifice. Earlier thought accepted Isaac but with several opinions. The Qur'an does not name either son but does relate the story of the sacrifice. Other Muslim views offer that God never really ordered the sacrifice, that it was only a dream that Abraham thought should be carried out, but that's not what this verse says.

VERSE 3

> **And Abraham rose up early in the morning, and**
> **saddled his ass, and took two of his young men**
> **with him, and Isaac his son, and clave the wood**

**for the burnt offering, and rose up, and went unto
the place of which God had told him.**

The faith of Abraham can hardly be questioned after this test. Although he was ready to follow God's instructions and sacrifice his son, he remembered God's promise that a nation would come through Isaac. So he trusted God to intervene or to raise Isaac from the dead after the offering. In either case, Abraham was prepared to follow God's command without question.

This story is important on two levels; it proved Abraham's faith and was a precursor of the crucifixion, which came many years later on the same mount.

VERSE 4

**Then on the third day Abraham lifted up his eyes,
and saw the place afar off.**

Mount Moriah is a hugely significant location not only in Genesis but throughout the Old and New Testaments. It's where King David built an altar (2 Samuel 24:18, 21) and where Solomon later built a glorious temple.

After Nebuchadnezzar's army destroyed that temple, the Jews rebuilt it when they returned from captivity in Babylonia. King Herod added to the temple, and it became known as Herod's Temple. Jesus had His confrontation with the money changers in this temple (John 2:15). In AD 70, the Romans destroyed the temple, and all that remains today is a portion of a wall known as the Western Wall or the Wailing Wall.

The Supreme Muslim Council (the *waqf*) controls most of the area atop the mount with several holy sites such as the Dome of the Rock and the Al-Aqsa Mosque.

There are prophecies regarding the building of a third temple, which would also be here on Mount Moriah.

VERSE 5

> **And Abraham said unto his young men, Abide ye
> here with the ass; and I and the lad will go yonder
> and worship, and come again for you.**

VERSE 6

> **And Abraham took the wood of the burnt offering,
> and laid** *it* **upon Isaac his son; and he took the fire
> in his hand, and a knife; and they went both of
> them together.**

The word translated as "fire" here is *'êsh*, from a root simply meaning "flame," "fiery," or "hot." How it was carried we are not told, but it can be assumed that what Abraham carried was probably burning coals in a container.

VERSE 7

> **And Isaac spake unto Abraham his father, and
> said, My father: and he said, here** *am* **I, my son.
> And he said, Behold the fire and the wood: but
> where** *is* **the lamb for a burnt offering?**

VERSE 8

> **And Abraham said, My son, God will provide
> himself a lamb for a burnt offering: so they went
> both of them together.**

Many see a symbolism here of Isaac's carrying the wood for his own offering and the prophetic answer given by Abraham that God Himself would provide a lamb with Jesus' having to carry His own cross and His being the Lamb of God provided for the offering of all humanity.

VERSE 9

> **And they came to the place which God had told
> him of; and Abraham built an altar there, and laid
> the wood in order, and bound Isaac his son, and
> laid him on the altar upon the wood.**

Abraham proved his faith here, and I think Isaac's also. They didn't question how God would keep His promise; they just trusted He would.

VERSE 10

And Abraham stretched forth his hand, and took the knife to slay his son.

VERSE 11

And the angel of the Lord called to him out of heaven, and said, Abraham, Abraham: and he said, Here *am* **I.**

VERSE 12

And he said, Lay not thine hand upon the lad, neither do thou any thing unto him: for now I know that thou fearest God, seeing thou hast not withheld thy son, thine only *son* **from me.**

Although technically, Isaac wasn't Abraham's only son, Ishmael had been sent away, so Isaac was the only remaining son and heir.

VERSE 13

And Abraham lifted up his eyes, and looked, and behold behind *him* **a ram caught in a thicket by his horns: and Abraham went and took the ram, and offered him up for a burnt offering in the stead of his son.**

Another similarity to the crucifixion is the ram caught by his horns in a thicket and Jesus having to wear a crown of thorns. And of course the ram (a male) was being compared to the Lamb of God.

In Hebrews 11:17, Paul made a specific reference to this offering; another example that the apostles of the New Testament knew, understood, and trusted Genesis.

VERSE 14

And Abraham called the name of that place Jehovahjireh: as it is said *to* this day, In the mount of the Lord it shall be seen.

Translated literally, the name means "God will see" or more often "God will provide."

VERSE 15

And the angel of the Lord called unto Abraham out of heaven the second time,

VERSE 16

And said, by myself have I sworn, saith the Lord, for because thou hast done this thing, and hast not withheld thy son, thine only *son*:

VERSE 17

That in blessing I will bless thee, and in multiplying I will multiply thy seed as the stars of the heaven, and as the sand which *is* upon the sea shore; and thy seed shall possess the gate of his enemies.

VERSE 18

And in thy seed shall all the nations of the earth be blessed; because thou hast obeyed my voice.

VERSE 19

So Abraham returned unto his young men, and they rose up and went together to Beer-sheba; and Abraham dwelt at Beer-sheba.

VERSE 20

And it came to pass after these things, that it was told Abraham, saying, Behold, Milcah, she hath also born children unto thy brother Nahor;

Milcah, daughter of Haran, was a woman of ancient Mesopotamia and an ancestor of the patriarch Jacob. Haran also had another daughter, Iscah, and a son, Lot. Milcah's father died in Ur before his father Terah. Milcah married her uncle Nahor, Haran's brother.

Although Leviticus later outlawed marriages between aunt and nephew (Leviticus 18:14, 20:19), it didn't rule out marriage between uncle and niece. In fact, the Talmud approved of a man who married his sister's daughter.

There is also another Milcah mentioned in the Bible; she was the daughter of Zelophehad, son of Hepher (Numbers 26:33). Zelophehad had five daughters but no sons. That Milcah was notable for having helped win the right for daughters to inherit their fathers' lands.

VERSE 21

Huz, his firstborn, and Buz his brother, and Kemuel the father of Aram,

Huz and Buz—another set of twins?

VERSE 22

And Chesed, and Hazo, and Pildash, and Jidlaph, and Bethuel.

VERSE 23

And Bethuel begat Rebekah; these eight Milcah did bear to Nahor, Abraham's brother.

VERSE 24

And his concubine, whose name was **Reumah, she bare also Tebah, and Gaham, and Thahash, and Maachah.**

CHAPTER TWENTY-THREE

VERSE 1

And Sarah was an hundred and seven and twenty years old: *these were* **the years of the life of Sarah.**

VERSE 2

And Sarah died in Kirjatharba; the same *is* **Hebron in the land of Canaan: and Abraham came to mourn for Sarah, and to weep for her.**

As the mother of the Hebrew nation, Sarah has the unique honor of being the only woman in all of Scripture whose age, death, and burial were specifically noted.

VERSE 3

And Abraham stood up from before his dead, and spake unto the sons of Heth, saying,

VERSE 4

I *am* **a stranger and a sojourner with you: give me a possession of a buryingplace with you, that I may bury my dead out of my sight.**

VERSE 5

And the children of Heth answered Abraham, saying unto him,

VERSE 6

Hear us, my lord: thou *art* **a mighty prince among us: in the choice of our sepulchres bury thy dead; none of us shall withhold from thee his sepulchre, but that thou mayest bury thy dead.**

VERSE 7

And Abraham stood up, and bowed himself to the people of the land, *even* to the children of Heth.

VERSE 8

And he communed with them, saying, If it be your mind that I should bury my dead out of my sight; hear me, and entreat for me to Ephron the son of Zohar,

VERSE 9

That he may give me the cave of Machpelah, which he hath, which *is* in the end of his field; for as much money as it is worth he shall give it me for a possession of a buryingplace amongst you.

Abraham didn't ask for the plot as a gift; he said he would pay Ephron's asking price.

VERSE 10

And Ephron dwelt among the children of Heth: and Ephron the Hittite answered Abraham in the audience of the children of Heth, *even* of all that went in at the gate of his city, saying,

VERSE 11

Nay, my lord, hear me: the field give I thee, and the cave that *is* therein, I give it thee; in the presence of the sons of my people give I it thee: bury thy dead.

A generous offer indeed. Ephron offered free of charge not only the cave but also the field where the cave was.

VERSE 12

And Abraham bowed down himself before the people of the land.

The people of the land—the sons of Heth—were Hittites. The

Hittites originated from Noah's great-grandson Heth, through Ham and Canaan, and were sometimes referred to as the "sons of Heth." Although not as well known as other ancient empires (e.g., Egypt, Assyria, Babylon, Greece, Persia, and Rome), at the peak of their power, the Hittites challenged the Egyptians and Assyrians for control of what is now Israel.

The Hittite Kingdom was at its peak from about 1750 BC to about 1180 BC. Hittites were known especially for their chariots and ironwork, though their weapons were made of bronze because iron was scarce and used almost exclusively for jewelry.

VERSE 13

And he spake unto Ephron in the audience of the people of the land, saying, But if thou *wilt give it*, **I pray thee, hear me: I will give thee money for the field; take** *it* **of me, and I will bury my dead there.**

For his own reasons, Abraham wanted to purchase the land rather than have it as a gift.

VERSE 14

And Ephron answered Abraham, saying unto him,

VERSE 15

My lord, hearken unto me: the land is *worth* **four hundred shekels of silver; what** *is* **that betwixt me and thee? Bury therefore thy dead.**

VERSE 16

And Abraham hearkened unto Ephron; and Abraham weighed to Ephron the silver, which he had named in the audience of the sons of Heth, four hundred shekels of silver, current *money* **with the merchant.**

An interesting exchange here: Ephron offered the cave and the field as gifts after Abraham had requested only the cave, and Abraham refused to take it for nothing (probably knowing the offer had been made with the expectation of something in return). Ephron then named a price for both field and cave. Ephron got top dollar for the sale, and Abraham got a family sepulcher and a field, which turned out to be the only land Abraham owned.

VERSE 17

> **And the field of Ephron, which** *was* **in Machpelah, which** *was* **before Mamre, the field, and the cave which** *was* **therein, and all the trees which** *were* **in the field, that** *were* **in all the borders round about, were made sure**

VERSE 18

> **Unto Abraham for a possession in the presence of the children of Heth, before all that went in at the gate of his city.**

This verse is a continuation of verse 17. There is no reason for the division.

VERSE 19

> **And after this, Abraham buried Sarah his wife in the cave of the field of Machpelah before Mamre: the same** *is* **Hebron in the field of Canaan.**

VERSE 20

> **And the field, and the cave that** *is* **therein, were made sure unto Abraham for a possession of a buryingplace by the sons of Heth.**

CHAPTER TWENTY-FOUR

VERSE 1

And Abraham was old, *and* well stricken in age: and the Lord had blessed Abraham in all things.

VERSE 2

And Abraham said unto his eldest servant of his house, that ruled over all that he had, Put, I pray thee, thy hand under my thigh:

VERSE 3

And I will make thee swear by the Lord, the God of heaven, and the God of the earth, that thou shalt not take a wife unto my son of the daughters of the Canaanites, among whom I dwell:

VERSE 4

But thou shalt go unto my country, and to my kindred, and take a wife unto my son Isaac.

Marriages were customarily arranged by the parents, often among first cousins, to preserve family bloodlines and traditions. Since Abraham was too old and feeble to make the journey himself, he relegated the responsibility to Eliezer. Though he entrusted Eliezer with the management of his estate, he made him swear an oath to do his bidding in this matter. He had a strong desire to see his son marry one of his own kind. He feared that if he didn't, his son could perhaps become influenced by his wife to stray from his father's faith.

This was a concern throughout the early development of Israel no doubt caused by the fact that very often then as now, one or the other in a marriage would abandon the faith in which he or she was raised and convert to that of the spouse.

VERSE 5

> And the servant said unto him, Peradventure the woman will not be willing to follow me unto this land: must I needs bring thy son again unto the land from whence thou camest?

VERSE 6

> And Abraham said unto him, Beware thou that thou bring not my son thither again.

VERSE 7

> The Lord God of heaven, which took me from my father's house, and from the land of my kindred, and which spake unto me, and that sware unto me, saying, Unto thy seed will I give this land; he shall send his angel before thee, and thou shalt take a wife unto my son from thence.

VERSE 8

> And if the woman will not be willing to follow thee, then thou shalt be clear from this my oath: only bring not my son thither again.

VERSE 9

> And the servant put his hand under the thigh of Abraham his master, and sware to him concerning that matter.

Abraham's faith was strong enough to assure him only one trip was necessary.

The next fifty-seven verses describe the journey of Eliezer to the city of Nahor with all the trappings and wedding gifts necessary for a ceremonial marriage arrangement. His meeting with Rebekah and her family and his dealings with Rebekah's brother Laban were so well detailed that they present a clear, vivid picture of what took place and confirm that much of what is in Genesis is the result of an eyewitness account. The writer may not have been the eyewitness, but it is obvious that he recorded the words of someone who had been.

VERSE 10

> And the servant took ten camels of the camels of his master, and departed; for all the goods of his master *were* in his hand: and he arose, and went to Mesopotamia, unto the city of Nahor.

Nahor was the city of Abraham's birth, named after his grandfather. A caravan of ten camels is large, so the gifts and goods Eliezer carried were many.

VERSE 11

> And he made his camels to kneel down without the city by a well of water at the time of the evening, *even* the time that women go out to draw *water*:

VERSE 12

> And he said, O Lord God of my master Abraham, I pray thee, send me good speed this day, and shew kindness unto my master Abraham.

Eliezer was from Damascus. According to the Targums, he was the son of Nimrod and obviously followed his own religion. But here he prayed to the God of Abraham because he was on Abraham's business. Eliezer means "Help of my God" in Hebrew.

He is one of three named Eliezer in the Bible. The second was the second son of Moses and his wife Zipporah (Exodus 18:4), and the third was a prophet who was a son of Dodavah, noted for his rebuke of King Jehosophat (2 Chronicles 20:37).

VERSE 13

> Behold, I stand *here* by the well of water; and the daughters of the men of the city come out to draw water:

The community well in those days was similar to the saloon in the Wild West; it was a gathering place for locals and a great place to obtain information. As in the Wild West, travelers could exchange information about the road ahead or learn about the residents. Oftentimes, they had only to observe and listen to gain whatever knowledge they desired.

VERSE 14

And let it come to pass, that the damsel to whom I shall say, Let down thy pitcher, I pray thee, that I may drink; and she shall say, Drink, and I will give thy camels drink also: *let the same be* **she** *that* **thou hast appointed for thy servant Isaac; and thereby shall I know that thou hast shewed kindness unto my master.**

VERSE 15

And it came to pass, before he had done speaking, that, behold, Rebekah came out, who was born to Bethuel, son of Milcah, the wife of Nahor, Abraham's brother, with her pitcher upon her shoulder.

VERSE 16

And the damsel *was* **very fair to look upon, a virgin, neither had any man known her: and she went down to the well, and filled her pitcher, and came up.**

VERSE 17

And the servant ran to meet her, and said, Let me, I pray thee, drink a little water of thy pitcher.

VERSE 18

And she said, Drink, my lord: and she hasted, and let down her pitcher upon her hand, and gave him drink.

VERSE 19

> And when she had done giving him drink, she said, I will draw *water* for thy camels also, until they have done drinking.

VERSE 20

> And she hasted, and emptied her pitcher into the trough, and ran again to the well to draw water, and drew for all his camels.

VERSE 21

> And the man wondering at her held his peace, to wit whether the Lord had made his journey prosperous or not.

VERSE 22

> And it came to pass, as the camels had done drinking, that the man took a golden earring of half a shekel weight, and two bracelets for her hands of ten *shekels* weight of gold;

VERSE 23

> And said, Whose daughter *art* thou? tell me, I pray thee: is there room *in* thy father's house for us to lodge in?

VERSE 24

> And she said unto him, I *am* the daughter of Bethuel the son of Milcah, which she bare unto Nahor.

VERSE 25

> She said moreover unto him, We have both straw and provender enough, and room to lodge in.

VERSE 26

And the man bowed down his head, and worshipped the Lord.

Although Eliezer was not of the same faith as Abraham, this experience seems to have converted him. At least he recognized the power of Abraham's God.

VERSE 27

And he said, blessed *be* **the Lord God of my master Abraham, who hath not left destitute my master of his mercy and his truth: I** *being* **in the way, the Lord led me to the house of my master's brethren.**

VERSE 28

And the damsel ran, and told *them* **of her mother's house these things.**

In the next verses, we meet Rebekah's brother Laban. He seems materialistic, but he and the rest of the family shared Abraham's faith. He was a gracious host.

The description of the marriage bargaining was typical except that Laban was involved as well as Bethuel, Rebekah's father, who under normal circumstances would have made the arrangements. We don't learn why Laban was involved, but it could have been that Bethuel was advanced in age and relied on Laban's help in family matters. At any rate, the negotiations were conducted by the men only without consultation with the mother or the prospective bride.

VERSE 29

And Rebekah had a brother, and his name *was* **Laban: and Laban ran out unto the man, unto the well.**

VERSE 30

And it came to pass, when he saw the earring and bracelets upon his sister's hands, and when he heard the words of Rebekah his sister, saying,

Thus spake the man unto me; that he came unto the man; and, behold, he stood by the camels at the well.

VERSE 31

And he said, Come in, thou blessed of the Lord; wherefore standest thou without? For I have prepared the house, and room for the camels.

VERSE 32

And the man came into the house: and he ungirded his camels, and gave straw and provender for the camels, and water to wash his feet, and the men's feet that *were* with him.

VERSE 33

And there was set *meat* before him to eat: but he said, I will not eat, until I have told mine errand. And he said, Speak on.

VERSE 34

And he said, I *am* Abraham's servant.

VERSE 35

And the Lord hath blessed my master greatly; and he is become great: and he hath given him flocks, and herds, and silver, and gold, and manservants, and maidservants, and camels, and asses.

VERSE 36

And Sarah my master's wife bare a son to my master when she was old: and unto him hath he given all that he hath.

VERSE 37

And my master made me swear, saying, Thou shalt not take a wife to my son of the daughters of the Canaanites, in whose land I dwell.

VERSE 38

But thou shalt go unto my father's house, and to my kindred, and take a wife unto my son.

VERSE 39

And I said unto my master, Peradventure the woman will not follow me.

VERSE 40

And he said unto me, the Lord, before whom I walk, will send his angel with thee, and prosper thy way; and thou shalt take a wife for my son of my kindred, and of my father's house:

VERSE 41

Then shalt thou be clear from *this* my oath, when thou comest to my kindred; and if they give not thee *one*, thou shalt be clear from my oath.

VERSE 42

And I came this day unto the well, and said, O Lord God of my master Abraham, if now thou do prosper my way which I go:

VERSE 43

Behold, I stand by the well of water; and it shall come to pass, that when the virgin cometh forth to draw *water*, and I say to her, Give me, I pray thee, a little water of thy pitcher to drink;

VERSE 44

And she say to me, Both drink thou, and I will also draw for thy camels; *let* the same *be* the woman whom the Lord hath appointed out for my master's son.

VERSE 45

And before I had done speaking in my heart, behold, Rebekah came forth with her pitcher on her shoulder; and she went down unto the well, and drew *water*: and I said unto her, Let me drink, I pray thee.

VERSE 46

And she made haste, and let down her pitcher from her *shoulder*, and said, Drink, and I will give thy camels drink also: so I drank, and she made the camels drink also.

VERSE 47

And I asked her, and said, Whose daughter *art* thou? And she said, The daughter of Bethuel, Nahor's son, whom Milcah bare unto him: and I put the earring on her face, and the bracelets on her hands.

VERSE 48

And I bowed down my head, and worshipped the Lord, and blessed the Lord God of my master Abraham, which had led me in the right way to take my master's brother's daughter unto his son.

VERSE 49

And now if ye will deal kindly and truly with my master, tell me: and if not, tell me; that I may turn to the right hand, or to the left.

VERSE 50

Then Laban and Bethuel answered and said, the thing proceedeth from the Lord: we cannot speak unto thee bad or good.

VERSE 51

Behold, Rebekah *is* **before thee, take** *her* **and go, and let her be thy master's son's wife, as the Lord hath spoken.**

VERSE 52

And it came to pass, that, when Abraham's servant heard their words, he worshipped the Lord, *bowing himself* **to the earth.**

VERSE 53

And the servant brought forth jewels of silver, and jewels of gold, and raiment, and gave *them* **to Rebekah: he gave also to her brother and to her mother precious things.**

VERSE 54

And they did eat and drink, he and the men that *were* **with him, and tarried all night.; and they rose up in the morning, and he said, Send me away unto my master.**

VERSE 55

And her brother and her mother said, Let the damsel abide with us a *few* **days, at the least ten; after that she shall go.**

VERSE 56

And he said unto them, Hinder me not, seeing the Lord hath prospered my way; send me away that I may go to my master.

VERSE 57

And they said, We will call the damsel, and inquire at her mouth.

VERSE 58

And they called Rebekah, and said unto her, Wilt thou go with this man? And she said, I will go.

VERSE 59

And they sent away Rebekah their sister, and her nurse, and Abraham's servant, and his men.

VERSE 60

And they blessed Rebekah, and said unto her, Thou art **our sister, be thou** the mother **of thousands of millions, and let thy seed possess the gate of those which hate them.**

VERSE 61

And Rebekah arose, and her damsels, and they rode upon the camels, and followed the man: and the servant took Rebekah, and went his way.

VERSE 62

And Isaac came from the way of the well Lahairoi; for he dwelt in the south country.

This is the well mentioned in 16:14 between Kadesh and Bered.

VERSE 63

And Isaac went out to meditate in the field at eventide: and he lifted up his eyes, and saw, and, behold, the camels were **coming.**

VERSE 64

And Rebekah lifted up her eyes, and when she saw Isaac, she lighted off the camel.

VERSE 65

For she had **said unto the servant, What man** is **this that walketh in the field to meet us? And the**

servant *had* said, It *is* my master: therefore she took a veil and covered herself.

VERSE 66

And the servant told Isaac all things that he had done.

VERSE 67

And Isaac brought her into his mother Sarah's tent, and took Rebekah, and she became his wife; and he loved her: and Isaac was comforted after his mother's *death*.

This is not only a beautiful story of Eliezer's dedication to carry out Abraham's wishes. The precise detail coupled with the repetition indicates the accuracy of the account as well as the importance the author placed on the events.

CHAPTER TWENTY-FIVE

VERSE 1

Then again Abraham took a wife, and her name *was* Keturah.

Richard Elliott Friedman (*Commentary on the Torah*, New York: HarperCollins, 2001) called Keturah "the most ignored significant person in the Torah." She was apparently a concubine of Abraham, and there is some controversy as to whether Abraham did in fact ever take her in marriage after Sarah's death. The word translated as "wife" is *ishshaw* and can have several general meanings that don't specifically mean "wife." It could have been translated merely as "woman," and that perhaps is more likely.

The timing may also be misleading; it suggests that all Keturah's children were born after the death of Sarah, when in all probability some or all had been born earlier, while Sarah was still his wife and Keturah was his concubine.

At Sarah's death, Abraham would have been about 137, but since he lived to be 175, there was still time if that's the way it happened. There are good arguments for both sides of the question as to whether Abraham actually married Keturah and if so, whether it was after Sarah's death or during her lifetime. It wasn't uncommon for the patriarchs of that day to have two wives in addition to concubines mainly for the purpose of childbearing.

Keturah is again listed in 1 Chronicles 1:32–33 with a listing of her sons and grandsons, and there she was listed as a concubine. It is believed that her descendants settled in areas farther south and east, in Arabia and parts of Africa.

The Midianites were the most prominent of Keturah's descendants, and they largely integrated with the descendants of Ishmael. Thus, Abraham did indeed become the "father of many nations" because of Sarah, Hagar, and Keturah.

VERSE 2

And she bare him Zimran, and Jokshan, and Medan, and Midian, and Ishbak, and Shuah.

According to the book of Jasher, the children of Zimran were Abihen, Molich, and Narim. With two prior sons, these six, an unmentioned number of daughters, and the additional odd sprinkling of children by concubines as mentioned in verse 6, Abraham seemed to have done his part to fulfill God's commission to spread out and fill the earth.

VERSE 3

And Jokshan begat Sheba, and Dedan. And the sons of Dedan were Asshurim, and Letushim, and Leummim.

VERSE 4

And the sons of Midian: Ephah, and Epher, and Hanoch, and Abidah, and Eldaah. All these *were* **the children of Keturah.**

VERSE 5

And Abraham gave all that he had unto Isaac.

VERSE 6

But unto the sons of the concubines, which Abraham had, Abraham gave gifts, and sent them away from Isaac his son, while he yet lived, eastward, unto the east country.

Josephus wrote, "Abraham contrived to settle them in colonies; and they took possession of Troglodytis and the country of Happy Arabia, as far as it reaches to the Red Sea." Happy Arabia (sometimes Felix Arabia) is modern-day Yemen. The area gets more rainfall and is much greener than the rest of the peninsula and is much more productive. Hence the term Happy Arabia, which originally meant fertile Arabia.

In all probability, Abraham tried to keep all these sons separated from Isaac to avoid conflict while fulfilling God's commission to spread out and inhabit the globe. For such reasons, Zimran, also known as Zambran, has also been tentatively identified by some with the Arabian town of Zabran, between Mecca and Medina.

It is thought that Jokshan peopled part of Arabia, specifically Yemen, and was the person Arabians called Qahtan and acknowledged as the head of their nation.

Not much known about Medan. There seems to be no known connection to the Madan people of Iran and Iraq.

Midian's five sons, Ephah, Epher, Enoch, Abida, and Eldaah, were the progenitors of the Midianites. We know a great deal about them. Their chief city was also named Midian. They became a large, wealthy tribe (Isaiah 60:6) that clashed with Israel on many occasions.

Ishbak is a mystery, with nothing but a vague reference in cuneiform to a people who may or may not have been his descendants.

Shuah is thought to have migrated northward into northern Mesopotamia to what is now part of Syria.

VERSE 7

And these *are* **the days of the years of Abraham's life which he lived, an hundred threescore and fifteen years.**

VERSE 8

Then Abram gave up the ghost, and died in a good old age, an old man, and full *of years***; and was gathered to his people.**

VERSE 9

And his sons Isaac and Ishmael buried him in the cave of Machpelah, in the field of Ephron the son of Zohar the Hittite, which *is* **before Mamre;**

All the other children of Abraham had been sent away before his death, probably to avoid any squabbles over inheritance. It is interesting that Ishmael was allowed to return.

VERSE 10

The field which Abraham purchased of the sons of Heth: there was Abraham buried, and Sarah his wife.

VERSE 11

And it came to pass after the death of Abraham, that God blessed his son Isaac; and Isaac dwelt by the well Lahairoi.

VERSE 12

Now these *are* the generations of Ishmael, Abraham's son, whom Hagar the Egyptian, Sarah's handmaid, bare unto Abraham:

VERSE 13

And these *are* the names of the sons of Ishmael, by their names, according to their generations: the firstborn of Ishmael, Nebajoth; and Kedar, and Adbeel, and Mibsam,

VERSE 14

And Mishma, and Dumah, and Massa,

VERSE 15

Hadar, and Tema, Jetur, Naphish, and Kedemah:

VERSE 16

These *are* the sons of Ishmael, and these *are* their names, by their towns, and by their castles; twelve princes according to their nations.

It's interesting that both Isaac and Ishmael had twelve sons, each of whom later became the leader of a separate group.

VERSE 17

And these *are* the years of the life of Ishmael, an hundred and thirty and seven years: and he gave

up the ghost and died; and was gathered unto his people.

VERSE 18

And they dwelt from Havilah unto Shur, that *is* before Egypt, as thou goest toward Assyria: *and* he died in the presence of all his brethren.

Apparently, Ishmael's family stayed together for a considerable time and grew larger and stronger in the area they occupied, a large, mostly desert area in the northern Sinai Peninsula on the northeastern border of Egypt, perhaps stretching into northwest Arabia.

VERSE 19

And *these are* the generations of Isaac, Abraham's son: Abraham begat Isaac:

VERSE 20

And Isaac was forty years old when he took Rebekah to wife, the daughter of Bethuel the Syrian of Padanaram, the sister to Laban the Syrian.

VERSE 21

And Isaac entreated the Lord for his wife, because she *was* barren: and the Lord was entreated of him, and Rebekah his wife conceived.

Here is a similar situation to that of Adam and Eve in that the result of the one conception was twins. I'm convinced Cain and Abel were twins, though probably not identical.

VERSE 22

And the children struggled together within her; and she said, If *it be* so, why *am* I thus? And she went to inquire of the Lord.

VERSE 23

And the Lord said unto her, Two nations *are* in thy womb, and two manner of people shall be

separated from thy bowels; and *the one* **people shall be stronger than** *the other* **people; and the elder shall serve the younger.**

VERSE 24

And when her days to be delivered were fulfilled, behold *there were* **twins in her womb.**

VERSE 25

And the first came out red, all over like an hairy garment; and they called his name Esau.

It was very important to establish which twin was born first; he would get a double inheritance and would become the family priest and head of the household upon the death of their father.

VERSE 26

And after that came his brother out, and his hand took hold of Esau's heel; and his name was called Jacob: and Isaac *was* **threescore years old when she bare them.**

VERSE 27

And the boys grew: and Esau was a cunning hunter, a man of the field; and Jacob *was* **a plain man, dwelling in tents.**

The word for "plain" is *tâm*, and I believe this is the only time it was translated as "plain." Its normal usage is "pure," "perfect," "pious," or "complete," any of which might have been a better translation. We are left to wonder exactly what Jacob's temperament and characteristics were. It's been speculated that he was a shepherd.

VERSE 28

And Isaac loved Esau, because he did eat of *his* **venison; but Rebekah loved Jacob.**

There's probably more involved here than just the eating of venison. I would guess that Esau was a little more virile and manly than Jacob, which would appeal to his father, while his mother would favor a less manly, possibly more studious son.

VERSE 29

And Jacob sod pottage: and Esau came from the field, and he *was* faint:

The term *sod pottage* is interesting. Pottage of course means simply a thick soup or stew. It comes from a root meaning *pot* and refers to anything cooked in a pot. The word *sod* causes confusion. As it was used here, it meant "to boil" or "cook." This is the only time the word *zûwd* was translated this way however; it usually means "to seethe" or "to be very proud." *Sod* is apparently an Old English word, and it's used only one other time in the King James translation (2 Chronicles 35:13); there, it also clearly means to cook as with a stew, although the word translated there as sod is *bûshal.*

VERSE 30

And Esau said to Jacob, Feed me, I pray thee, with that same red *pottage*; for I *am* faint: therefore was his name called Edom.

Esau's name in Hebrew means "hairy," and according to Genesis 25:25, it's a reference to his hairiness at birth. He is also called Edom, which means red. The land of Edom is said to be mostly a red dirt or clay, so perhaps the name was derived from that.

VERSE 31

And Jacob said, Sell me this day thy birthright.

VERSE 32

And Esau said, Behold, I *am* at the point to die: and what profit shall this birthright do to me?

VERSE 33

And Jacob said, Swear to me this day; and he sware unto him: and he sold his birthright unto Jacob.

VERSE 34

Then Jacob gave Esau bread and pottage of lentils; and he did eat and drink, and rose up, and went his way: thus Esau despised *his* birthright.

The word for despised here is *bâzâh*; it would probably be better translated as "scorned" or "treated with contempt." Jacob later complained that Esau had taken his birthright, so we know he valued it even though he had let it go in a time of weakness.

CHAPTER TWENTY-SIX

VERSE 1

And there was a famine in the land, beside the first famine that was in the days of Abraham. And Isaac went unto Abimelech king of the Philistines unto Gerar.

Famines were fairly common in those days due mainly to lack of proper irrigation in times of little rainfall, and, of course, pest infestations and other natural hardships. The cycle of feast and famine repeated itself.

This is not the same Abimelech with whom Abraham dealt. The name translates as "my father is king" and was used by many Philistine kings of that era. The Haggada identifies the two references to Abimelech as two separate people, the second being the first Abimelech's son.

VERSE 2

And the Lord appeared unto him, and said, Go not down into Egypt; dwell in the land which I shall tell thee of:

VERSE 3

Sojourn in this land, and I will be with thee, and will bless thee; for unto thee, and unto thy seed, I will give all these countries, and I will perform the oath which I sware unto Abraham thy father;

VERSE 4

And I will make thy seed to multiply as the stars in heaven, and will give unto thy seed all these countries; and in thy seed shall all the nations of the earth be blessed;

VERSE 5

Because that Abraham obeyed my voice, and kept my charge, my commandments, my statutes, and my laws.

VERSE 6

And Isaac dwelt in Gerar:

Gerar was in the western Negev Desert about nine miles southeast of Gaza and fifteen miles northwest of Beersheba. It was near the southern end of the Philistine coastal plain on the inland route of the International Coastal Highway.[8] Its specific location is controversial; the most likely site is Tel Haror.

VERSE 7

And the men of the place asked *him* **of his wife; and he said, She** *is* **my sister, for he feared to say,** *She is* **my wife; lest,** *said he,* **the men of the place should kill me for Rebekah; because she** *was* **fair to look upon.**

Here, Isaac used the same ruse Abraham had used twice, but not with the same king; this was nearly a century later. Aa mentioned previously, Abimelech was the name of at least two kings of Philistia, one a contemporary of Abraham, and the other probably son of the former in the days of Isaac. It's also possible that Abimelech was the royal title rather than the personal name, much the same as Pharaoh was the title in Egypt.

This becomes one of the earliest recorded instances of the application of the adage "If it ain't broke, don't fix it" because in every instance after the subterfuge was discovered, good things happened, first to Abraham and then to Isaac, and no punishment for either deception was meted out. In fact, both turned out very profitably.

VERSE 8

And it came to pass, when he had been there a long time, that Abimelech king of the Philistines

looked out at a window, and saw, and, behold, Isaac *was* sporting with Rebekah his wife.

The word used here for "sporting" is *tsâchaq*, to "play" or "laugh." It's also the root word of the name Isaac.

VERSE 9

And Abimelech called Isaac, and said, Behold, of a surety she *is* thy wife: and how saidst thou, She *is* my sister? And Isaac said unto him, Because I said, Lest I die for her.

VERSE 10

And Abimelech said, What *is* this thou hast done unto us? One of the people might lightly have lien with thy wife, and thou shouldest have brought guiltiness upon us.

VERSE 11

And Abimelech charged all *his* people, saying, He that toucheth this man or his wife shall surely be put to death.

VERSE 12

Then Isaac sowed in that land, and received in the same year an hundredfold: and the Lord blessed him.

VERSE 13

And the man waxed great, and went forward, and grew until he became very great.

VERSE 14

For he had possession of flocks, and possession of herds, and great store of servants: and the Philistines envied him.

184 | PHILLIP M. BRANSON

VERSE 15

For all the wells which his father's servants had digged in the days of Abraham his father, the Philistines had stopped them, and filled them with earth.

It is difficult to understand why something like this would have been done in a land where water was so precious a commodity, especially in light of the present knowledge based on archaeological evidence that shows the Philistines were a highly advanced culture with political, technological, and artistic superiority.

However, according to the *Commentary on the Whole Bible* by Jamieson, Fausset, and Brown, "The same base stratagem for annoying those against whom they have taken an umbrage is practiced still by choking the wells with sand or stones, or defiling them with putrid carcasses."

The origin of the Philistines seems to be somewhat in doubt, but most scholars believe they were part of the nomadic group that became known as the Sea Peoples, who were originally part of the Mycenaean civilization of Greece, which existed from c.1600 BC to c.1100 BC. They were nomadic sailors who roamed the Mediterranean. They tried to settle in Egypt, but Ramses III drove them out. They finally settled in this area between Egypt and Judah.

VERSE 16

And Abimelech said unto Isaac, Go from us; for thou art much mightier than we.

I believe the word translated as "mightier," *'âwtsam*, could have better been translated as "more prosperous." Either that or the meaning is that individually Isaac and his family were stronger than Abimelech's people. They were certainly no threat collectively to the Philistines.

VERSE 17

And Isaac departed thence, and pitched his tent in the valley of Gerar, and dwelt there.

It's unclear just how far Gerar was from the Valley of Gerar, but we can assume it was relatively close. Isaac may have been living in the city and simply moved out to where he kept his flocks and herds. The Valley of Gerar was probably the modern Wadi el-Jerdr. The area was a rich pastoral country (2 Chronicles 14:12–18).

VERSE 18

And Isaac digged again the wells of water, which they had digged in the days of Abraham his father; for the Philistines had stopped them after the death of Abraham: and he called their names after the names by which his father had called them.

VERSE 19

And Isaac's servants digged in the valley, and found there a well of springing water.

VERSE 20

And the herdmen of Gerar did strive with Isaac's herdmen, saying, The water *is* ours: and he called the name of the well Esek; because they strove with him.

So apparently, some of the subjects of Abimelech realized the value of the wells. Perhaps the king had the wells stopped up out of spite or malice without regard for his own people's welfare.

VERSE 21

And they digged another well, and strove for that also: and he called the name of it Sitnah.

The name is derived from a root word *satam*, meaning "to attack," "accuse," "be in opposition to."

VERSE 22

And he removed from thence, and digged another well; and for that they strove not: and he called the name of it Rehoboth; and he said, For now

the Lord hath made room for us, and we shall be fruitful in the land.

Rehoboth is apparently a word derived from a combination of words whose roots mean "avenue" or "broad place."

VERSE 23

And he went up from thence to Beersheba.

VERSE 24

And the Lord appeared unto him the same night, and said, I am **the God of Abraham thy father: fear not, for I** am **with thee, and I will bless thee, and multiply thy seed for my servant Abraham's sake.**

VERSE 25

And he builded an altar there, and called upon the name of the Lord, and pitched his tent there: and there Isaac's servants digged a well.

VERSE 26

Then Abimelech went to him from Gerar, and Ahuzzath one of his friends, and Phichol the chief captain of his army.

VERSE 27

And Isaac said unto them, Wherefore come ye to me, seeing ye hate me, and have sent me away from you?

VERSE 28

And they said, We saw certainly that the Lord was with thee: and we said, Let there be now an oath betwixt us, even **betwixt us and thee, and let us make a covenant with thee;**

VERSE 29

> That thou wilt do us no hurt, as we have not touched thee, and as we have done unto thee nothing but good, and have sent thee away in peace: thou *art* now the blessed of the Lord.

VERSE 30

> And he made them a feast, and they did eat and drink.

VERSE 31

> And they rose up betimes in the morning, and sware one to another: and Isaac sent them away, and they departed from him in peace.

VERSE 32

> And it came to pass the same day, that Isaac's servants came, and told him concerning the well which they had digged, and said unto him, We have found water.

VERSE 33

> And he called it Shebah: therefore the name of the city *is* Beersheba unto this day.

Shebah means "seven" or "seventh." This was apparently the seventh well Isaac's servants had dug for him.

VERSE 34

> And Esau was forty years old when he took to wife Judith the daughter of Beeri the Hittite, and Bashemath the daughter of Elon the Hittite:

VERSE 35

> Which were a grief of mind unto Isaac and to Rebekah.

Isaac was then a hundred. Not much had been said about Esau or

Jacob from the time they were young boys until this point, when they were 40. The marriage of Esau to two women who were considered heathens in the sight of Isaac and Rebekah had to have been a severe blow to Isaac even though Esau was his favorite.

CHAPTER TWENTY-SEVEN

VERSE 1

And it came to pass, that when Isaac was old, and his eyes were dim, so that he could not see, he called Esau his eldest son, and said unto him, My son: and he said unto him, Behold, *here am* **I.**

VERSE 2

And he said, Behold now, I am old, I know not the day of my death:

VERSE 3

Now therefore take, I pray thee, thy weapons, thy quiver and thy bow, and go out to the field, and take me *some* **venison;**

VERSE 4

And make me savoury meat, such as I love, and bring *it* **to me, that I may eat; that my soul may bless thee before I die.**

Isaac was about 137 at the time of the blessings. That would have meant Esau was about 77. Other calculations put Isaac at about 123, making Jacob and Esau about 63. At any rate, Esau and Jacob were no longer children. But their parents still maintained their favoritism, the mother for Jacob and the father for Esau.

What happened next was a complicated scheme of deception and trickery planned by Rebekah and perpetrated by Jacob. Rebekah firmly believed Jacob should receive Isaac's blessing and the inheritance. She apparently also believed that to achieve this goal, the end justified the means.

While Jacob was somewhat reluctant to go through with the deception (more from the fear of being discovered than because of moral or ethical inhibitions), he agreed after a rather feeble protest.

Was there divine intervention here? Who knows? But we do know two things. First, God knew what was going to take place, because He had told Rebekah before the twins had been born (25:23) that the older son would serve the younger. Second, God loved the works of the Israelites—the descendants of Jacob—and hated the works of the Edomites—the descendants of Esau (Malachi 1:3; Romans 9:13). In Hebrews 12:16, Paul described Esau as profane.

The rest of the chapter deals with the deception and its consequences.

VERSE 5

And Rebekah heard when Isaac spoke to Esau his son. And Esau went to the field to hunt *for* **venison,** *and* **to bring** *it.*

VERSE 6

And Rebekah spake unto Jacob her son, saying, Behold, I heard thy father speak unto Esau thy brother, saying,

VERSE 7

Bring me venison, and make me savoury meat, that I may eat, and bless thee before the Lord before my death.

VERSE 8

Now therefore, my son, obey my voice according to that which I command thee.

VERSE 9

Go now to the flock, and fetch me from thence two good kids of the goats; and I will make them savoury meat for thy father, such as he loveth:

VERSE 10

And thou shalt bring *it* **to thy father, that he may eat, and that he may bless thee before his death.**

VERSE 11

> And Jacob said to Rebekah his mother, Behold, Esau my brother *is* a hairy man, and I *am* a smooth man:

VERSE 12

> My father peradventure will feel me, and I shall seem to him a deceiver; and I shall bring a curse upon me, and not a blessing.

VERSE 13

> And his mother said unto him, Upon me *be* thy curse, my son: only obey my voice, and go fetch me *them*.

VERSE 14

> And he went, and fetched, and brought *them* to his mother: and his mother made savoury meat, such as his father loved.

VERSE 15

> And Rebekah took goodly raiment of her eldest son Esau, which *were* with her in the house, and put them upon Jacob her younger son:

VERSE 16

> And she put the skins of the kids of the goats upon his hands, and upon the smooth of his neck:

VERSE 17

> And she gave the savoury meat and the bread, which she had prepared, into the hand of her son Jacob.

VERSE 18

> And he came unto his father, and said, my father: and he said, Here *am* I; who *art* thou, my son?

VERSE 19

And Jacob said unto his father, I *am* **Esau thy firstborn; I have done according as thou badest me: arise, I pray thee, sit and eat of my venison, that thy soul may bless me.**

VERSE 20

And Isaac said unto his son, How *is it* **that thou hast found** *it* **so quickly, my son? And he said, Because the Lord thy God brought** *it* **to me.**

Jacob worshiped the same god Isaac did, but here, he used the expression "your God," which is probably what Esau would have said. This is further proof that Esau had adopted the idol worship of his wives.

VERSE 21

And Isaac said unto Jacob, Come near, I pray thee, that I may feel thee, my son, whether thou *be* **my very son Esau or not.**

Perhaps Isaac noticed a difference in the voice or some other strangeness, because he seemed to suspect he was speaking to someone other than Esau.

VERSE 22

And Jacob went near unto Isaac his father; and he felt him, and said, The voice *is* **Jacob's voice, but the hands** *are* **the hands of Esau.**

VERSE 23

And he discerned him not, because his hands were hairy, as his brother Esau's hands: so he blessed him.

VERSE 24

And he said, *Art* **thou my very son Esau? And he said, I** *am.*

VERSE 25

> And he said, bring *it* near to me, and I will eat of my son's venison, that my soul may bless thee. And he brought *it* near to him, and he did eat: and he brought him wine, and he drank.

It must have been that the method of cooking venison and kid were so similar that it was impossible to tell one from the other.

VERSE 26

> And his father Isaac said unto him, Come near now, and kiss me, my son.

VERSE 27

> And he came near, and kissed him: and he smelled the smell of his raiment, and blessed him, and said, See, the smell of my son *is* as the smell of a field which the Lord hath blessed:

VERSE 28

> Therefore God give thee of the dew of heaven, and the fatness of the earth, and plenty of corn and wine:

The first part of the blessing was for personal success and prosperity.

VERSE 29

> Let people serve thee, and nations bow down to thee: be lord over thy brethren, and let thy mother's sons bow down to thee: cursed *be* every one that curseth thee, and blessed *be* he that blesseth thee.

The second half of the blessing was more for future generations.

VERSE 30

> And it came to pass, as soon as Isaac had made an end of blessing Jacob, and Jacob was yet scarce

gone out from the presence of Isaac his father, that Esau his brother came in from his hunting.

VERSE 31

And he also had made savoury meat, and brought it unto his father, and said unto his father, Let my father arise, and eat of his son's venison, that thy soul may bless me.

VERSE 32

And Isaac his father said unto him, Who *art* thou? And he said, I *am* thy son, thy firstborn Esau.

VERSE 33

And Isaac trembled very exceedingly, and said, Who? Where *is* he that hath taken venison, and bought *it* me, and I have eaten of all before thou camest, and have blessed him? yea, *and* he shall be blessed.

VERSE 34

And when Esau heard the words of his father, he cried with a great and exceeding bitter cry, and said unto his father, Bless me, *even* me also, O my father.

VERSE 35

And he said, Thy brother came with subtilty, and hath taken away thy blessing.

VERSE 36

And he said, Is not he rightly named Jacob? for he hath supplanted me these two times: he took away my birthright; and, behold, now he hath taken away my blessing. And he said, Hast thou not reserved a blessing for me?

VERSE 37

And Isaac answered and said unto Esau, Behold, I have made him thy lord, and all his brethren have I given to him for servants; and with corn and wine have I sustained him: and what shall I do now unto thee, my son?

VERSE 38

And Esau said unto his father, Hast thou but one blessing, my father? Bless me, *even* **me also, O my father. And Esau lifted up his voice and wept.**

VERSE 39

And Isaac his father answered and said unto him, Behold, thy dwelling shall be the fatness of the earth, and of the dew of heaven from above,

VERSE 40

And by thy sword shalt thou live, and shalt serve thy brother; and it shall come to pass when thou shalt have the dominion, that thou shalt break his yoke from off thy neck.

VERSE 41

And Esau hated Jacob because of the blessing wherewith his father blessed him: and Esau said in his heart, The days of mourning for my father are at hand; then will I slay my brother Jacob.

VERSE 42

And these words of Esau her elder son were told to Rebekah: and she sent and called Jacob her younger son, and said unto him, Behold, thy brother Esau, as touching thee, doth comfort himself, *purposing* **to kill thee.**

VERSE 43

Now therefore, my son, obey my voice; and arise, flee thou to Laban my brother to Haran;

VERSE 44

And tarry with him a few days, until thy brother's fury turn away:

VERSE 45

Until thy brother's anger turn away from thee, and he forget *that* **which thou hast done to him: then I will send, and fetch thee from thence: why should I be deprived also of you both in one day?**

VERSE 46

And Rebekah said to Isaac, I am weary of life because of the daughters of Heth: if Jacob take a wife of the daughters of Heth, such as these *which are* **of the daughters of the land, what good shall my life do me?**

The daughters of Heth, of course, were the Hittite women Esau had married. While Esau's marriages obviously vexed Rebekah, the real reason for this conversation appears to have been her concern for Jacob's safety. By a somewhat subtle means, she was able to persuade Isaac he should send Jacob away to find a suitable wife for himself. In fact, she said just enough so that Isaac was convinced that sending Jacob away was his own idea, a stratagem I believe that is still practiced by many wives to this day.

CHAPTER TWENTY-EIGHT

VERSE 1

And Isaac called Jacob, and blessed him, and charged him, and said unto him, Thou shalt not take a wife of the daughters of Canaan.

VERSE 2

Arise, go to Padanaram, to the house of Bethuel thy mother's father; and take thee a wife from thence of the daughters of Laban thy mother's brother.

A marriage to a first cousin was deemed quite appropriate at that time.

VERSE 3

And God Almighty bless thee, and make thee fruitful, and multiply thee, that thou mayest be a multitude of people;

VERSE 4

And give thee the blessing of Abraham, to thee, and to thy seed with thee; that thou mayest inherit the land wherein thou art a stranger, which God gave unto Abraham.

This is the completion of Isaac's blessing, passing on God's promise to Abraham through Jacob rather than through Esau. This is after Isaac had learned of Jacob's deceit.

VERSE 5

And Isaac sent away Jacob: and he went to Padanaram unto Laban, son of Bethuel the Syrian, the brother of Rebekah, Jacob's and Esau's mother.

VERSE 6

When Esau saw that Isaac had blessed Jacob, and sent him away to Padanaram, to take him a wife from thence; and that as he blessed him he gave him a charge, saying, Thou shalt not take a wife of the daughters of Canaan;

VERSE 7

And that Jacob obeyed his father and mother, and was gone to Padanaram;

VERSE 8

And Esau seeing that the daughters of Canaan pleased not Isaac his father;

VERSE 9

Then went Esau unto Ishmael, and took unto the wives which he had Mahalath the daughter of Ishmael Abraham's son, the sister of Nebajoth, to his wife.

In an attempt to gain back some favor from his parents, Esau took a third wife, this time from Abraham's line. She was his cousin, but more important, she was from Ishmael's side of the family. If Isaac and Rebekah did in fact approve of this union, the approval was never recorded.

VERSE 10

And Jacob went out from Beersheba, and went toward Haran.

VERSE 11

And he lighted upon a certain place, and tarried there all night, because the sun was set; and he took of the stones of that place, and put *them for* his pillows, and lay down in that place to sleep.

VERSE 12

> **And he dreamed, and behold a ladder set up on the earth, and the top of it reached to heaven: and behold the angels of God ascending and descending on it.**

There have been a great many interpretations of this passage and of the meaning of the ladder. It's one of the most recognizable stories from the Old Testament, but it was after all a dream, probably prophetic of what was to come. In the New Testament (John 1:51), Jesus spoke to Nathaniel: "Hereafter ye shall see Heaven open, and the angels of God ascending and descending upon the son of man." This would indicate to me that the meaning was that Jesus was Himself the ladder that ascended to heaven.

VERSE 13

> **And, behold, the Lord stood above it, and said, I** *am* **the Lord God of Abraham thy father, and the God of Isaac: the land whereon thou liest, to thee will I give it and to thy seed;**

VERSE 14

> **And thy seed shall be as the dust of the earth, and thou shalt spread abroad to the west, and to the east, and to the north, and to the south: and in thee and in thy seed shall all the families of the earth be blessed.**

There certainly can be no denying that this prophecy has been fulfilled and is continuing to be satisfied when one considers the enormous number of contributions in every field of science and the humanities made by the Jewish people.

VERSE 15

> **And, behold, I** *am* **with thee, and will keep thee in all** *places***, whither thou goest, and will bring thee again into this land; for I will not leave thee, until I have done** *that* **which I have spoken to thee of.**

This prophecy was fulfilled on May 14, 1948, with the birth of Israel as a nation.

VERSE 16

And Jacob awaked out of his sleep, and he said, Surely the Lord is in this place; and I knew *it* not.

VERSE 17

And he was afraid, and said, How dreadful *is* this place! This *is* none other but the house of God, and this *is* the gate of heaven.

The word translated as dreadful is *yawray* from a root meaning to fear or dread. But it can also mean to revere, and I believe that is closer to what is meant here.

VERSE 18

And Jacob rose up early in the morning, and took the stone that he had put *for* his pillows, and set it up *for* a pillar, and poured oil upon the top of it.

VERSE 19

And he called the name of that place Beth-el: but the name of the city *was called* Luz at the first.

Bethel (sometimes spelled Beth-el) literally translated means "House of God." Luz was the name left over from the Canaanite occupation and was either in the same location or very nearby. According to this passage and also Judges 1:23, they are the same city. There was a later city built in the land of the Hittites (Judges 1:26) also named Luz.

VERSE 20

And Jacob vowed a vow, saying, If God will be with me, and will keep me in this way that I go, and will give me bread to eat, and raiment to put on,

VERSE 21

**So that I come again to my father's house in peace;
then shall the Lord be my God:**

VERSE 22

And this stone, which I have set *for* **a pillar, shall
be God's house: and of all that thou shalt give me
I will surely give the tenth unto thee.**

These last three verses sound a little condescending on Jacob's part and make him sound as if he were listing a precondition for his faith, but that wasn't the case. The word translated as "if" in Verse 20 is *eem*, a word used in a multitude of ways and would better have been translated as "seeing that" or "since." In that context, the passages make perfect sense and convey the true feelings of Jacob, which were a profound acceptance and faith. This is another instance where the Bible means what it says and says what it means but presents the opportunity for misinterpretation.

CHAPTER TWENTY-NINE

**Then Jacob went on his journey, and came into the
land of the people of the east.**

The land of the people of the east was most likely the land formerly
known as Mesopotamia, the region of the Tigris and Euphrates Rivers
in southwestern Asia. The region extends northwestward from the
Persian Gulf through the center of modern Iraq. It includes the eastern
part of Syria and a small part of southeastern Turkey, where the two
rivers have their sources. Alexander the Great gave Mesopotamia—
Greek for "land between the rivers"—its name. Jacob's journey then
was a trek of approximately four hundred miles.

VERSE 2

**And he looked, and behold a well in the field, and,
lo, there *were* three flocks of sheep lying by it;
for out of that well they watered the flocks: and a
great stone *was* upon the well's mouth.**

The water table is high in this area, so wells would have been
common, as they still are. That the water was used for animal
husbandry rather than crop cultivation is a matter of choice that
continues to this day in most of the region. Agriculture takes a great
deal more effort and requires greater knowledge than tending flocks.
And if you include the necessity for machinery, it also becomes more
expensive.

VERSE 3

**And thither were all the flocks gathered: and
they rolled the stone from the well's mouth, and
watered the sheep, and put the stone again upon
the well's mouth in his place.**

VERSE 4

> And Jacob said unto them, My brethren, whence
> *be* ye? And they said, Of Haran *are* we.

VERSE 5

> And he said unto them, Know ye Laban the son of
> Nahor? And they said, We know *him*.

VERSE 6

> And he said unto them, *Is* he well? And they said,
> *He is* well: and behold, Rachel his daughter cometh
> with the sheep.

VERSE 7

> And he said, Lo, *it is* yet high day, neither *is it* time
> that the cattle should be gathered together: water
> ye the sheep, and go *and* feed *them*.

VERSE 8

> And they said, We cannot, until all the flocks be
> gathered together, and *till* they roll the stone from
> the well's mouth; then we water the sheep.

VERSE 9

> And while he yet spake with them, Rachel came
> with her father's sheep: for she kept them.

VERSE 10

> And it came to pass, when Jacob saw Rachel
> the daughter of Laban his mother's brother, and
> the sheep of Laban his mother's brother, that
> Jacob went near, and rolled the stone from the
> well's mouth, and watered the flock of Laban his
> mother's brother.

The wording of this passage makes me wonder if Jacob was more enamored of Rachel or the sheep. I suppose that's unfair considering what Jacob had to go through to finally get Rachel.

204 | PHILLIP M. BRANSON

VERSE 11

And Jacob kissed Rachel, and lifted up his voice, and wept.

VERSE 12

And Jacob told Rachel that he *was* **her father's brother, and that he** *was* **Rebekah's son: and she ran and told her father.**

VERSE 13

And it came to pass, when Laban heard the tidings of Jacob his sister's son, that he ran to meet him, and embraced him, and kissed him, and brought him to his house. And he told Laban all these things.

VERSE 14

And Laban said to him, Surely thou *art* **my bone and my flesh. And he abode with him the space of a month.**

VERSE 15

And Laban said unto Jacob, Because thou *art* **my brother, shouldest thou therefore serve me for nought? Tell me, what** *shall* **thy wages** *be***?**

VERSE 16

And Laban had two daughters: the name of the elder *was* **Leah, and the name of the younger** *was* **Rachel.**

VERSE 17

Leah *was* **tender eyed; but Rachel was beautiful and well favoured.**

The word translated as "tender" here is *rak,* used elsewhere to mean "physically tender" or "soft" or "weak" as in soft hearted or weak willed. The usage here implies some real or imagined deficiency and could be anything from blue eyes (which were considered unattractive) to being cross-eyed or having a wandering eye to a simple case of near- or farsightedness. The fact that it was mentioned here indicated Jacob was inclined toward Rachel chiefly because of her beauty.

VERSE 18

And Jacob loved Rachel; and said, I will serve thee seven years for Rachel thy younger daughter.

VERSE 19

And Laban said, *It is* better that I give her to thee, than that I should give her to another man: abide with me.

VERSE 20

And Jacob served seven years for Rachel; and they seemed unto him *but* a few days, for the love he had to her.

VERSE 21

And Jacob said unto Laban, Give *me* my wife, for my days are fulfilled, that I may go in unto her.

VERSE 22

And Laban gathered together all the men of the place, and made a feast.

VERSE 23

And it came to pass in the evening, that he took Leah his daughter, and brought her to him; and he went in unto her.

It's not clear how this deception was accomplished. It may have been with the help of much liquor during the feast or possibly in the darkness with the help of a heavy wedding veil. At any rate, it was an obvious case of fraud on Laban's part, which he tried to justify with a very lame explanation of family customs he related about seven years too late.

VERSE 24

And Laban gave his daughter Leah Zilpah his maid *for* **an handmaid.**

VERSE 25

And it came to pass, that in the morning, behold, it *was* **Leah: and he said to Laban, What** *is* **this thou hast done unto me? Did not I serve with thee for Rachel? Wherefore then hast thou beguiled me?**

VERSE 26

And Laban said, It must not be done so in our country, to give the younger before the firstborn.

This is still the custom among some eastern people, but Laban certainly should have apprised Jacob of it at the start of the agreement instead of at the end.

VERSE 27

Fulfill her week, and we will give thee this also for the service which thou shalt serve with me yet seven other years.

So at the end of the weeklong wedding celebration, Jacob was to receive another bride. This time, he finally got his beloved Rachel, but it cost him another seven years of herding sheep and whatever else Laban required.

It was a harsh deception on Laban's part, but Jacob was no stranger to deception and this is perhaps proof that what goes around comes around. He was, after all, in Haran as a result of having to flee for his safety from his own deception of Esau.

VERSE 28

And Jacob did so, and fulfilled her week: and he gave him Rachel his daughter to wife also.

Apparently, the practice of marrying sisters was still condoned at that point. It was not officially made unlawful until Leviticus 18:18.

VERSE 29

And Laban gave to Rachel his daughter Bilhah his handmaid to be her maid.

VERSE 30

And he went in also unto Rachel, and he loved also Rachel more than Leah, and served with him yet seven other years.

VERSE 31

And when the Lord saw that Leah *was* hated, he opened her womb: but Rachel *was* barren.

VERSE 32

And Leah conceived, and bare a son, and she called his name Rueben: for she said, Surely the Lord hath looked upon my affliction; now therefore my husband will love me.

VERSE 33

And she conceived again, and bare a son; and said, Because the Lord hath heard that I *was* hated, he hath therefore given me this *son* also: and she called his name Simeon.

VERSE 34

And she conceived again, and bare a son; and said, Now this time will my husband be joined unto me, because I have born him three sons: therefore was his name called Levi.

VERSE 35

And she conceived again, and bare a son: and she said, Now will I praise the Lord: therefore she called his name Judah; and left bearing.

Jacob may have loved Rachel more, but he obviously found some time for Leah too.

CHAPTER THIRTY

VERSE 1

And when Rachel saw that she bare Jacob no children, Rachel envied her sister; and said unto Jacob, Give me children, or else I die.

VERSE 2

And Jacob's anger was kindled against Rachel: and he said, *Am* I in God's stead, who hath withheld from thee the fruit of the womb?

VERSE 3

And she said, Behold my maid Bilhah, go in unto her; and she shall bear upon my knees, that I may also have children by her.

Rachel entered into a similar situation as the one with Sarah and Hagar. We aren't told whether it was the strong desire for motherhood alone that was made stronger by her rivalry with her sister or whether she had knowledge of Jacob's blessing and the promise to Abraham and Isaac of a great nation to come forth from their seed.

VERSE 4

And she gave him Bilhah her handmaid to wife: and Jacob went in unto her.

No mention is made of Jacob protesting this arrangement on moral grounds or otherwise, but judging from his past and future conduct, it would seem unlikely.

VERSE 5

And Bilhah conceived, and bare Jacob a son.

VERSE 6

> And Rachel said, God hath judged me, and hath also heard my voice, and hath given me a son: therefore called she his name Dan.

VERSE 7

> And Bilhah Rachel's maid conceived again, and bare Jacob a second son.

Apparently, the question of whether Jacob was averse to this plan is now moot.

VERSE 8

> And Rachel said, With great wrestlings have I wrestled with my sister, and I have prevailed: and she called his name Naphtali.

VERSE 9

> When Leah saw that she had left bearing, she took Zilpah her maid, and gave her Jacob to wife.

VERSE 10

> And Zilpah Leah's maid bare Jacob a son.

VERSE 11

> And Leah said, A troop cometh: and she called his name Gad.

VERSE 12

> And Zilpah Leah's maid bare Jacob a second son.

VERSE 13

> And Leah said, Happy am I, for the daughters will call me blessed: and she called his name Asher.

At this point, I believe we can leave off wondering if Jacob had any moral objections to his wives' schemes and conclude that he was an enthusiastic participant.

Notice that nothing was written about daughters. There must have been some, but as in the case of most of the other genealogies, we are left to guess how many.

VERSE 14

> **And Rueben went in the days of wheat harvest, and found mandrakes in the field, and brought them unto his mother Leah. Then Rachel said unto Leah, Give me, I pray thee, of thy son's mandrakes.**

Mandrake in Hebrew is *dûdā'im*, meaning "love plant." Among certain Asian cultures, it's believed to ensure conception. The mandrake root has long played a role in magic and cultish rituals and is still used to this day by some practitioners of Wicca and Odinism.

VERSE 15

> **And she said unto her, *Is it* a small matter that thou hast taken my husband? And wouldest thou take away my son's mandrakes also? And Rachel said, Therefore he shall lie with thee to-night for thy son's mandrakes.**

VERSE 16

> **And Jacob came out of the field in the evening, and Leah went out to meet him, and said, Thou must come in unto me; for surely I have hired thee with my son's mandrakes. And he lay with her that night.**

Once again, Jacob seemed ever willing to go along with the program of the day.

VERSE 17

> **And God hearkened unto Leah, and she conceived, and bare Jacob the fifth son.**

VERSE 18

And Leah said, God hath given me my hire, because I have given my maiden to my husband: and she called his name Issachar.

VERSE 19

And Leah conceived again, and bare Jacob a sixth son.

VERSE 20

And Leah said, God hath endued me *with* **a good dowry; now will my husband dwell with me, because I have born him six sons: and she called his name Zebulun.**

The more sons a wife was able to provide, the higher the respectability and standing of the husband. Leah was justified in her belief that Jacob would favor her over Rachel. But the birth of a daughter was not nearly as exciting, and the good fortune stopped with the next child.

VERSE 21

And afterwards, she bare a daughter, and called her name Dinah.

This is the first mention of a daughter, but it seems likely there were others. I believe Dinah was mentioned here because of the role she played later in chapter 34.

VERSE 22

And God remembered Rachel, and God hearkened to her, and opened her womb.

VERSE 23

And she conceived, and bare a son; and said, God hath taken away my reproach.

VERSE 24

And she called his name Joseph; and said, the Lord shall add to me another son.

VERSE 25

And it came to pass, when Rachel had born Joseph, that Jacob said unto Laban, Send me away, that I may go unto mine own place, and to my country.

Jacob had at that point served out all the time he owed Laban, some fourteen years. He was no doubt eager to get home and begin building his own fortune and leave Laban and his tricks behind.

VERSE 26

Give *me* my wives and children, for whom I have served thee, and let me go: for thou knowest my service which I have done thee.

VERSE 27

And Laban said unto him, if I have found favor in thine eyes, *tarry*: *for* I have learned by experience that the Lord hath blessed me for thy sake.

Laban didn't give up easily. He was well aware of how much he had prospered with Jacob tending his flocks and herds, and true to his nature, he was unwilling to see Jacob leave. Notice he didn't mention that he would miss Jacob, his own daughters, or his grandchildren. He was concerned only with what Jacob's departure would mean to his holdings.

VERSE 28

And he said, Appoint me thy wages, and I will give it.

Laban was forced to try to hire Jacob to stay since he has nothing more to hold over his head.

VERSE 29

> **And he said unto him, Thou knowest how I have served thee, and how thy cattle was with me.**

VERSE 30

> **For it** *was* **little which thou hadst before I** *came,* **and it is** *now* **increased into a multitude; and the Lord hath blessed thee since my coming: and now when shall I provide for mine own house also?**

I believe Jacob at that point would have left empty-handed and been glad to just take his family and get away. However, because of Laban's penchant for conniving and trickery, Jacob was able not only to leave but also to get a little of his own back.

VERSE 31

> **And he said, What shall I give thee? And Jacob said, Thou shalt not give me any thing: if thou wilt do this thing for me, I will again feed** *and* **keep thy flock.**

VERSE 32

> **I will pass through all thy flock today, removing from thence all the speckled and spotted cattle, and all the brown cattle among the sheep, and the spotted and speckled among the goats: and** *of such* **shall be my hire.**

This passage would read more easily if the second use of the word "cattle" ("all the brown cattle among the sheep") had been translated as "animals," as it could well have been. The original word was *she,* or *sêy,* taken from a root meaning simply "to push out to graze" or a small animal that grazes. It also applied to the goats.

VERSE 33

> **So shall my righteousness answer for me in time to come, when it shall come for my hire before thy face: every one that** *is* **not speckled and spotted**

> **among the goats, and brown among the sheep,
> that shall be counted stolen with me.**

Jacob offered to take only the blemished animals off Laban's hands in return for once more tending Laban's cattle.

VERSE 34

> **And Laban said, Behold, I would it might be
> according to thy word.**

Of course Laban would jump at that offer, thinking to lose only the poorest and weakest of his cattle and flocks and not too many of them at that. He wouldn't, after all, have had a very high opinion of Jacob's ability to bargain based on his previous experience of gaining fourteen years of indentured service as the price of his two daughters.

VERSE 35

> **And he removed that day the he goats that were
> ringstraked and spotted, and all the she goats that
> were speckled and spotted, *and* every one that
> had *some* white in it, and all the brown among the
> sheep, and gave *them* into the hands of his sons.**

So Laban went away and left Jacob to tend to the cattle and flocks.

VERSE 36

> **And he set three days' journey betwixt himself and
> Jacob; and Jacob fed the rest of Laban's flocks.**

Jacob kept his word about feeding the stock, but he was also doing a little conniving of his own.

VERSE 37

> **And Jacob took his rods of green poplar, and
> of the hazel and chestnut tree; and pilled white
> strakes in them, and made the white appear which
> *was* in the rods.**

VERSE 38

And he set the rods which he had pilled before the flocks in the gutters in the watering troughs when the flocks came to drink, that they should conceive when they came to drink.

VERSE 39

And the flocks conceived before the rods, and brought forth cattle ringstraked, speckled, and spotted.

There is no scientific evidence that this would work to influence the color or makeup of any animal. The best guess for why it worked here is that God had a hand in it.

VERSE 40

And Jacob did separate the lambs, and set the faces of the flocks toward the ringstraked, and all the brown in the flock of Laban; and he put his own flocks by themselves, and put them not unto Laban's cattle.

VERSE 41

And it came to pass, whenever the stronger cattle did conceive, that Jacob laid the rods before the eyes of the cattle in the gutters, that they might conceive among the rods.

VERSE 42

But when the cattle were feeble, he put *them* not in: so the feebler were Laban's, and the stronger Jacob's.

VERSE 43

And the man increased exceedingly, and had much cattle, and maidservants, and menservants, and camels, and asses.

Jacob certainly lived up to the letter of his agreement and didn't do anything wrong or commit any theft (although a modern cattleman might argue the point in regard to the breeding process). And you have to admire the way he was able to come away with something to show for his labors.

CHAPTER THIRTY-ONE

VERSE 1

And he heard the words of Laban's sons, saying, Jacob hath taken away all that *was* **our father's; and of** *that* **which** *was* **our father's hath he gotten all this glory.**

Laban had departed from Jacob and moved off three days' journey. Apparently, Laban's sons remained behind with Jacob or came back to check up on him. Either way, Jacob became aware that the sons were unhappy with the contract between Laban and him. In the next verse, we see that the sons influenced Laban so that he was also unhappy with the arrangement even though he'd been eager to accept it when he thought he was getting the best of the deal.

VERSE 2

And Jacob beheld the countenance of Laban, and, behold, it *was* **not toward him as before.**

VERSE 3

And the Lord said unto Jacob, Return unto the land of thy fathers, and to thy kindred; and I will be with thee.

Jacob undoubtedly asked God for guidance mainly because he was a righteous man but partially perhaps out of fear that Laban would either renege on the bargain or do him bodily harm.

VERSE 4

And Jacob sent and called Rachel and Leah to the field unto his flock,

VERSE 5

And said unto them, I see your father's countenance, that it *is* not toward me as before; but the God of my father hath been with me.

VERSE 6

And ye know that with all my power I have served your father.

VERSE 7

And your father hath deceived me, and changed my wages ten times; but God suffered him not to hurt me.

VERSE 8

If he said thus, The speckled shall be thy wages; then all the cattle bare speckled: and if he said thus, The ringstraked shall be thy hire; then bare all the cattle ringstraked.

VERSE 9

Thus God hath taken away the cattle of your father, and given *them* to me.

Jacob gave God the credit for the idea behind the wage agreement, and in the next verse, he gave Him credit for implementing it so that he was finally given a fair wage for his years of service.

In so doing, Jacob also paved the way for his departure and convinced the two sisters that everything was happening according to God's will and thereby allayed any feelings of mixed loyalty the two women might have had between their father and their husband.

VERSE 10

And it came to pass at the time that the cattle conceived, that I lifted up mine eyes, and saw in a dream, and, behold, the rams which leaped upon the cattle *were* ringstraked, speckled, and grisled.

VERSE 11

And the angel of God spake unto me in a dream, *saying*, **Jacob: And I said, Here** *am* **I.**

VERSE 12

And he said, Lift up now thine eyes, and see, all the rams which leap upon the cattle *are* **ringstraked, speckled, and grisled: for I have seen all Laban doeth unto thee.**

VERSE 13

I *am* **the god of Beth-el, where thou anointedst the pillar,** *and* **where thou vowedst a vow unto me: now arise, get thee out from this land, and return unto the land of thy kindred.**

VERSE 14

And Rachel and Leah answered and said unto him, *Is there* **yet any portion or inheritance for us in our father's house?**

VERSE 15

Are we not counted of him strangers? for he hath sold us, and hath quite devoured also our money.

VERSE 16

For all the riches which God hath taken from our father, that *is* **ours, and our children's: now then, whatsoever God hath said unto thee, do.**

As it turned out, Jacob needn't have worried about Rachel and Leah's reaction. They were in agreement with him regarding what he was due from the standpoint of the wages for his labor and the inheritance that should have been theirs; they were more than willing to leave their father and go with him.

VERSE 17

Then Jacob rose up, and set his sons and his wives upon camels;

Once his mind was made up, it didn't take him long to pack up and leave.

VERSE 18

And he carried away all his cattle, and all his goods which he had gotten, the cattle of his getting, which he had gotten in Padanaram, for to go to Isaac his father in the land of Canaan.

VERSE 19

And Laban went to shear his sheep: and Rachel had stolen the images that *were* her father's.

The word for "images" here is *teraphiym*, from which our word 'teraphim' comes. The problem is that the meaning of the word is unclear. Teraphim are thought to have been images of household gods or domestic idols used for worship in the home. Teraphim were called "givers of prosperity," "guardians of comfort," and "nourishers." The images were probably small, perhaps intricately carved and very likely valuable or at least of considerable sentimental value for their owners.

VERSE 20

And Jacob stole away unawares to Laban the Syrian, in that he told him not that he fled.

It's interesting to note the use of the title "Laban the Syrian" when he had until then just been called Laban. He was after all Jacob's uncle. The new appellation would seem to further emphasize the rift between the two.

COMMON SENSE AND GENESIS | 221

VERSE 21

So he fled with all that he had; and he rose up, and passed over the river, and set his face *toward* the mount Gilead.

The writer could have used "started out for" or "began his journey to," but I think the phrase "set his face toward" is much more descriptive.

VERSE 22

And it was told Laban on the third day that Jacob was fled.

VERSE 23

And he took his brethren with him, and pursued after him seven days' journey; and they overtook him in the mount of Gilead.

Jacob had a three-day head start, but Laban caught up with him after only seven days. Of course Jacob was encumbered with flocks, family, and belongings, and Laban's party no doubt traveled light. The fact that Laban pursued Jacob at all indicated his degree of anger.

VERSE 24

And God came to Laban the Syrian in a dream by night, and said unto him, Take heed that thou speak not to Jacob either good or bad.

VERSE 25

Then Laban overtook Jacob. Now Jacob had pitched his tent in the mount: and Laban with his brethren pitched in the mount of Gilead.

The mount of Gilead is a mountainous region on the eastern side of the Jordan River in what is today Jordan. The Arabic word *jilead* means rough or rugged. It's also sometimes called the Land of Gilead; it refers to a rough, mountainous region rather than to a single hill or mountain. So the two parties camped in the same general area, but not side by side.

VERSE 26

And Laban said to Jacob, What hast thou done, that thou hast stolen away unawares to me, and carried away my daughters, as captives *taken* with the sword?

VERSE 27

Wherefore didst thou flee away secretly, and steal away from me; and didst not tell me, that I might have sent thee away with mirth, and with songs, with tabret, and with harp?

The meaning of the word *tabret* is unclear. There are several possible definitions, the most popular of which is that it was a type of small drum shaped much like a handheld tambourine and played mostly by girls or women.

VERSE 28

And hast not suffered me to kiss my sons and my daughters? thou hast now done foolishly in *so* doing.

Even after being warned, Laban could not resist becoming involved in an argument.

VERSE 29

It is in the power of my hand to do you hurt: but the God of your father spake unto me yesternight, saying, Take thou heed that thou speak not to Jacob either good or bad.

VERSE 30

And now, *though* thou wouldst needs be gone, because thou sore longedst after thy father's house, *yet* wherefore hast thou stolen my goods?

VERSE 31

And Jacob answered and said to Laban, Because I was afraid: for I said, Peradventure thou wouldest take by force thy daughters from me.

VERSE 32

With whomsoever thou findest thy goods, let him not live: before our brethren discern thou what *is* thine with me, and take *it* to thee. For Jacob knew not that Rachel had stolen them.

VERSE 33

And Laban went into Jacob's tent, and into Leah's tent, and into the two maidservants' tents; but he found *them* not. Then went he out of Leah's tent, and entered into Rachel's tent.

VERSE 34

Now Rachel had taken the images, and put them in the camel's furniture, and sat upon them. And Laban searched all the tent, but found *them* not.

VERSE 35

And she said to her father, Let it not displease my lord that I cannot rise up before thee; for the custom of women *is* upon me. And he searched, but found not the images.

VERSE 36

And Jacob was wroth, and chode with Laban: and Jacob answered and said to Laban, What *is* my trespass? What *is* my sin, that thou hast so hotly pursued after me?

Chode is an old form (16th-17th century) of the past tense for chide. The meaning is that Jacob spoke out in anger.

VERSE 37

Whereas thou hast searched all my stuff, what hast thou found of all thy household stuff? set *it* here before my brethren and thy brethren, that they may judge betwixt us both.

VERSE 38

This twenty years *have* I *been* with thee; thy ewes and thy she goats have not cast their young, and the rams of thy flock have I not eaten.

VERSE 39

That which was torn *of beasts* I brought not to thee; I bare the loss of it; of my hand didst thou require it, *whether* stolen by day, or stolen by night.

VERSE 40

Thus I was; in the day the drought consumed me, and the frost by night; and my sleep departed from mine eyes.

VERSE 41

Thus have I been twenty years in thy house; I have served thee fourteen years for thy two daughters, and six years for thy cattle; and thou hast changed my wages ten times.

VERSE 42

Except the God of my father, the God of Abraham, and the fear of Isaac, had been with me, surely thou hadst sent me away now empty. God hath seen my affliction and the labour of my hands, and rebuked *thee* yesternight.

Jacob pled his case eloquently. Before all the witnesses, Laban could do little but acquiesce.

COMMON SENSE AND GENESIS | 225

VERSE 43

> **And Laban answered and said unto Jacob,** *These*
> **daughters** *are* **my daughters, and** *these* **children**
> *are* **my children, and** *these* **cattle** *are* **my cattle,**
> **and all that thou seest** *is* **mine: and what can I do**
> **this day unto these my daughters, or unto their**
> **children which they have born?**

VERSE 44

> **Now therefore come thou, let us make a covenant,**
> **I and thou; and let it be for a witness between me**
> **and thee.**

VERSE 45

> **And Jacob took a stone, and set it up** *for* **a pillar.**

VERSE 46

> **And Jacob said unto his brethren, Gather stones;**
> **and they took stones, and made an heap: and they**
> **did eat there upon the heap.**

Jacob used the practice of setting up a stone or stones to form a
pillar to mark the sites where something significant happened to him.
Jacob used it in 28:18–22 and again in 35:14–15.

VERSE 47

> **And Laban called it Jegarsahadutha: but Jacob**
> **called it Galeed.**

Jegarsahadutha means "pile of testimony" or "witness pile."
Galeed's meaning is much the same: "heap of testimony" or "witness
heap." It appears that there were two markers; Jacob marked his with
a single large stone, while Laban built a pile of stones.

VERSE 48

> **And Laban said, This heap is a witness between**
> **me and thee this day. Therefore was the name of**
> **it called Galeed.**

VERSE 49

And Mizpah; for he said, The Lord watch between me and thee, when we are absent one from another.

This is now used as a blessing in churches all over the world when people are departing from one another. But I doubt that was what was meant here. I think he was saying that this was a final good-bye and that there were to be no further dealings between the two.

VERSE 50

If thou shalt afflict my daughters, or if thou shat take *other* wives beside my daughters, no man *is* with us; see, God *is* witness betwixt me and thee;

VERSE 51

And Laban said to Jacob, Behold this heap, and behold *this* pillar, which I have cast betwixt me and thee;

VERSE 52

This heap *be* witness, and *this* pillar *be* witness, that I will not pass over this heap to thee, and that thou shalt not pass over this heap and this pillar unto me, for harm.

VERSE 53

The God of Abraham, and the God of Nahor, and the God of their father, judge betwixt us. And Jacob sware by the fear of his father Isaac.

VERSE 54

Then Jacob offered sacrifice unto the mount, and called his brethren to eat bread: and they did eat bread, and tarried all night in the mount.

VERSE 55

And early in the morning Laban rose up, and kissed his sons and his daughters, and blessed them: and Laban departed, and returned to his place.

CHAPTER THIRTY-TWO

VERSE 1

And Jacob went on his way, and the angels of God met him.

VERSE 2

And when Jacob saw them, he said, This *is* God's host: and he called the name of that place Mahanaim.

The word for Mahanaim in Hebrew means "two camps." It was near Jabbok, either near the Jordan or the Jabbok River. It's mentioned thirteen times in the Old Testament.

VERSE 3

And Jacob sent messengers before him to Esau his brother unto the land of Seir, the country of Edom.

Jacob remembered that Esau had sworn to do him harm and was no doubt fearful of his reception. He sent an envoy ahead to smooth the way and developed a plan for survival if the messengers didn't succeed.

The "land of Seir" was named after Seir the Horite, who first settled there. The land was later occupied by Edom and the Edomites. Reference to the area can be found in the Harris Egyptian papyrus dating to c. 1200 BC.

VERSE 4

And he commanded them, saying, Thus shall ye speak unto my lord Esau; Thy servant Jacob saith thus, I have sojourned with Laban, and stayed there until now.

VERSE 5

And I have oxen, and asses, flocks, and menservants, and womenservants: and I have sent to tell my lord, that I may find grace in thy sight.

VERSE 6

And the messengers returned to Jacob, saying, We came to thy brother Esau, and also he cometh to meet thee, and four hundred men with him.

VERSE 7

Then Jacob was greatly afraid and distressed: and he divided the people that *was* with him, and the flocks, and herds, and the camels, into two bands;

VERSE 8

And said, If Esau come to the one company, and smite it, then the other company which is left shall escape.

VERSE 9

And Jacob said, O God of my father Abraham, and God of my father Isaac, the Lord which saith unto me, Return unto thy country, and to thy kindred, and I will deal with thee:

VERSE 10

I am not worthy of the least of all the mercies, and of all the truth, which thou hast showed unto thy servant; for with my staff I passed over this Jordan; and now I am become two bands.

VERSE 11

Deliver me, I pray thee, from the hand of my brother, from the hand of Esau: for I fear him, lest

he will come and smite me, *and* the mother with the children.

VERSE 12

And thou sadist, I will surely do thee good, and make thy seed as the sand of the sea, which cannot be numbered for multitude.

This is the first recorded example of prayer in the Bible.

VERSE 13

And he lodged there that same night; and took of that which came to his hand a present for Esau his brother;

VERSE 14

Two hundred she goats, and twenty he goats, two hundred ewes, and twenty rams,

VERSE 15

Thirty milch camels with their colts, forty kine, and ten bulls, twenty she asses, and ten foals.

VERSE 16

And he delivered *them* unto the hand of his servants, every drove by themselves; and said unto his servants, Pass over before me, and put a space betwixt drove and drove.

VERSE 17

And he commanded the foremost, saying, When Esau my brother meeteth thee, and asketh thee, saying, Whose *art* thou? And whither goest thou? And whose *are* these before thee?

VERSE 18

Then thou shalt say, *They be* thy servant Jacob's; it *is* a present sent unto my lord Esau: and, behold, also he *is* behind us.

VERSE 19

And so commanded he the second, and the third, and all that followed the droves, saying, On this manner shall ye speak unto Esau, when ye find him.

VERSE 20

And say ye moreover, Behold, thy servant Jacob *is* **behind us. For he said, I will appease him with the present that goeth before me, and afterward I will see his face; peradventure he will accept me.**

VERSE 21

So went the present over before him: and himself lodged that night in the company.

VERSE 22

And he rose up that night, and took his two wives, and his two womenservants, and his eleven sons, and passed over the ford Jabbok.

This is the first mention of the Jabbok River. The modern Arabic name for the Jabbok River, Nahr ez-Zarqa, means "the blue river," so called because of the deep blue color of the water. It played an important part in the coming history of Israel. It was mentioned in Numbers 21:24, Deuteronomy 3:16, Judges 11:13, and Joshua 12:2. The river empties into the Jordan River about halfway between the Sea of Galilee and the Dead Sea. Because of its location in a deep gorge, the river has always formed a natural boundary.

There were at least twelve children with Jacob counting his daughter Dinah, and I believe there were many more daughters. It's illogical to believe there would have been eleven sons but only one girl.

Dinah was listed because she played an important role in the next chapter, and that seems to be the general practice in all the genealogies in the Old Testament: to list those who were important to the main story, that is, the development of the nation of Israel and the line leading subsequently to the birth of Jesus.

VERSE 23

And he took them, and sent them over the brook, and sent over that he had.

VERSE 24

And Jacob was left alone; and there wrested a man with him until the breaking of day.

VERSE 25

And when he saw that he prevailed not against him, he touched the hollow of his thigh; and the hollow of Jacob's thigh was out of joint, as he wrestled with him.

This is somewhat difficult to understand at first because of the use of "he" and "him'" without identification. It becomes easier when one assigns the "he" to the man with whom Jacob wrestled, that is, the Lord or the angel of the Lord. The "him" then becomes Jacob, and it's clear what took place.[9]

VERSE 26

And he said, Let me go, for the day breaketh. And he said, I will not let thee go, except thou bless me.

Again, the first "he" was the Lord and the second was Jacob. At that point, Jacob had realized with whom he was wrestling, was humbled, and sought his Lord's blessing.

VERSE 27

And he said unto him, What *is* thy name? And he said, Jacob.

VERSE 28

> **And he said, Thy name shall be called no more Jacob, but Israel: for as a prince thou hast power with God and with men, and hast prevailed.**

VERSE 29

> **And Jacob asked** *him*, **and said, Tell** *me*, **I pray thee, thy name. And he said, Wherefore** *is* **it** *that* **thou dost ask after my name? And he blessed him there.**

VERSE 30

> **And Jacob called the name of the place Peniel: for I have seen God face to face, and my life is preserved.**

Peniel is also Penuel, as seen in the next verse. They are one and the same place. A town was afterward built on this location (Judges 8:8; 1 Kings 12:25). Later, the men of this place refused to help Gideon and his little army when they were in pursuit of the Midianites (Judges 8:1–21). On his return, Gideon slew the men of this city and razed its lofty watchtower.

VERSE 31

> **And as he passed over Penuel the sun rose upon him, and he halted upon his thigh.**

VERSE 32

> **Therefore the children of Israel eat not** *of* **the sinew which shrank, which** *is* **upon the hollow of the thigh, unto this day; because he touched the hollow of Jacob's thigh in the sinew that shrank.**

The shrinkage of this sinew (the one that holds the hip joint in place) would have caused Jacob to walk with a limp for the rest of his life. It was a reminder to him of the incident and a means of keeping him humble lest he should ever boast of his encounter.

CHAPTER THIRTY-THREE

VERSE 1

And Jacob lifted up his eyes, and looked, and behold, Esau came, and with him four hundred men. And he divided the children unto Leah, and unto Rachel, and unto the two handmaids.

That is, Jacob divided his family in case one party should be attacked.

VERSE 2

And he put the handmaids and their children foremost, and Leah and her children after, and Rachel and Joseph hindermost.

VERSE 3

And he passed over before them, and bowed himself to the ground seven times, until he came near his brother.

After each bow, Jacob would have taken a few steps toward Esau before bowing again. After the last bow, he would presumably have been directly in front of Esau or very nearly so. This was and is a common custom of the East to show respect.

VERSE 4

And Esau ran to meet him, and embraced him, and fell on his neck, and kissed him: and they wept.

All of Jacob's worry and fear had been for nothing. Or had it been? Might it have been a different reunion if God hadn't been watching over Jacob?

VERSE 5

And he lifted up his eyes, and saw the women and the children; and said, Who *are* those with thee? And he said, The children which God hath graciously given thy servant.

VERSE 6

Then the handmaidens came near, they and their children, and they bowed themselves.

VERSE 7

And Leah also with her children came near, and bowed themselves: and after came Joseph near and Rachel, and they bowed themselves.

VERSE 8

And he said, What *meanest* thou by all this drove which I have met? And he said, *These are* to find grace in the sight of my lord.

Esau was speaking of the herd of cattle Jacob had set aside for a gift, those mentioned in verses 14, 15, and 16 of the previous chapter.

VERSE 9

And Esau said, I have enough, my brother; keep that thou hast unto thyself.

VERSE 10

And Jacob said, Nay, I pray thee, if now I have found grace in thy sight, then receive my present at my hand: for therefore I have seen thy face, as though I had seen the face of God, and thou wast pleased with me.

Jacob had an ulterior motive for wanting Esau to accept the gift, for if Esau accepted, it would become a proof of friendship. And if Esau still considered himself to have been wronged by Jacob, accepting the gift would signify that all had been forgiven.

VERSE 11

> **Take, I pray thee, my blessing that is brought to thee; because God hath dealt graciously with me, and because I have enough. And he urged him, and he took** *it*.

It is interesting that Jacob would use the word *blessing* here and use the same word that was used in chapter 27 when Jacob disguised himself as Esau to receive his father's blessing. He might better have chosen different terminology.

VERSE 12

> **And he said, Let us take our journey, and let us go, and I will go before thee.**

A generous offer from Esau to escort Jacob and his entourage; it offered both safety and prestige.

VERSE 13

> **And he said unto him, My lord knoweth that the children** *are* **tender, and the flocks and herds with young** *are* **with me: and if men should overdrive them one day, all the flock will die.**

VERSE 14

> **Let my lord, I pray thee, pass over before his servant: and I will lead on softly, according as the cattle that goeth before me and the children be able to endure, until I come unto my lord unto Seir.**

Jacob offered a logical and persuasive argument for not traveling together. It was also likely that he just didn't want to push the new relationship with Esau. They were still very different and could easily have again become estranged due to some slight—real or imagined—during the journey. It was a prudent decision on Jacob's part to leave well enough alone for the time being.

VERSE 15

And Esau said, Let me now leave with thee *some* **of the folk that** *are* **with me. And he said, What needeth it? let me find grace in the sight of my lord.**

Apparently Jacob is still apprehensive about Esau's intentions.

VERSE 16

So Esau returned that day on his way unto Seir.

Seir is a town and a mountain range. It was also sometimes used as a synonym for a goat. It actually meant "rough" or "hairy" and described the Horite people, who were the first inhabitants of the region, and then later the Edomites. The area was later given to the descendants of Esau.

VERSE 17

And Jacob journeyed to Succoth, and built him a house, and made booths for his cattle: therefore the name of the place is called Succoth.

Succoth's location is unknown today. It was apparently situated to the east of the Jordan and north of the Jabbok River and was close to the Jordan valley. It was the first stop for the Israelites on the Exodus from Egypt (Exodus 12:37).

VERSE 18

And Jacob came to Shalem, a city of Shechem, which *is* **in the land of Canaan, when he came from Padanaram; and pitched his tent before the city.**

VERSE 19

And he bought a parcel of a field, where he had spread his tent, at the hand of the children of Hamor, Shechem's father, for an hundred pieces of money.

VERSE 20

**And he erected there an altar, and called it
El-elohe-Israel.**

El-elohe-Israel means simply "the mighty one," "the God of Israel."

CHAPTER THIRTY-FOUR

VERSE 1

And Dinah, the daughter of Leah, which she bare unto Jacob, went out to see the daughters of the land.

VERSE 2

And when Shechem, the son of Hamor the Hivite, prince of the country, saw her, he took her, and lay with her, and defiled her.

The Hivites were one group of the descendants of Canaan, son of Ham, according to the Table of Nations in Genesis 10:17.

VERSE 3

And his soul clave unto the daughter of Jacob, and he loved the damsel, and spake kindly unto the damsel.

VERSE 4

And Shechem spake unto his father Hamor, saying, Get me this damsel to wife.

VERSE 5

And Jacob heard that he had defiled Dinah his daughter: now his sons were with his cattle in the field; and Jacob held his peace until they were come.

Jacob was understandably distraught by what had happened to Dinah. However, he didn't immediately take any action. When a man had more than one wife at that time, the custom was for him to let the full brothers of the injured woman defend her honor. Therefore, Jacob would have left it to Simeon and Levi to avenge Leah's defilement.

VERSE 6

And Hamor the father of Shechem went out unto Jacob to commune with him.

VERSE 7

And the sons of Jacob came out of the field when they heard *it:* **and the men were grieved, and they were very wroth, because he had wrought folly in Israel in lying with Jacob's daughter; which thing ought not to be done.**

VERSE 8

And Hamor communed with them, saying, The soul of my son Shechem longeth for your daughter: I pray you give her him to wife.

VERSE 9

And make ye marriages with us, *and* **give your daughters unto us, and take our daughters unto you.**

VERSE 10

And ye shall dwell with us: and the land shall be before you; dwell and trade ye therein, and get you possessions therein.

VERSE 11

And Shechem said unto her father and unto her brethren, Let me find grace in your eyes, and what ye shall say unto me I will give.

VERSE 12

Ask me never so much dowry and gift, and I will give according as ye shall say unto me: but give me the damsel to wife.

Shechem offers to make amends by paying a tribute, but doesn't show any remorse or apologize for his actions.

VERSE 13

And the sons of Jacob answered Shechem and Hamor his father deceitfully, and said, because he had defiled Dinah their sister:

VERSE 14

And they said unto them, We cannot do this thing, to give our sister to one that is uncircumcised; for that *were* **a reproach unto us;**

VERSE 15

But in this will we consent unto you: If ye shall be as we *be***, that every male of you be circumcised;**

VERSE 16

Then will we give our daughters unto you, and we will take your daughters unto us, and we will dwell with you, and we will become one people.

It would appear on the surface that Simeon and Levi had reached an amicable compromise that would lead to a peaceful resolution. But neither Shechem nor Hamor had shown the slightest remorse or contrition for Shechem's act of defilement, so the brothers were dealing with them in kind. They were setting a very cunning trap and didn't intend for a minute to resolve the situation peacefully. Nothing had been said about adopting Jacob's religion. If the Hivites had known that circumcision was merely an outward token of their religion, they might have been more suspicious.

VERSE 17

But if ye will not harken unto us, to be circumcised; then will we take our daughter, and we will be gone.

VERSE 18

And their words pleased Hamor, and Shechem Hamor's son.

VERSE 19

And the young man deferred not to do this thing, because he had delight in Jacob's daughter: and he *was* **more honourable than all the house of his father.**

VERSE 20

And Hamor and Shechem his son came unto the gate of their city, and communed with the men of their city, saying,

VERSE 21

These men *are* **peaceable with us; therefore let them dwell in the land, and trade therein; for the land, behold,** *it is* **large enough for them; let us take their daughters to us for wives, and let us give them our daughters.**

VERSE 22

Only herein will the men consent unto us for to dwell with us, to be one people, if every male among us be circumcised, as they *are* **circumcised.**

VERSE 23

Shall **not their cattle and their substance and every beast of theirs** *be* **ours? only let us consent unto them, and they will dwell with us.**

Hamor's argument is that the Hivites will eventually own or control all of Jacob's possessions.

VERSE 24

And unto Hamor and unto Shechem his son hearkened all that went out of the gate of his city; and every male was circumcised, all that went out of the gate of his city.

VERSE 25

> **And it came to pass on the third day, when they were sore, that two of the sons of Jacob, Simeon and Levi, Dinah's brethren, took each man his sword, and came upon the city boldly, and slew all the males.**

VERSE 26

> **And they slew Hamor and Shechem his son with the edge of the sword, and took Dinah out of Shechem's house, and went out.**

VERSE 27

> **The sons of Jacob came upon the slain, and spoiled the city, because they had defiled their sister.**

VERSE 28

> **They took their sheep, and their oxen, and their asses, and that which *was* in the city, and that which *was* in the field,**

VERSE 29

> **And all their wealth, and all their little ones, and their wives took they captive, and spoiled even all that *was* in the house.**

VERSE 30

> **And Jacob said to Simeon and Levi, Ye have troubled me to make me stink among the inhabitants of the land, among the Canaanites and the Perizites: and I *being* few in number, they shall gather themselves together against me, and slay me; and I shall be destroyed, I and my house.**

Jacob rightfully concluded that the Canaanites would seek revenge and seemed more concerned with the consequences of the massacre than with its morality.

VERSE 31

And they said, Should he deal with our sister as with an harlot?

CHAPTER THIRTY-FIVE

VERSE 1

**And God said unto Jacob, Arise, go up to Beth-el,
and dwell there; and make there an altar unto God,
that appeared unto thee when thou fleddest from
the face of Esau thy brother.**

Beth-el means literally "House of El" or "House of God." The
original name for the city was Luz, a Canaanite name. This was the
same city where Jacob had his ladder dream, after which he renamed
it Beth-El.

The original name Luz has two meanings. One is "almond tree,"
and the other is "turning aside" or "twisting." Almonds were native to
the Middle East and are still a major commodity there.

The only other mention of a city named Luz is in Judges 1:26. That
was a new city founded by the lone survivor from the sack of Beth-el
by the tribe of Joseph.

VERSE 2

**Then Jacob said unto his household, and to all
that _were_ with him, Put away the strange gods that
are among you, and be clean, and change your
garments:**

A better translation would be "gods of the strangers." This would
include much of the spoils from Shalem, the city of Shechem, and
perhaps idols and other items brought along by the various people
added to Jacob's retinue from Mesopotamia.

VERSE 3

**And let us arise, and go up to Beth-el; and I will
make there an altar unto God, who answered me
in the day of my distress, and was with me in the
way which I went.**

VERSE 4

> **And they gave unto Jacob all the strange god which** *were* **in their hand, and** *all their* **earrings which** *were* **in their ears; and Jacob hid them under the oak which** *was* **by Shechem.**

Note that along with the idols, special mention was given to earrings, which were also used as religious symbols and in idolatrous practices.

VERSE 5

> **And they journeyed: and the terror of God was upon the cities that** *were* **round about them, and they did not pursue after the sons of Jacob.**

We're not told how many cities were involved here, only that the inhabitants outnumbered Jacob's people. There probably wouldn't have been that many cities, however, because Beth-el was only thirty or so miles from Shechem.

VERSE 6

> **So Jacob came to Luz, which** *is* **in the land of Canaan, that** *is,* **Beth-el, he and all the people that** *were* **with him.**

VERSE 7

> **And he built there an altar, and called the place El-beth-el: because there God appeared unto him, when he fled from the face of his brother.**

Bethel was an important city for the northern Kingdom of Israel after the days of Solomon and David. Like many other ancient cities, it was occupied, destroyed, and rebuilt several times over the centuries until it finally disappeared from all records.

The ruins of Beitin have long thought to be the remains of Bethel, but positive identification has not yet been made.

Bethel was also mentioned in Amos 5:5: "But do not seek Bethel, Nor enter Gilgal, Nor pass over to Beersheba; For Gilgal shall surely go into captivity, And Bethel shall come to nothing." This prophecy has proven true, since no further records have been found.

VERSE 8

But Deborah Rebekah's nurse died, and she was buried beneath Beth-el under an oak: and the name of it was called Allonbachuth.

The insertion of this information into the account of Jacob's return to Beth-el indicated the importance and esteem in which Deborah was held. Having originally been sent by Laban to care for Rebekah, his sister, she would have been honored and loved by Jacob's family for many years. She would have been about 180 years old at the time of her death.

VERSE 9

And God appeared unto Jacob again, when he came out of Padanaram, and blessed him.

Padanaram was apparently a field or plain rather than a city. It bordered the Euphrates River in what is now modern day Syria. It was the same place later called Padan (Genesis 48:7). Both Isaac and Jacob got their wives from Padanaram.

VERSE 10

And God said unto him, Thy name *is* Jacob; thy name shall not be called any more Jacob, but Israel shall be thy name; and he called his name Israel.

VERSE 11

And God said unto him, I *am* God Almighty: be fruitful and multiply; a nation and a company of nations shall be of thee, and kings shall come out of thy loins;

This was the sixth and last time God issued the directive to be fruitful and multiply. While the others were generalities issued to men in general as well as to wildlife, this one was specifically to the founder of the nation that became Israel.

VERSE 12

And the land which I gave Abraham and Isaac, to thee I will give it, and to thy seed after thee will I give the land.

VERSE 13

And God went up from him in the place where he talked with him.

VERSE 14

And Jacob set up a pillar in the place where he talked with him, *even* **a pillar of stone; and he poured a drink offering thereon, and he poured oil thereon.**

VERSE 15

And Jacob called the name of the place where God spake with him, Beth-el.

VERSE 16

And they journeyed from Beth-el; and there was but a little way to come to Ephrath: And Rachel travailed, and she had hard labour.

This is the first mention of Ephrath, also called Ephratah. The inhabitants were called Ephrathites. The city or area that encompasses the city was later called Bethlehem. Here it is said that Rachel had almost reached Ephrath when she went into a very hard labor.[10]

VERSE 17

And it came to pass, when she was in hard labour, that the midwife said unto her, Fear not; thou shalt have this son also.

Rachel had been barren for many years after her marriage to

Jacob, but she was finally granted a son, Joseph. Here, she was about to give birth to her second and last child.

VERSE 18

And it came to pass, as her soul was in departing, (for she died) that she called his name Benoni: but his father called him Benjamin.

Benoni is of Hebrew origin and means "son of my sorrow."

VERSE 19

And Rachel died, and was buried in the way to Ephrath, which is Bethlehem.

The site of Rachel's tomb "on the way to Bethlehem," "a little way to come to Ephrath," "in the border of Benjamin," has been and still is disputed. There are actually two possible locations, and good evidence exists for either. The traditional location recognized today is about two miles south of Jerusalem and one mile north of Bethlehem.

VERSE 20

And Jacob set a pillar upon her grave: that is the pillar of Rachel's grave unto this day.

According to the Jewish sages, the original monument was a pillar of thirteen stones. Each of Jacob's twelve sons placed a stone on Rachel's grave, with Jacob's stone on top. The pillar remained there on the side of the road for hundreds of years.

From the Byzantine period until the 1800s, according to the Jewish Press (JewishPress.com), Rachel's tomb was the third holiest site in Judaism after the Temple Mount and the Tomb of the Patriarchs in Hebron. For the past 1,700 years, the site has been identified as the burial place of the Jewish matriarch, and Jews were known to pray at the site for over the past 3,000 years.

VERSE 21

And Israel journeyed, and spread his tent beyond the tower of Edar.

The translation is "tower of the flock." We aren't told if this was a town with a tower in it or simply a single tower in a field. It was a watchtower built to protect the flocks from robbers. There were probably many such towers throughout the area. According to Jerome (c.347 – 420, a theologian, historian and son of Eusebius) this tower was one thousand paces from Bethlehem.

VERSE 22

And it came to pass, when Israel dwelt in that land, that Reuben went and lay with Bilhah his father's concubine: and Israel heard *it*. **Now the sons of Jacob were twelve:**

Here is a good example of how the separation and numbering of the chapters and verses can be confusing. Verse 21 would seem to stand alone or at least with the first part of 22. In the last half of this verse and the balance of chapter 35 the narrative shifts and is devoted to the genealogy of Jacob.

VERSE 23

The sons of Leah; Reuben, Jacob's firstborn, and Simeon, and Levi, and Judah, and Issachar, and Zebulun:

VERSE 24

The Sons of Rachel; Joseph and Benjamin:

VERSE 25

And the sons of Bilhah, Rachel's handmaid; Dan, and Naphtali:

VERSE 26

And the sons of Zilpah, Leah's handmaid; Gad, and Asher; these *are* **the sons of Jacob, which were born to him in Padanaram.**

Twelve sons in all. It is interesting that again no mention is made of daughters except Dinah. It is certainly reasonable to assume that

Jacob had many daughters. In fact, there is a Daughters of Jacob bridge across the Jordan, straddling the border between Israel and the Israeli-occupied portion of the Golan Heights.

VERSE 27

And Jacob came unto Isaac his father unto Mamre, unto the city of Arbah, which *is* Hebron, where Abraham and Isaac sojourned.

VERSE 28

And the days of Isaac were an hundred and four score years.

VERSE 29

And Isaac gave up the ghost, and died, and was gathered unto his people; *being* old and full of days; and his sons Esau and Jacob buried him.

CHAPTER THIRTY-SIX

VERSE 1

Now these *are* the generations of Esau, who is Edom.

As is the case with several other chapters of Genesis, this chapter is mainly about genealogies.

The word for Edom translates as "red" or "ruddy"' and may have been given to the area because of its red-colored soil. It is also said to have been given to Esau because of his ruddy complexion, and by some even as a result of his having eaten the red pottage of his brother Jacob (25:30), though that seems a bit of a stretch.

VERSE 2

Esau took his wives of the daughters of Canaan; Adah the daughter of Elon the Hittite, and Aholibamah the daughter of Anah the daughter of Zibeon the Hivite;

VERSE 3

And Bashemath Ismael's daughter, sister of Nebajoth.

VERSE 4

And Adah bare to Esau Eliphaz; and Bashemath bare Reuel;

VERSE 5

And Aholibamah bare Jeush, and Jaalam, and Korah: These *are* the sons of Esau, which were born unto him in the land of Caanan.

Esau had a total of three wives and five sons with probably at least as many daughters. With these, he founded the Kingdom of Edom, and the inhabitants were called Edomites. They moved into the area south of the Dead Sea—mostly the Negev Desert—and displaced the Horites, who had settled there. From about 1000 BC to about 200 BC, Edom was a prosperous kingdom due mainly to its location on the principal trade routes (the King's Highway and the Incense Route) and because of its copper mining.

They didn't have much tillable land, but they were said to have done some trading by sea, perhaps as far as India. Their religion would have been the worship of fertility gods such as El, Baal, Kaus, and Asherah. Although they were distantly related, there was constant warfare and strife between the Jews and the descendants of Esau that continues to this day.

VERSE 6

And Esau took his wives, and his sons, and his daughters, and all the persons of his house, and his cattle, and all his beasts, and all his substance, which he had got in the land of Canaan; and went into the country from the face of his brother Jacob.

VERSE 7

For their riches were more than that they might dwell together; and the land wherein they were strangers could not bear them because of their cattle.

As was case with Abraham and Lot, the herds and flocks of the two men eventually got too big for the area in which they were located. The time that Jacob and Esau spent together may or may not have been considerable depending on whether Esau's marriages and the increase of his herds took place before or after Jacob arrived. Time spans and ages were listed only when they related directly to the story.

VERSE 8

Thus dwelt Esau in Mount Seir: Esau *is* Edom.

There is both the "land of Seir," mentioned in 32:3 and "Mount Seir," mentioned in 14:6. There should be no disagreement as to whether these were one and the same. Chapter 32 specifically mentioned the land of Seir as being "the country of Edom." They both refer to the original name of the mountain range extending along the east side of the valley of Arabah from the Dead Sea to the Elanitic Gulf (also known as the Gulf of Aqaba).

The balance of chapter 36 is a listing of the genealogy of the descendants of the children of Seir, who inhabited the land before Esau and his descendants conquered it.

The genealogy can be confusing on several levels. First are the three wives of Esau. They were listed here with different names from those given earlier, but they are the same people. Genealogies necessarily cover several generations, in this case probably several centuries, as the lifetimes were still somewhat longer than what are common today. And the accounts may have been from more than one source.

The genealogy listed in 35:22–26 lists the sons of Jacob according to the mothers, as is the listing here for the sons of Esau. But the wives of Esau were called by different names from those in chapter 26. The difference is explained by taking into account the custom of giving surnames based on events that took place in that person's life and the fact that women often received new names upon being married. Hence, Basemath became Adah, still listed as the daughter of Elon the Hittite. Judith became Oholibamah, daughter of Anah, and Mahalath became Basemath, which makes it even more confusing because that was the original name of his first wife. So although the names differ, Esau had only three wives.

VERSE 9

And these *are* **the generations of Esau the father of the Edomites in mount Seir:**

VERSE 10

These *are* **the names of Esau's sons; Eliphaz the son of Adah the wife of Esau, Reuel the son of Bashemath the wife of Esau.**

VERSE 11

And the sons of Eliphaz were Teman, Omar, Zepho, and Gatam, and Kenaz.

VERSE 12

And Timna was concubine to Eliphaz Esau's son; and she bare to Eliphaz Amalek: these *were* **the sons of Adah Esau's wife.**

When the people of Israel left Egypt under the leadership of Moses, the first opposition they encountered was from the Amalekites, descendants of Amalek. Here we see that Amalek was the grandson of Esau.

VERSE 13

And these *are* **the sons of Reuel; Nahath, and Zerah, Shammah, and Mizzah: these were the sons of Bashemath Esau's wife.**

VERSE 14

And these were the sons of Aholibamah, the daughter of Anah the daughter of Zibeon, Esau's wife: and she bare to Esau Jeush, and Jaalam, and Korah.

VERSE 15

These *were* **dukes of the sons of Esau: the sons of Eliphaz the firstborn** *son* **of Esau; duke Teman, duke Omar, duke Zepho, duke Kenaz,**

The Hebrew word translated as "duke" is *aluf*, *'allûwph*, or *allûf*, used to describe the chieftains of Edom and Moab, also later translated as "chief," "general," or sometimes "clan." It indicated that each son would go his own way and become a chieftain of his own clan. Today, aluf is a description of a high rank in the Israeli Defense Force, corresponding to our general or admiral.

VERSE 16

Duke Korah, duke Gatam, *and* **duke Amalek: these** *are* **the dukes** *that came* **of Eliphaz in the land of Edom, these** *were* **the sons of Adah.**

VERSE 17

And these *are* **the sons of Reuel Esau's son; duke Nahath, duke Zerah, duke Shammah, duke Mizzah: these are the dukes** *that came* **of Reuel in the land of Edom; these** *are* **the sons of Bashemath Esau's wife.**

VERSE 18

And these *are* **the sons of Aholibamah Esau's wife; duke Jeush, duke Jaalam, duke Korah: these** *were* **the dukes** *that came* **of Aholibamah the daughter of Anah, Esau's wife.**

VERSE 19

These *are* **the sons of Esau, who** *is* **Edom, and these** *are* **their dukes.**

VERSE 20

These *are* **the sons of Seir the Horite, who inhabited the land; Lotan, and Shobal, and Zibeon, and Annah.**

This should have been the beginning of a new chapter because the genealogy switched here to a completely different family, the children of Seir.

"And Seir the son of Hur, son of Hivi, son of Canaan, went and found a valley opposite to Mount Paran, and he built a city there, and he and his seven sons and his household dwelt there, and he called the city which he built Seir, according to his name; that is the land of Seir unto this day."[11]

The only logical explanation for including the listing here is that these were the people who inhabited Seir before the arrival of Esau.

VERSE 21

And Dishon, and Ezer, and Dishan: These *are* **the dukes of the Horites, the children of Seir in the land of Edom.**

As mentioned before, the Horites were the original inhabitants of Edom. Not too much is known about them except that they were also called Hurrians in other writings. The name Horite meant cave dweller, and there were many caves in the mountains of Seir. When the Edomites came into the land, most of the Horites were destroyed, but some were assimilated into the new culture as exemplified by Timna, the concubine of Eliphaz, who was Esau's son, and Oholibamah, who was one of Esau's wives.

VERSE 22

And the children of Lotan were Hori and Hemam; and Lotan's sister *was* **Timna.**

VERSE 23

And the children of Shobal *were* **these; Alvan, and Manahath, and Ebal, Shepho, and Onam.**

VERSE 24

And these *are* **the children of Zibeon; both Ajah, and Anah: this** *was that* **Anah that found the mules in the wilderness, as he fed the asses of Zibeon his father.**

VERSE 25

And the children of Anah *were* **these; Dishon, and Aholibamah the daughter of Anah.**

VERSE 26

And these *are* **the children of Dishon; Hemdan, and Eshban, and Ithran, and Cheran.**

VERSE 27

The children of Ezer *are* **these; Bilhan, and Zaavan and Akan.**

VERSE 28

The children of Dishan *are* **these; Uz and Aran.**

VERSE 29

These *are* **the dukes** *that came* **of the Horites; duke Lotan, duke Shobal, duke Zibeon, duke Anah,**

VERSE 30

Duke Dishon, duke Ezer, duke Dishan: these *are* **the dukes** *that came* **of Hori, among their dukes in the land of Seir.**

VERSE 31

And these *are* **the kings that reigned in the land of Edom, before there reigned any king over the children of Israel.**

VERSE 32

And Bela the son of Beor reigned in Edom; the name of his city *was* **Dinhabah.**

Again, many of these kingdoms were merely cities or city-states and were not similar to the kingdoms of later history.

VERSE 33

And Bela died, and Jobab the son of Zerah of Bozrah reigned in his stead.

Apparently, the kingships were not hereditary. We don't learn whether they were elected, taken by force, or selected in some other way.

VERSE 34

And Jobab died, and Husham of the land of Temani reigned in his stead.

Teman was a clan (and then a district) of Edom, getting its name from Teman, the first son of Eliphaz and grandson of Esau. The inhabitants were called Temani. One of Job's three friends, Eliphaz (probably named after the grandson of Esau), was a Temanite (Job 2:11).

VERSE 35

And Husham died, and Hadad the son of Bedad, who smote Midian in the field of Moab, reigned in his stead: and the name of his city was **Avith.**

VERSE 36

And Hadad died, and Samlah of Masrekah reigned in his stead.

VERSE 37

And Samlah died, and Saul of Rehoboth by **the river reigned in his stead.**

VERSE 38

And Saul died, and Baalhanan the son of Achbor reigned in his stead.

VERSE 39

And Baalhanan the son of Achbor died, and Hadar reigned in his stead: and the name of his city was **Pau; and his wife's name** was **Mehetabel, the daughter of Matred, the daughter of Mezahab.**

Note the unusual naming of women here. It's probably a result of directly copying Edomite records. Ordinarily, women weren't named unless they had a direct bearing on the story.

VERSE 40

And these *are* **the names of the dukes** *that came* **of Esau, according to their families, after their places, by their names; duke Timnah, duke Alvah, duke Jetheth.**

Here we switch back to the descendants of Esau. This would have been less confusing if it had been added after verse 19.

VERSE 41

Duke Aholibamah, duke Elah, duke Pinon,

VERSE 42

Duke Kenaz, duke Teman, duke Mibzar,

VERSE 43

Duke Magdiel, duke Iram: these *be* **the dukes of Edom, according to their habitations in the land of their possession: he** *is* **Esau the father of the Edomites.**

The prophecies concerning the Edomites are many: Isaiah 34:1–17, Jeremiah 49:7– 22, Ezekiel 35:1–15, Malachi 1:1–4, and the entire book of Obadiah tell us why God hated Esau but loved Jacob. There is some debate as to whether those prophecies were fulfilled when the Kingdom of Edom was defeated by the Nabateans in the fifth century BC and wiped out in AD 70 or whether judgment is yet forthcoming for the rest of the descendants of Esau.

CHAPTER THIRTY-SEVEN

VERSE 1

And Jacob dwelt in the land wherein his father was a stranger, in the land of Canaan,

After Esau took his family and possessions and went up to the hill country of Seir, Jacob was left in the valley. Canaan was the region between the Jordan River and the Mediterranean, corresponding roughly to Israel, the Promised Land of the Israelites. It was named after Canaan, the fourth son of Ham (Genesis 10:6). His descendants were the ones cursed in consequence of the transgression of his father, Ham (9:22–27). His eldest son, Zidon, was the father of the Sidonians and Phoenicians. He had eleven sons, who founded as many tribes (Genesis 10:15–18). The name Canaan signifies "the lowlands" as distinguished from the land of Gilead to the east of what is now Jordan, a mountainous district. The extent and boundaries of Canaan were set forth fully in different parts of Scripture (Genesis 10:19, 17:8 and Numbers 13:29, 34:8 for example).

VERSE 2

These *are* the generations of Jacob. Joseph, *being* seventeen years old, was feeding the flock with his brethren; and the lad *was* with the sons of Bilhah, and with the sons of Zilpah, his father's wives: and Joseph brought unto his father their evil report.

This starts out like a genealogy, but in fact, the rest of chapter 37 is the story of Jacob's son Joseph and his trouble with his brothers, which resulted in Joseph being sold into slavery in Egypt.

We aren't told what exactly the evil report was. It could have been that the other sons were lax in their duties concerning the flock, or it may have been something else. We can assume it was something more than just malicious gossip.

VERSE 3

> **Now Israel loved Joseph more than all his children, because he *was* the son of his old age: and he made him a coat of *many* colours.**

There is a problem with the translation of the Hebrew phrase *kethoneth passim*. Bible translations have used phrases such as "a long robe with sleeves," "a richly ornamented robe," "a full sleeved robe," "a coat reaching to his feet," "an ornamented tunic," "a silk robe," or "a fine woolen cloak." This is the King James Version, so I have used "coat of (many) colors." It is possible that any one of the above is more accurate.

In Joseph's day, everyone had a coat or cloak to keep warm, carry belongings, and even serve as security for a loan. Most were very plain and about knee length; they were merely functional. In contrast, the coat Jacob gave his son was colorful and may have been ankle length and probably more in keeping with what royalty wore, perhaps more of a robe than a coat. It was probably very beautiful.

VERSE 4

> **And when his brethren saw that their father loved him more than all his brethren, they hated him, and could not speak peaceably unto him.**

VERSE 5

> **And Joseph dreamed a dream, and he told *it* his brethren: they hated him yet the more.**

VERSE 6

> **And he said unto them, Hear, I pray you, this dream which I have dreamed:**

VERSE 7

> **For, behold, we *were* binding sheaves in the field, and, lo, my sheaf arose, and also stood upright; and, behold, your sheaves stood round about, and made obeisance to my sheaf.**

VERSE 8

And his brethren said to him, Shalt thou indeed reign over us? Or shalt thou indeed have dominion over us? And they hated him yet the more for his dreams, and for his words.

VERSE 9

And he dreamed yet another dream, and told it his brethren, and said, Behold, I have dreamed a dream more; and, behold, the sun and the moon and the eleven stars made obeisance to me.

The sun, moon, and eleven stars refer to Joseph's family: his father, mother, and eleven brothers.

VERSE 10

And he told *it* to his father; and to his brethren: and his father rebuked him, and said unto him, What *is* this dream that thou hast dreamed? Shall I and thy mother and thy brethren indeed come to bow down ourselves to thee to the earth?

VERSE 11

And his brethren envied him; but his father observed the saying.

Dreams were considered important, and Jacob believed what Joseph said would come true.

VERSE 12

And his brethren went to feed their father's flock in Shechem.

Shechem was in the next valley over, a rich pastureland.

VERSE 13

And Israel said unto Joseph, Do not thy brethren feed *the flock* in Shechem? come, and I will send thee unto them. And he said unto him, Here *am* I.

This verse leads me to believe Joseph's evil report to his father in verse 2 pertained to his half-brothers not taking care of business while watching the flock. Remember it wasn't only Joseph who carried the report. There were five people altogether; the two sons of Bilhah and the two sons of Zilpah were with Joseph as well.

Jacob seems to have been worried that something might have been amiss with either the men or the animals.

VERSE 14

And he said unto him, Go, I pray thee, see whether it be well with thy brethren, and well with the flocks; and bring me word again. So he sent him out of the vale of Hebron, and he came to Shechem.

VERSE 15

And a certain man found him, and, behold, *he was* **wandering in the field: and the man asked him, saying, What sleekest thou?**

The flocks had been moved and were not where they were supposed to be.

VERSE 16

And he said, I seek my brethren: tell me, I pray thee, where they feed *their flocks***.**

VERSE 17

And the man said, they are departed hence; for I heard them say, Let us go to Dothan, And Joseph went after his brethren, and found them in Dothan.

Dothan means "two wells." It's north of Shechem and is also rich pastureland. It is identified with the modern Tell-Dothan, about 12 miles north of Samaria, in the hills of Gilboa. The 'two wells' are still in existence, and one of them bears the name of the 'pit of Joseph' (Jubb Yusuf)."

VERSE 18

And when they saw him afar off, even before he came near unto them, they conspired against him to slay him.

VERSE 19

And they said one to another, Behold, this dreamer cometh.

This is literally "master of dreams," spoken as a term of derision.

VERSE 20

Come now therefore, and let us slay him, and cast him into some pit, and we will say, Some evil beast hath devoured him: and we shall see what will become of his dreams.

VERSE 21

And Reuben heard *it*, and he delivered him out of their hands; and said, Let us not kill him.

VERSE 22

And Reuben said unto them, shed no blood, *but* cast him into this pit that *is* in the wilderness, and lay no hand upon him; that he might rid him out of their hands, to deliver him to his father again.

Rueben's plan was to hide Joseph safely until he could return and rescue him. The word used for "pit" here is *bôwr*, most commonly used for "well" or "cistern" although sometimes "dungeon" or just a hole in the ground. But since they were out in the fields, it's safe to assume Reuben was referring to a well. Verse 24 tells us it was a dry well.

VERSE 23

And it came to pass when Joseph was come unto his brethren, that they stripped Joseph out of his coat, *his* coat of *many* colours that *was* on him;

VERSE 24

And they took him, and cast him into a pit: and the pit *was* **empty,** *there was* **no water in it.**

VERSE 25

And they sat down to eat bread: and they lifted up their eyes and looked, and, behold, a company of Ishmeelites came from Gilead with their camels bearing spicery and balm and myrrh, going to carry *it* **down to Egypt.**

The spelling here should be Ishmaelites They were the descendants of Ishmael, the son of Abraham and Hagar who was cast out from the family and later founded the Arab nations. Here, they were also associated with the Midianites, who were descended from Midian, also a son of Abraham but with Keturah. The two groups were most probably joined as part of a group of Bedouin tribes.

VERSE 26

And Judah said unto his brethren, What profit *is it* **if we slay our brother, and conceal his blood?**

VERSE 27

Come, and let us sell him to the Ishmeelites, and let not our hand be upon him, for he *is* **our brother** *and* **our flesh. And his brethren were content.**

VERSE 28

Then there passed by Midianites merchantmen; and they drew and lifted up Joseph out of the pit, and sold Joseph to the Ishmeelites for twenty *pieces* **of silver: and they brought Joseph into Egypt.**

VERSE 29

And Reuben returned unto the pit; and, behold, Joseph *was* **not in the pit; and he rent his clothes.**

Reuben, who had prevented Joseph's slaying a short while earlier, had planned all along to return and save Joseph from the pit. He was distraught when he got there too late.

VERSE 30

And he returned unto his brethren, and said, The child *is* not; and I, whither shall I go?

VERSE 31

And they took Joseph's coat, and killed a kid of the goats, and dipped the coat in the blood;

VERSE 32

And they sent the coat of *many* colours, and they brought *it* to their father; and said, This we have found: know now whether it *be* thy son's coat or no.

I thought that the word *sent* here might have been a typographical error, and that it was meant to read "rent," which would be logical. But the translation is from the word *shālach*, which definitely means "to send."

VERSE 33

And he knew it, and said, *It is* my son's coat; an evil beast hath devoured him; Joseph is without doubt rent in pieces.

VERSE 34

And Jacob rent his clothes, and put sackcloth upon his loins, and mourned for his son many days.

Sackcloth was a rough garment usually made from the hair of a goat or later the hair of a camel. It was specifically worn as a symbol of mourning or penitence.

VERSE 35

And all his sons and all his daughters rose up to comfort him; but he refused to be comforted; and he said, For I will go down into the grave unto my son mourning. Thus his father wept for him.

VERSE 36

And the Midianites sold him into Egypt unto Potiphar, an officer of Pharaoh's, *and* **captain of the guard.**

This concludes the story of Joseph's betrayal by his brothers and his being sold into slavery in Egypt. The story picks up again in chapter 39.

As with the Edomites, God's wrath against the Midianites was severe. They, along with the Kenites, a clan within the Midianites and the Amalakites, continued to oppress and wage war with the Israelites until Gideon virtually annihilated them (Judges 6:33–40, 7:1–25).

The story of Gideon's battle is fascinating. He started with an army of 32,000 men against the Midianites, who numbered about 135,000. God told Gideon he had too many men and pared the army down to a mere 300. He gave Gideon the plan of battle. The reason for the small number was so Gideon would know God had facilitated the victory, not the army. It's a great story.

CHAPTER THIRTY-EIGHT

VERSE 1

And it came to pass at that time, that Judah went down from his brethren, and turned in to a certain Adullamite, whose name *was* Hirah.

That is, Judah went to see a friend named Hirah in Adullam. The ruins of Adullam are quite accessible today, although much is overgrown with olive trees. It's on a hill above the Elah Valley in Israel. The city's history (and that of the Cave of Adullum, where David sought refuge from King Saul) is well recorded. The historicity of the Bible is proven again and again by geological, geographical, and archaeological documentation as well as the earliest writings of historians.

VERSE 2

And Judah saw there a daughter of a certain Canaanite, whose name *was* Shuah; and he took her, and went in unto her.

VERSE 3

And she conceived, and bare a son; and he called his name Er.

VERSE 4

And she conceived again, and bare a son; and she called his name Onan.

Judah named the firstborn, but his wife named the other two.

VERSE 5

And she yet again conceived, and bare a son; and called his name Shelah: and he was at Chezib, when she bare him.

This is the only mention of Chezib in the Bible, but it's probably the same city as Achzib in Joshua 15:44, 19:29; Micah 1:14; and Judges 1:31. It is also probably the same as Chozeba in 1 Chronicles 4:22. The city's name is from a root word meaning "to lie," or "to deceive."

VERSE 6

And Judah took a wife for Er his firstborn, whose name *was* **Tamar.**

Some time lapse here, as Er had just been born in verse 3. The name Tamar means "date palm" or "source of food." Tamar is listed as one of the four female ancestors of Jesus in the gospel of Matthew.

VERSE 7

And Er, Judah's firstborn, was wicked in the sight of the Lord; and the Lord slew him.

In Hebrew, *Er* spelled backward is "evil," Er (עֵר) and Er's character (רַע). We aren't told of the exact form of Er's wickedness or in what manner he died. However, as we shall see, Er and Onan didn't want Tamar to become pregnant (but for very different reasons,) and since she was in the direct line that would lead to Jesus, that may have been reason enough.

VERSE 8

And Judah said unto Onan, Go in unto thy brother's wife, and marry her, and raise up seed to thy brother.

This was according to the custom of the day (*levirate* marriage, from the Latin *levir*, meaning "husband's brother"; see Deuteronomy 25:5–10). If a man died and his wife had not yet had a child by him, his brother was obligated to marry the widow. The first child from that union would be considered the child and heir of the deceased husband. The practice is still used today is some cultures with mixed benefits for the widow.

COMMON SENSE AND GENESIS | 271

VERSE 9

And Onan knew that the seed should not be his; and it came to pass, when he went in unto his brother's wife, that he spilled *it* on the ground, lest that he should give seed to his brother.

This is the origin of "onanism," a commonly used method today to prevent pregnancy. It is also called "coitus interruptus" or simply withdrawal. Whether it is still considered a sin depends on who's defining it.

VERSE 10

And the thing which he did displeased the Lord: wherefore he slew him also.

VERSE 11

Then said Judah to Tamar his daughter in law, Remain a widow at thy father's house, till Shelah my son be grown: for he said, Lest peradventure he die also, as his brethren *did*. And Tamar went and dwelt in her father's house.

VERSE 12

And in process of time the daughter of Shuah Judah's wife died; and Judah was comforted, and went up unto his sheep-shearers to Timnath, he and his friend Hirah the Adullamite.

This is the same Timnath that was under Philistine control when Samson went there, saw a woman, took her for a wife, and slew a lion with his bare hands (Judges 14:1–30).

VERSE 13

And it was told Tamar, saying, Behold thy father in law goeth up to Timnath to shear his sheep.

VERSE 14

And she put her widow's garments off from her, and covered her with a veil, and wrapped herself, and sat in an open place, which *is* by the way to Timnath; for she saw that Shelah was grown, and she was not given unto him to wife.

VERSE 15

When Judah saw her, he thought her *to be* an harlot; because she had covered her face.

Judah had recently lost his wife and was no doubt still in mourning. Plus, there are two different words used here for "harlot." One is *zânâh*, used to describe a common prostitute; the other is *qedeshah*, usually reserved for a cult or sacred prostitute. We're not told which one Judah thought Tamar was since both words were used (here and again in verses 21 and 22.)

VERSE 16

And he turned unto her by the way, and said, Go to, I pray thee, let me come in unto thee; (for he knew not that she *was* his daughter in law.) And she said, What wilt thou give me, that thou mayest come in unto me?

VERSE 17

And he said, I will send *thee* a kid from the flock. And she said, Wilt thou give *me* a pledge, till thou send it?

VERSE 18

And he said, What pledge shall I give thee? And she said, Thy signet, and thy bracelets, and thy staff that *is* in thine hand, And he gave *it* her, and came in unto her, and she conceived by him.

This was apparently the first opportunity Tamar had to conceive a child. As mentioned before, it's thought that one of the reasons God was so displeased with Er was that he didn't want a child, possibly because he was afraid of spoiling Tamar's good looks.

Onan was slain also for not fathering a child by her, probably because the first child would have inherited Er's portion of any estate. Since Er had had no child, the first portion would have fallen to Onan unless he had fathered a child by Tamar.

VERSE 19

And she arose, and went away, and laid by her veil from her, and put on the garments of her widowhood.

VERSE 20

And Judah sent the kid by the hand of his friend the Adullamite, to receive *his* pledge from the woman's hand; but he found her not.

VERSE 21

Then he asked the men of that place, saying, Where *is* the harlot, that *was* openly by the way side? And they said, There was no harlot in this *place*.

VERSE 22

And he returned to Judah, and said, I cannot find her; and also the men of the place said, *that* there was no harlot in this *place*.

VERSE 23

And Judah said, Let her take *it* to her, lest we be shamed: behold, I sent this kid, and thou hast not found her.

Judah was willing to let her keep the things he had given her because he didn't want the embarrassment of trying to locate her again and having the locals laugh at him. He had fulfilled his part of the bargain by sending the kid, and to him, that was enough.

VERSE 24

And it came to pass about three months after, that it was told Judah, saying, Tamar thy daughter in law hath played the harlot; and also, behold, she *is* with child by whoredom. And Judah said, Bring her forth, and let her be burnt.

In those days, Judah would have had the authority to order Tamar's death, and he chose the particularly harsh one of burning, which was a common punishment for adultery even though Tamar was no longer married. She was pregnant out of wedlock, which was apparently considered to be equally bad.

VERSE 25

When she *was* brought forth, she went to her father in law, saying, By the man, whose these *are, am* I with child: and she said, Discern, I pray thee, whose *are* these, the signet, the bracelets, and staff.

VERSE 26

And Judah acknowledged *them*, and said, She hath been more righteous than I; because that I gave her not Shelah my son. And he knew her again no more.

Judah didn't marry Tamar, nor did he have any further relations with her.

VERSE 27

And it came to pass, in the time of her travail, that, behold, twins *were* in her womb.

Twins seem to have been pretty common, going back as far as Cain and Abel.

VERSE 28

And it came to pass, when she travailed, that *the* **one put out** *his* **hand: and the midwife took and bound upon his hand a scarlet thread, saying, This came out first.**

VERSE 29

And it came to pass, as he drew back his hand, that, behold, his brother came out: and she said, How hast thou broken forth? *this* **breach** *be* **upon thee: therefore his name was called Pharez.**

The name Pharez, or Perez, meant "breach," "breakthrough," or "burst forth." His descendants included David, Solomon, and Jesus.

VERSE 30

And afterward came out his brother, that had the scarlet thread upon his hand: and his name was called Zerah.

The meaning of the name Zerah is "bright red." This concluded the genealogy of Judah at that point. He (along with Reuben) was chiefly responsible for saving Joseph's life, having suggested he be sold into slavery. The story of Joseph resumed in the next chapter.

CHAPTER THIRTY-NINE

VERSE 1

And Joseph was brought down to Egypt; and Potiphar, an officer of Pharoah, captain of the guard, an Egyptian, bought him of the hands of the Ishmeelites, which had brought him down thither.

Potiphar, or Potiphera, was an Egyptian name meaning "he to whom the god Ra has given."

The word used here for "officer" is the Hebrew *cârîyc*, which derives from a root word meaning "to castrate." It was therefore often used to signify a eunuch, and since many high court officers were eunuchs, the words became interchangeable. But it could also mean one who was impotent or even celibate.

There is some debate as to whether Potiphar was a physical eunuch, but I doubt it. Eunuchs were usually employed in matters of harems, and Potiphar was the head of some sort of police department or the palace guard. And he was married. It's more logical to assume he either didn't want or couldn't have children.

VERSE 2

And the Lord was with Joseph, and he was a prosperous man; and he was in the house of his master the Egyptian.

It was common for those captured in battle to be put to work as slaves at hard labor, usually in the fields or other such physical tasks. But slaves who were purchased were treated much better and often employed as secretaries or scribes or used for other domestic purposes.

VERSE 3

And his master saw that the Lord *was* **with him, and that the Lord made all that he did to prosper in his hand.**

VERSE 4

And Joseph found grace in his sight, and he served him: and he made him overseer over his house, and all *that* **he had he put into his hand.**

VERSE 5

And it came to pass from the time *that* **he had made him overseer in his house, and over all that he had, that the Lord blessed the Egyptian's house for Joseph's sake; and the blessing of the Lord was upon all that he had in the house, and in the field.**

VERSE 6

And he left all that he had in Joseph's hand; and he knew not aught he had, save the bread which he did eat. And Joseph was a goodly *person*, **and well favoured.**

It's difficult to pinpoint the time frame of Joseph's slavery in Egypt, but we know his time in Potiphar's house and in prison totaled about thirteen years; he was seventeen when he was sold into slavery and thirty when he was made overseer to the king. Of those thirteen years, at least two were spent in prison.

According to the Jewish calendar, Joseph was purchased by Potiphar in the year 2216, (1544 BC), which would have been toward the end of the Middle Kingdom (c. 2030 BC–1640 BC) or the beginning of the Second Intermediate Period. If so, Potiphar might have been Ptahwer, an officer of Pharaoh Ahmenemhet III.

VERSE 7

> **And it came to pass after these things, that his master's wife cast her eyes upon Joseph; and she said, Lie with me.**

Remember that Potiphar was either celibate or impotent whether by choice or otherwise.

VERSE 8

> **But he refused, and said unto his master's wife, behold, my master wotteth not what *is* with me in the house, and he hath committed all that he hath to my hand;**

VERSE 9

> ***There is* none greater in this house than I; neither hath he kept back any thing from me but thee, because thou *art* his wife: how can I do this great wickedness, and sin against God?**

The Egyptians at that time were sun worshipers and also very promiscuous, men and women alike. But Joseph had obviously not let that influence him. Note that he was even more concerned about sinning against God than against his master.

VERSE 10

> **And it came to pass, as she spake to Joseph day by day, that he hearkened not unto her, to lie by her, *or* be with her.**

VERSE 11

> **And it came to pass about that time, that *Joseph* went into the house to do his business; and *there was* none of the men of the house there within.**

VERSE 12

And she caught him by his garment, saying, Lie with me; and he left his garment in her hand, and fled, and got him out.

VERSE 13

And it came to pass, when she saw that he had left his garment in her hand, and was fled forth,

VERSE 14

That she called unto the men of her house, and spake unto them, saying, See, he hath brought in an Hebrew unto us to mock us; he came in unto me to lie with me, and I cried with a loud voice:

VERSE 15

And it came to pass, when he heard that I lifted up my voice and cried, that he left his garment with me, and fled, and got him out.

VERSE 16

And she laid up his garment by her, until his lord came home.

VERSE 17

And she spake unto him, according to these words, saying, The Hebrew servant, which thou hast brought unto us, came in unto me to mock me:

VERSE 18

And it came to pass, as I lifted up my voice and cried, that he left his garment with me, and fled out.

Talk about no fury like a woman scorned. This was possibly the first recorded mention of that.

VERSE 19

And it came to pass, when his master heard the words of his wife, which she spake unto him, saying, After this manner did thy servant to me; that his wrath was kindled.

VERSE 20

And Joseph's master took him, and put him into the prison, a place where the king's prisoners *were* **bound: and he was there in the prison.**

The laws of Hammurabi concerning women were drawn up several centuries before this happened. They detailed the punishments for adultery and the treatment of women in general, so it might be that Potiphar doubted his wife's story or at least thought there might have been two sides to it. He undoubtedly could have had Joseph put to death for his crime, but he had him imprisoned instead, and so saved his life.

It's also interesting that this is the first mention of a prison in the Bible. Normal punishment for a crime was a specific action—maybe a fine for a lesser offense, bodily mutilation of some sort (still practiced today in some parts of the Middle East), or death. In the laws of the Old Testament, there's no mention of imprisonment for any crime or sin. This was apparently a special facility reserved for particular prisoners and particular offenses.

VERSE 21

But the Lord was with Joseph, and shewed him mercy, and gave him favour in the sight of the keeper of the prison.

VERSE 22

And the keeper of the prison committed to Joseph's hand all the prisoners there *were* **in the prison; and whatsoever they did there, he was the doer** *of it.*

Joseph quickly became what we would call a trustee, earning

probably the title of "scribe of the prison," a chief assistant to the keeper, the warden or overseer.

VERSE 23

The keeper of the prison looked not to any thing *that was* **under his hand, because the Lord was with him, and that which he did, the Lord made** *it* **prosper.**

CHAPTER FORTY

And it came to pass after these things, *that* **the butler of the king of Egypt and** *his* **baker had offended their lord the king of Egypt.**

That is, after Joseph was promoted to his position of trust in prison. The word used here for "butler" is *mashqeh*, often translated as "cupbearer," and the word for "baker," *âphah*, signified the chief cook. Both of these were very high offices held by princes of the realm or other important personages. Each man would have been in charge of many people, perhaps hundreds. We are not told here what the offenses were that had angered the king, but the book of Jasher in the Apocrypha 46 states,

> "In those days, Joseph was still confined in the prison house in the land of Egypt.
> 1. At that time, the attendants of Pharaoh, the chief of the butlers and the chief of the bakers who belonged to the king of Egypt, were standing before him.
> 2. The butler placed wine before the king to drink, and the baker placed bread before the king to eat. The king drank the wine and ate the bread, he and his servants and ministers that ate at the king's table.
> 3. And while they were eating and drinking, the butler and the baker remained there, and Pharaoh's ministers found many flies in the wine the butler had brought, and stones of niter were found in the baker's bread. (Niter is the mineral form of potassium nitrate.)
> 4. And the captain of the guard placed Joseph as an attendant on Pharaoh's officers, and Pharaoh's officers were in confinement one year."

VERSE 2

And Pharaoh was wroth against two _of_ his officers, against the chief of the butlers and against the chief of the bakers.

VERSE 3

And he put them in ward in the house of the captain of the guard, into the prison, the place where Joseph _was_ bound.

The prison was evidently a cellblock or jail of some sort attached to Potiphar's house. To be put in ward was to be confined until their case was decided, which in this case took about a year.

VERSE 4

And the captain of the guard charged Joseph with them, and he served them: and they continued a season in ward.

The word used for ward throughout this chapter in _mishmâr,_ best translated as "prison," although it could also mean "to guard," "watch," or "secure."

VERSE 5

And they dreamed a dream both of them, each man his dream in one night, each man according to the interpretation of his dream, the butler and the baker of the king of Egypt, which _were_ bound in the prison.

VERSE 6

And Joseph came in unto them in the morning, and looked upon them, and, behold, they _were_ sad.

VERSE 7

And he asked Pharaoh's officers that _were_ with him in the ward of his lord's house, saying, Wherefore look ye _so_ sadly to-day?

VERSE 8

And they said unto him, We have dreamed a dream, and *there is* **no interpreter of it. And Joseph said unto them,** *Do* **not interpretations** *belong* **to God? Tell me** *them***, I pray you.**

VERSE 9

And the chief butler told his dream to Joseph, and said to him, In my dream, behold, a vine *was* **before me;**

VERSE 10

And in the vine *were* **three branches: and it** *was* **as though it budded,** *and* **her blossoms shot forth; and the clusters thereof brought forth ripe grapes:**

VERSE 11

And Pharaoh's cup *was* **in my hand: and I took the grapes, and pressed them into Pharaoh's cup, and I gave the cup into Pharaoh's hand.**

VERSE 12

And Joseph said unto him, This *is* **the interpretation of it: The three branches** *are* **three days:**

VERSE 13

Yet within three days shall Pharaoh lift up thine head, and restore thee unto thy place: and thou shalt deliver Pharaoh's cup into his hand, after the former manner when thou wast his butler.

VERSE 14

But think on me when it shall be well with thee, and shew kindness, I pray thee, unto me, and make mention ot me unto Pharaoh, and bring me out of this house:

VERSE 15

For indeed I was stolen away out of the land of the Hebrews: and here also have I done nothing that they should put me into the dungeon.

VERSE 16

When the chief baker saw that the interpretation was good, he said unto Joseph, I also *was* **in my dream, and behold, I** *had* **three white baskets on my head:**

VERSE 17

And in uppermost basket *there* **was all manner of bakemeats for Pharaoh; and the birds did eat them out of the basket upon my head.**

VERSE 18

And Joseph answered and said, This *is* **the interpretation thereof: The three baskets** *are* **three days:**

VERSE 19

Yet within three days shall Pharaoh lift up thine head from off thee, and shall hang thee on a tree, and the birds shall eat thy flesh from off thee.

This was a terrible form of punishment practiced then and today in some parts of the Muslim world.

VERSE 20

And it came to pass the third day, *which* **was Pharaoh's birthday, that he made a feast unto all his servants: and he lifted up the head of the chief butler and of the chief baker among his servants.**

VERSE 21

And he restored the chief butler unto his butlership again; and he gave the cup into Pharaoh's hand.

VERSE 22

But he hanged the chief baker: as Joseph had interpreted to them.

VERSE 23

Yet did not the chief butler remember Joseph, but forgat him.

CHAPTER FORTY-ONE

VERSE 1

And it came to pass at the end of two full years, that Pharaoh dreamed: and, behold, he stood by the river.

The two full years could have indicated the duration of Joseph's imprisonment, or it could have been two years since the incidents described in the last chapter. If the latter were the case, Joseph's time in prison would have been something over three years.

The story of Pharaoh's dream is well known, and I will give most of it without comment. However, a little background might be helpful. The word *pharaoh* means "great house." Pharaoh sat in the great house, a descriptive term. It was not until some three hundred years later that the title was used to specifically name or address a king. Therefore, the Bible does not name the pharaoh who was king at the time, so there is some debate as to who that Pharaoh was.

Many scholars put Joseph's time in the Hyksos rule (ca. 1650–1560 BC) with perhaps Apopsis, the last of the Hyksos kings, being the one who dreamed. Others prefer to date Joseph to the Middle Kingdom, ca. 2000 BC–1700 BC), with pharaohs as late as Amenemhet III of the Twelfth Dynasty. Good evidence is available for both sides of the debate, as will be discussed later.

The Hyksos people were of mixed Semitic-Asiatic descent who had come to Egypt during the eighteenth century BC and ruled over Egypt in the Fifteenth Dynasty. The name itself derives from the Egyptian words for "rulers of foreign countries." Many cultural improvements were instituted under the Hyksos rule such as new musical instruments, improved bronze- and pottery-working methods, and new farming methods and crops.

Militarily, the introduction of the horse and chariot, the improvement of the battle ax, the composite bow, and improved methods of fortification were a few of the Hyksos's innovations that became important in Egypt's later dynasties.

The Hyksos, Hurian, and Hittite Kingdoms (among others such as the Minoan) are rarely mentioned when studying ancient and medieval history, nor are the various migrations of the earliest tribes and peoples as they repopulated the world. For a better understanding of where we came from and how the people in the Bible fit into the history of the world, I recommend research that includes some history of as many as possible of the early civilizations, from Mu (Lemuria) on down. They make fascinating reading and help the student fit together the pieces of our ancestral puzzle to show the real picture of our origins and how we got to where we are today.

Here is Pharaoh's dream:

VERSE 2

And, behold, there came up out of the river seven well favoured kine and fatfleshed; and they fed in a meadow.

VERSE 3

And, behold, seven other kine came up after them out of the river, ill favoured and leanfleshed; and stood by the *other* kine upon the brink of the river.

VERSE 4

And the ill favoured and leanfleshed kine did eat up the seven well favoured and fat kine. So Pharaoh awoke.

VERSE 5

And he slept and dreamed the second time: and, behold, seven ears of corn came up upon one stalk, rank and good.

VERSE 6

And, behold, seven thin ears and blasted with the east wind sprung up after them.

VERSE 7

And the seven thin ears devoured the seven rank and full ears. And Pharaoh awoke, and, behold, it *was* **a dream.**

VERSE 8

And it came to pass in the morning that his spirit was troubled; and he sent and called for all the magicians of Egypt, and all the wise men thereof: and Pharaoh told them his dream; but *there was* **none that could interpret them unto Pharaoh.**

A distinction is made between magicians and wise men. Although not clarified here, it can be assumed that the wise men dealt with matters of state and day-to-day governing, while magicians dealt with matters of the occult and such things as dream interpretations. Both groups were wise enough not to try to guess at the meaning of Pharaoh's dreams.

VERSE 9

Then spake the chief butler unto Pharaoh, saying, I do remember my faults this day:

VERSE 10

Pharaoh was wroth with his servants, and put me in ward in the captain of the guard's house, *both* **me and the chief baker:**

VERSE 11

And we dreamed a dream one night, I and he; we dreamed each man according to the interpretation of his dream.

VERSE 12

And *there was* **there with us a young man, an Hebrew, servant to the captain of the guard, and we**

told him, and he interpreted to us our dreams; to each man according to his dream he did interpret.

VERSE 13

And it came to pass, and he interpreted to us, so it was; me he restored unto mine office, and him he hanged.

Joseph had asked the butler to remember him to Pharaoh, and he finally did—two years later—not so much to thank Joseph, I suspect, as to ingratiate himself with Pharaoh.

Interesting too is the fact that the butler credited Joseph with restoring him to office and with hanging the baker. Apparently, he was not quite comfortable with reminding Pharaoh that Pharaoh had had the baker beheaded and hanged.

VERSE 14

Then Pharaoh sent and called Joseph, and they brought him hastily out of the dungeon: and he shaved *himself*, and changed his raiment, and came in unto Pharaoh.

We don't know whether he shaved his head or beard or both, but it was probably both since the Egyptian custom was to shave both and sometimes (especially for the priests) to completely remove all body hair up to and including the eyebrows. The change of clothes was probably provided by Potiphar or perhaps by Pharaoh himself.

VERSE 15

And Pharaoh said unto Joseph, I have dreamed a dream, and *there is* none that can interpret it: and I have heard say of thee, *that* thou canst understand a dream and interpret it.

VERSE 16

And Joseph answered Pharaoh, saying, *It is* not in me: God shall give Pharaoh an answer of peace.

VERSE 17

And Pharaoh said unto Joseph, In my dream, behold, I stood on the bank of a river:

VERSE 18

And, behold, there came up out of the river seven kine, fatfleshed and well favoured; and they fed in a meadow:

VERSE 19

And, behold, seven other kine came up after them, poor and very ill favoured and leanfleshed, such as I never saw in all the land of Egypt for badness:

VERSE 20

And the lean and the ill favoured kine did eat up the first seven fat kine:

VERSE 21

And when they had eaten them up, it could not be known that they had eaten them; but they *were* still ill favoured, as at the beginning. So I awoke.

VERSE 22

And I saw in my dream, and, behold, seven ears came up in one stalk, full and good:

VERSE 23

And, behold, seven ears, withered, thin, *and* blasted with the east wind, sprung up after them:

VERSE 24

And the thin ears devoured the seven good ears: and I told *this* unto the magicians; but *there was* none that could declare *it* to me

VERSE 25

And Joseph said unto Pharaoh, The dream of Pharaoh *is* **one: God hath shewed Pharaoh what he** *is* **about to do.**

VERSE 26

The seven good kine *are* **seven years; and the seven good ears** *are* **seven years: the dream** *is* **one.**

VERSE 27

And the seven thin and ill favoured kine that came after them *are* **seven years; and the seven empty ears blasted with the east wind shall be seven years of famine.**

VERSE 28

This *is* **the thing which I have spoken unto Pharaoh: What God** *is* **about to do he sheweth unto Pharaoh.**

VERSE 29

Behold, there come seven years of great plenty throughout all the land of Egypt:

VERSE 30

And there shall arise after them seven years of famine; and all the plenty shall be forgotten in the land of Egypt; and the famine shall consume the land;

VERSE 31

And the plenty shall not be known in the land by reason of the famine following; for it *shall be* **very grievous.**

VERSE 32

And for that the dream was doubled unto Pharaoh twice; *it is* because the thing *is* established by God, and God will shortly bring it to pass.

VERSE 33

Now therefore let Pharaoh look out a man discreet and wise, and set him over the land of Egypt.

A less-confusing translation would be "seek out a man" or "look for a man." We don't know if Joseph had himself in mind when he made this suggestion, but it certainly was possible.

VERSE 34

And let Pharaoh do *this*, and let him appoint officers over the land, and take up the fifth part of the land of Egypt in the seven plenteous years.

That was, take one-fifth of the land's produce.

VERSE 35

And let them gather all the food of those good years that come, and lay up corn under the hand of Pharaoh, and let them keep food in the cities.

VERSE 36

And that food shall be for store to the land against the seven years of famine, which shall be in the land of Egypt; that the land perish not through the famine.

This was an excellent plan, one that would seem obvious today but was no doubt a radically new concept at that time. It's probable that people then lived from day to day without much thought to the future and without the concerns of modern life. That it hadn't been done before is evidenced by the fact that they had to build the storehouses that were to hold the grain and foodstuff.

VERSE 37

And the thing was good in the eyes of Pharaoh, and in the eyes of all his servants.

VERSE 38

And Pharaoh said unto his servants, Can we find *such a one* **as this** *is***, a man in whom the spirit of God** *is***?**

VERSE 39

And Pharaoh said unto Joseph, Forasmuch as God hath shewed thee all this, *there is* **none so discreet and wise as thou** *art***;**

VERSE 40

Thou shalt be over my house, and according unto thy word shall all my people be ruled: only in the throne will I be greater than thou.

VERSE 41

And Pharaoh said unto Joseph, See, I have set thee over all the land of Egypt.

VERSE 42

And Pharaoh took off his ring from his hand, and put it upon Joseph's hand, and arrayed him in vestures of fine linen, and put a gold chain around his neck;

VERSE 43

And he made him to ride in the second chariot which he had, and they cried before him, Bow the knee: and he made him *ruler* **over all the land of Egypt.**

This was a huge concession by Pharaoh. While he still retained the overall power of the throne, he gave the day-to-day running of his kingdom to Joseph, even presenting him with the ring, necklace, and vestments of his office.

There are several theories about the time all this took place. One is that the pharaoh mentioned here is Djoser (Netjererkhet), who ruled from 2628 BC to 2609 BC (Third Egyptian Dynasty) based on translated ancient Egyptian texts. It has been speculated that Joseph was the person named Imhotep, a highly skilled second in command of Djoser. I believe this is unlikely because Imhotep is said to have been an architect and engineer, a physician, perhaps the real "father of medicine," a nobleman, and a high priest of the sun god Ra, none of which fits the character or history of Joseph.

That's probably the earliest of all the dates suggested as possible for the time of Joseph's famine, but famines weren't rare. Thomas Mann retold the stories surrounding Joseph in his four-novel omnibus, *Joseph and His Brothers*. He identified Joseph with the figure of Osarseph, known from the writings of Manetho, and the pharaoh with Akhenaten (c. 1385 BC–c. 1350 BC). Manetho was a Greco-Egyptian priest who lived during the third century BC; his writings have mostly not survived except as related by the historian Josephus Flavius from the first century AD.

The writings included much that was obtained from documents that no longer exist, and some were no doubt factual, but they also contained many myths and legends. According to this particular story, Osarseph later changed his name to Moses, and the story has been completely discredited and relegated to anti-Jewish propaganda from the first and second centuries BC.

It could also be argued that the "new king" who came after Joseph's Pharaoh was one of the Hyksos kings, perhaps Khyan (c. 1620 BC) or Apophis (c. 1595 BC–c. 1565 BC), and that was the reason he "did not know Joseph" (Exodus 1:8).

The mention of Pharaoh's second chariot leads one to believe that the time could have been later in the Hyksos rule of Egypt. The horse-drawn chariot appeared in Egypt during the Hyksos period, whether or not the Hyksos had brought it there.

A good case could be made for the pharaoh here being the last of the Hyksos kings, who also took the title of Pharaoh, and the "new king" would have been one of the Egyptian princes who claimed power immediately after the Hyksos were driven out soon after 1530 BC.

That would explain how Joseph, a foreigner, had been elevated to such a high position; the Hyksos had been foreigners themselves. That would also explain why the new king did not recognize not only Joseph but also his title to the land of Goshen and why he undertook the immediate enslavement of the Israelites, who could possibly have been seen as a potential threat to reinstate a foreign rule.

When the Hyksos were driven out, many of their records were purposely destroyed, and very little record was left of them. That would perhaps explain why there is no historical record of Joseph. If this last theory is accurate, that would place the time of Joseph's release from prison and subsequent promotion somewhere between 1600 BC and 1550 BC and would agree with the theory that Ahmose I (Amosis I, Aahmes I, c. 1539 BC–1514 BC) was the "new king." Recent discoveries also suggest it may have been Seti I (c. 1290 BC–1279 BC), which would put Joseph's dates considerably later.

As with all dates in ancient history, especially with ancient Egypt, the dates are speculative; there are simply not enough records to pinpoint times. The best estimates are based on Egyptian dynasties, of which there may have been as many as thirty-three along with other periods called intermediary periods as well as some that were labeled only by an event or personage.

It's safe to say we just don't know when this took place, so we also don't know the dates for the Israelites' stay in Egypt or the dates for the Exodus. We do know they left Egypt after 430 years (Exodus 12:40). I have seen the dates mentioned for the arrival of Jacob's family at about 1880 BC, and therefore the dates for the Exodus at about 1450 BC, but again, I believe these are very speculative.

There is also much debate as to just who the Hyksos people were. The name was first used by the historian Manetho (c. 300 BC). Josephus Flavius (first century AD) translated Hyksos as "shepherd kings" or "captive kings." So Josephus thought this might have been a reference to the Hebrews themselves, but that theory has been discounted by modern scholars.

The only certainty is that they were a Semitic group of mixed origin that probably comprised several different nationalities. There are arguments that they included a Hurrian element, or that they were the Edomites, the Amalekites, the Amu, the Hittites, and even that all of the above were all mixed into one people.

What is known for sure is that the Hyksos brought considerable benefits to Egypt that lasted long after they had gone. They made Egypt a stronger power militarily as well as culturally. They introduced the humpbacked zebu cattle, new crops of fruits and vegetables, and improvements in pottery making, metalworking (bronze) and weaving among others. Possibly one of their greatest contributions was the preservation of famous Egyptian literary and scientific documents. During the reign of Apophis, scribes were commissioned to copy Egyptian texts so they wouldn't be lost. Texts such as the Edwin Smith Surgical Papyrus (dating from c. 3000 BC), the Westcar Papyrus, and the Rhind Mathematical Papyrus are among those restored.

VERSE 44

> **And Pharaoh said unto Joseph, I *am* Pharaoh, and without thee shall no man life up his hand or foot in all the land of Egypt.**

VERSE 45

> **And Pharaoh called Joseph's name Zaphnathpaaneah; and he gave him to wife Asenath the daughter of Potipherah the priest of On. And Joseph went out over *all* the land of Egypt.**

Maybe this is why there is no written record of Joseph. Can you imagine how hard it would have been to carve this name in stone? Seriously, I believe the reason is a simple one: he was known by another name, perhaps Zafntipaankh (Zaphenath-paneah), an Egyptian name meaning "nourisher of the living one," or "savior of the world," or Saba Sabani, a name given to him by Pharaoh when he became treasurer.

Many coins made of differing materials and of different sizes and denominations have been found bearing Joseph's name and likeness as well as the likeness of ancient Pharaohs and of Egyptian gods.

Some of the coins even depict the fat cows of the pharaoh's dream. But of course they carry no dates.

It has been theorized that Potipherah was a prince as well as a priest and that he may have been the same man as the Potiphar who was Joseph's jailer, but I believe that's a stretch. The name means "to whom Ra has given," and it could have been a common name considering the chief religion of the Egyptians at that time was the worship of Ra, the sun god.

VERSE 46

> **And Joseph was thirty years old when he stood before Pharaoh king of Egypt, And Joseph went throughout all the land of Egypt.**

VERSE 47

> **And in the seven plenteous years, the earth brought forth handfuls.**

VERSE 48

> **And he gathered up all the food of the seven years, which were in the land of Egypt, and laid up the food in the cities: the food of the field, which** *was* **round about every city, laid he up in the same.**

VERSE 49

> **And Joseph gathered corn as the sand of the sea, very much, until he left numbering, for** *it was* **without number.**

VERSE 50

> **And unto Joseph were born two sons before the years of famine came, which Asenath the daughter of Potiphera priest of On bare unto him.**

From this and from verses 45 and 46, we can conclude that some time was given Joseph before the start of the years of plenty, probably two or three years at least if his sons weren't twins. He would have had time to build the storehouses and make the other arrangements necessary for transferring and storing the vast amount of food and supplies that would be needed in the years of famine.

VERSE 51

> **And Joseph called the name of his firstborn Manasseh: For God,** *said he*, **hath made me forget all my toil, and all my father's house.**

VERSE 52

> **And the name of the second called he Ephraim: For God hath caused me to be fruitful in the land of my affliction.**

VERSE 53

> **And the seven years of plenteousness, that was in the land of Egypt, were ended.**

VERSE 54

> **And the seven years of dearth began to come, according as Joseph had said: and the dearth was in all lands; but in all the land of Egypt there was bread.**

VERSE 55

> **And when all the land of Egypt was famished, the people cried to Pharaoh for bread; and Pharaoh said unto all the Egyptians, Go unto Joseph; what he saith to you, do.**

VERSE 56

> **And the famine was over all the face of the earth: and Joseph opened all the storehouses, and sold unto the Egyptians; and the famine waxed sore in the land of Egypt.**

VERSE 57

And all countries came into Egypt to Joseph for to buy *corn*; **because that the famine was so sore in all lands.**

Famines were common in the ancient world (see Genesis 12:10.) While they were rarer in Egypt, they weren't unknown there. Irrigation of most of the farmland in Egypt depended on the Nile River's overflowing each year. If for some reason the floods either weren't forthcoming or were too strong, the crops would fail. Other areas depended on rainfall for irrigation with no real means to offset the damages of uncooperative weather.

Nearly all worldwide famines have been related to the lack of water or too much of it. The Byzantine Empire suffered a severe famine in about AD 927 due to four months of frost. The worst famine in Japan's history, from AD 1229 to 1232, and one in Indonesia in 1815 were caused by volcanic eruptions. There were another seven years of famine in Egypt from AD 1064 to 1071. And of course there was the drought of the 1930s in the United States, commonly known as the Dust Bowl.

Throughout history, there have been famines causing hundreds of thousands and in some cases even millions of deaths. Even today, California and the western part of the United States are in the throes of a four-year drought that could well become a famine of biblical proportions.

CHAPTER FORTY-TWO

VERSE 1

> **Now when Jacob saw that there was corn in Egypt, Jacob said unto his sons, Why do ye look one upon another?**

There are moral lessons to be learned from the story of Joseph in the preceding chapters and those that follow, and there are countless teachers who can do a much better job of explaining them than I could. So for the most part, I will just let the story tell itself. For the purpose of this work, I am concerned with the historicity of the writing and the accuracy of the translation.

VERSE 2

> **And he said, behold, I have heard that there is corn in Egypt: get you down thither, and buy for us from thence; that we may live, and not die.**

VERSE 3

> **And Joseph's ten brethren went down to buy corn in Egypt.**

VERSE 4

> **But Benjamin, Joseph's brother, Jacob sent not with his brethren; for he said, Lest peradventure mischief befall him.**

Benjamin was the youngest of Joseph's eleven brothers, and his only full brother, the others all being half-brothers. In the Qur'an, Benjamin is called a righteous child; he remained with Jacob when the other brothers plotted against Joseph.

VERSE 5

And the sons of Israel came to buy *corn* among those that came: for the famine was in the land of Canaan.

VERSE 6

And Joseph *was* the governor over the land, *and* he *it was* that sold to all the people of the land: and Joseph's brethren came, and bowed down themselves before him *with* their faces to the earth.

VERSE 7

And Joseph saw his brethren, and he knew them, but made himself strange unto them, and spake roughly unto them; and he said unto them, Whence come ye? And they said, From the land of Canaan to buy food.

There was little chance that Joseph's brothers would have recognized him even if he hadn't disguised his voice and spoken through an interpreter. He was, after all, now thirty years old. In addition, his brothers no doubt presumed him dead or in some form of slavery, certainly not in a position of power. And he was clean shaven whereas his brothers would have expected him to have a full beard.

VERSE 8

And Joseph knew his brethren, but they knew not him.

VERSE 9

And Joseph remembered the dreams which he dreamed of them, and said unto them, Ye *are* spies; to see the nakedness of the land ye are come.

In 37:1–11, Joseph dreamed that his mother, father, and brothers would bow down to him.

VERSE 10

And they said unto him, Nay, my lord, but to buy food are thy servants come.

VERSE 11

We *are* **all one man's sons;** *we are* **true men, thy servants are no spies.**

The brothers profess to be honest men, which they were for the purpose of this particular mission. They probably wouldn't have spoken so if they had known to whom they were talking.

VERSE 12

And he said unto them, Nay, but to see the nakedness of the land ye are come.

VERSE 13

And they said, Thy servants *are* **twelve brethren, the sons of one man in the land of Canaan; and, behold, the youngest** *is* **this day with our father, and one** *is* **not.**

VERSE 14

And Joseph said unto them, That *is it* **that I spake unto you, saying Ye** *are* **spies.**

VERSE 15

Hereby ye shall be proved: By the life of Pharaoh ye shall not go forth hence, except your youngest brother come hither.

Benjamin, aside from being Joseph's only full brother, was the only brother who had not been involved in the plot to sell Joseph into slavery in the beginning, so it was natural that Joseph wanted to see him.

VERSE 16

Send one of you, and let him fetch your brother; and ye shall be kept in prison, that your words may be proved, whether *there* **be** *any* **truth in you: or else by the life of Pharaoh surely ye** *are* **spies.**

VERSE 17

And he put them all together into ward three days.

Remember that being "put in ward" was their way of saying put in jail or held in some form of bondage.

VERSE 18

And Joseph said unto them the third day, This do, and live; *for* **I fear God.**

VERSE 19

If ye *be* **true** *men***, let one of your brethren be bound in the house of your prison: go ye, carry corn for the famine of your houses:**

VERSE 20

But bring your youngest brother unto me; so shall your words be verified, and ye shall not die. And they did so.

VERSE 21

And they said one to another, We *are* **verily guilty concerning our brother, in that we saw the anguish of his soul, when he besought us, and we would not hear; therefore is this distress come upon us.**

The brothers believed they were being punished for their earlier treatment of Joseph even though they still had no idea it was Joseph himself doing the punishing.

VERSE 22

And Reuben answered them, saying, Spake I not unto you, saying, Do not sin against the child; and ye would not hear? Therefore, behold, also his blood is required.

VERSE 23

And they knew not that Joseph understood *them*, **for he spoke unto them by an interpreter.**

Joseph learned that Reuben at least was not in favor of the actions of the others. He knew it was Reuben who had suggested the well instead of outright murder, but until then, he wouldn't have known that Reuben had been trying to spare him altogether.

VERSE 24

And he turned himself about from them, and wept; and returned to them again, and communed with them, and took from them Simeon, and bound him before their eyes.

By "turning about," he would have left the room and gotten completely out of their sight.

VERSE 25

Then Joseph commanded to fill their sacks with corn, and to restore every man's money into his sack, and to give them provision for the way: and thus he did unto them.

Joseph not only filled the requests for corn; he also returned the money they had brought to pay for it.

VERSE 26

And they laded their asses with the corn, and departed thence.

VERSE 27

And as one of them opened his sack to give his ass provender in the inn, he espied his money; for, behold, it *was* in his sack's mouth.

VERSE 28

And he said unto his brethren, My money is restored; and, lo, *it is* even in my sack: and their heart failed *them*, and they were afraid, saying one to another, What is this *that* God hath done unto us?

VERSE 29

And they came unto Jacob their father unto the land of Canaan, and told him all that befell unto them; saying.

VERSE 30

The man, *who is* the lord of the land, spake roughly to us, and took us for spies of the country.

VERSE 31

And we said unto him, We *are* true *men*; we are no spies:

VERSE 32

We *be* twelve brethren, sons of our father; one *is* not, and the youngest *is* this day with our father in the land of Canaan.

VERSE 33

And the man, the lord of the country, said unto us, Hereby shall I know that ye *are* true *men*; leave one of your brethren *here* with me, and take *food for* the famine of your households, and be gone:

VERSE 34

And bring your youngest brother unto me: then shall I know that ye *are* **no spies, but** *that* **ye** *are* **true** *men*: *so* **will I deliver your brother, and ye shall traffick in the land.**

VERSE 35

And it came to pass as they emptied their sacks, that, behold, every man's bundle of money *was* **in his sack: and when** *both* **they and their father saw the bundles of money, they were afraid.**

VERSE 36

And Jacob their father said unto them, Me have ye bereaved *of my children*: **Joseph** *is* **not, and Simeon** *is* **not, and ye will take Benjamin** *away*: **all these things are against me.**

VERSE 37

And Reuben spake unto his father, saying, Slay my two sons, if I bring him not to thee: deliver him into my hand, and I will bring him to thee again.

It's hard to believe Reuben really thought Jacob would kill his sons (Jacob's grandsons) in any case, but it shows that Reuben was sincere in his desire to complete the mission Joseph had given him.

VERSE 38

And he said, My son shall not go down with you; for his brother is dead, and he is left alone: if mischief befall him by the way in the which ye go, then shall ye bring down my gray hairs with sorrow to the grave.

CHAPTER FORTY-THREE

VERSE 1

And the famine *was* **sore in the land.**

VERSE 2

And it came to pass, when they had eaten up the corn which they had brought out of Egypt, their father said unto them, Go again, buy us a little food.

VERSE 3

And Judah spake unto him, saying, The man did solemnly protest unto us, saying, Ye shall not see my face, except your brother *be* **with you.**

VERSE 4

If thou wilt send our brother with us, we will go down and buy thee food:

VERSE 5

But if thou wilt not send *him***, we will not go down: for the man said unto us, Ye shall not see my face, except your brother** *be* **with you.**

VERSE 6

And Israel said, Wherefore dealt *ye so* **ill with me,** *as* **to tell the man whether ye had yet a brother?**

Note that the name was switched from Jacob to Israel. It may just indicate a time lapse from the last chapter, or it might be that the name was used for emphasis because he was angry over having to send Benjamin, the way a mother or father uses a child's full given name at times of stress or discipline.

VERSE 7

> **And they said, The man asked us straitly of our state, and of our kindred, saying, *Is* your father yet alive? Have ye *another* brother? and we told him according to the tenor of these words: could we certainly know that he would say, Bring your brother down?**

VERSE 8

> **And Judah said unto Israel his father, Send the lad with me, and we will arise and go; that we may live, and not die, both we, and thou, *and* also our little ones.**

The famine was so severe that Judah was telling Jacob that if they didn't get the food, they would all die anyway.

VERSE 9

> **I will be surety for him; of my hand shalt thou require him; if I bring him not unto thee, and set him before thee, then let me bear the blame for ever:**

VERSE 10

> **For except we had lingered, surely now we had returned this second time.**

An awkward translation; it merely meant that if we hadn't wasted so much time, we would have been back there by now. I suspect Simeon would also have appreciated a little more haste as he was waiting in prison.

VERSE 11

> **And their father Israel said unto them, If *it must be* so now, do this, take of the best fruits in the land in your vessels, and carry down the man a present, a little balm, and a little honey, spices, and myrrh, nuts, and almonds:**

The famine, probably caused by a lack of rain, had apparently hurt the production of the ground crops such as corn, wheat if they had it, and whatever fodder they raised for the animals more than the things Jacob had instructed the brothers to take as gifts. The honey, spices, and nuts (especially almonds) were very plentiful at that time and are significant cash crops to this day.

VERSE 12

And take double money in your hand; and the money that was brought again in the mouth of your sacks, carry *it* **again in your hand; peradventure it** *was* **an oversight:**

Jacob's advice was good on two levels. It could have been by mistake that the money was returned to them, and also, returning it would have helped establish the brothers' honesty.

VERSE 13

Take also your brother, and arise, go again unto the man.

A difficult decision for Jacob. He was deathly afraid for Benjamin's safety, but at the same time, he realized that without food, all his family and animals would have perished. He reached the only logical conclusion since Benjamin would probably have died anyway without food.

VERSE 14

And God Almighty give you mercy before the man, that he may send away your other brother, and Benjamin. If I be bereaved *of my children*, **I am bereaved.**

VERSE 15

And the men took that present, and they took double money in their hand, and Benjamin; and rose up, and went down to Egypt, and stood before Joseph.

VERSE 16

And when Joseph saw Benjamin with them, he said to the ruler of his house, Bring *these* men home, and slay, and make ready; for *these* men shall dine with me at noon.

Joseph ordered the majordomo of his house to prepare a feast to honor his brothers. The animal to be slain was most likely a goat, and the time for the day's main meal was typically at midday.

VERSE 17

And the man did as Joseph bade; and the man brought the men into Joseph's house.

VERSE 18

And the men were afraid, because they were brought into Joseph's house; and they said, Because of the money that was returned in our sacks at the first time are we brought in; that he may seek occasion against us, and fall upon us, and take us for bondmen, and our asses.

VERSE 19

And they came near to the steward of Joseph's house, and they communed with him at the door of the house,

VERSE 20

And said, O sir, we came indeed down at the first time to buy food;

VERSE 21

And it came to pass, when we came to the inn, that we opened our sacks, and, behold, *every* man's money *was* in the mouth of his sack, our money in full weight: and we have brought it again in our hand.

VERSE 22

And other money have we brought down in our hands to buy food: we cannot tell who put our money in our sacks.

VERSE 23

And he said, Peace *be* **to you, fear not: your God, and the God of your father, hath given you treasure in your sacks: I had your money. And he brought Simeon out unto them.**

Joseph's house manager quieted their fears and told them he got their money on the first trip. He told them their God must have put money in their sacks.

VERSE 24

And the man brought the men into Joseph's house, and gave *them* **water, and they washed their feet; and he gave their asses provender.**

VERSE 25

And they made ready the present against Joseph came at noon: for they heard that they should eat bread there.

"Bread" here was used in the same way we use the phrase "to break bread;" simply to eat a meal.

VERSE 26

And when Joseph came home, they brought him the present which *was* **in their hand into the house, and bowed themselves to him to the earth.**

VERSE 27

And he asked them of *their* **welfare, and said,** *Is* **your father well, the old man of whom ye spake?** *Is* **he yet alive?**

VERSE 28

And they answered, Thy servant our father *is* in good health, he *is* yet alive. And they bowed down their heads, and made obeisance.

VERSE 29

And he lifted up his eyes, and saw his brother Benjamin, his mother's son, and said, *Is* this your younger brother, of whom ye spake unto me? And he said, God be gracious unto thee, my son.

VERSE 30

And Joseph made haste; for his bowels did yearn upon his brother: and he sought where to weep; and he entered into *his* chamber, and wept there.

An interesting translation here. The word translated as "bowels" is *sheteph,* a root word originally meaning to "gush" or "overflow." The more modern translations of the Bible do a better job with phrases such as "overcome with affection," "deeply moved," and "his heart yearned." It was not the same word translated as "bowels" in Genesis 15:4 and 25:23, where the meaning clearly indicates the physical body as opposed to the usage here, where the word indicates an attitude or mental state.

VERSE 31

And he washed his face, and went out, and refrained himself, and said, Set on bread.

The word used here for "bread" is *lechem,* a generality meaning "food." The modern translation would be "set the table" or "put the food on the table."

VERSE 32

And they set out for him by himself, and for them by themselves, and for the Egyptians, which did eat with him, by themselves: because the Egyptians

> **might not eat bread with the Hebrews; for that** *is*
> **an abomination unto the Egyptians.**

Note the seating order specified here. The master of the house ate at a table by himself; the guests had their separate table (or tables, as there were usually only three or four to a table), and the local guests sat apart at their own tables.

Some of the pictures painted by the early masters show one large table for this type of meal, but that wasn't the case. They may have been seated on individual mats on the floor or at tables that were probably rather small and no taller than a footstool.

VERSE 33

> **And they sat before him, the firstborn according**
> **to his birthright, and the youngest according to**
> **his youth; and the men marveled one at another.**

VERSE 34

> **And he took** *and sent* **messes unto them from**
> **before him: but Benjamin's mess was five times**
> **so much as any of theirs. And they drank, and**
> **were merry with him.**

All the food was placed before Joseph, who would then send servings to each guest. And he showed his partiality by sending a much larger portion to Benjamin. It would really be interesting to know just what foods they were served and what they drank. We know that ancient Egyptians had a great variety of fruits and vegetables. They also had plenty of meats, including fish, duck, goose, stork, pigeon, goats, sheep, calves, and oxen. Notice there was no mention of pork and though pigs were raised and eaten in the delta; it was considered an abominable animal by the Egyptians even then.

For drink, they had wine and a beer made from barley, which was a common drink for everyone, including children. They could put on a real feast when the occasion suited. However, the quality was often sacrificed for quantity and variety.

CHAPTER FORTY-FOUR

VERSE 1

And he commanded the steward of his house, saying, Fill the men's sacks *with* **food, as much as they can carry, and put every man's money in his sack's mouth.**

VERSE 2

And put my cup, the silver cup, in the sack's mouth of the youngest, and his corn money. And he did according to the word that Joseph had spoken.

VERSE 3

As soon as the morning was light, the men were sent away, they and their asses.

Wouldn't you think they would have checked their packs before leaving after what had happened on the last trip?

VERSE 4

And **when they were gone out of the city,** *and* **not** *yet* **far off, Joseph said unto his steward, Up, follow after the men; and when thou dost overtake them, say unto them, Wherefore have ye rewarded evil for good?**

VERSE 5

Is **not this** *it* **in which my lord drinketh, and whereby indeed he divineth? Ye have done evil in so doing.**

VERSE 6

And he overtook them, and he spake unto them these same words.

Joseph didn't actually say he had used the cup for divining, although it was a common thing among Egyptians and Persians. Some famous people, including Alexander the Great, used sacred goblets or sometimes bowls for the purpose of divination. It's doubtful, however, that Joseph actually used his cup for this purpose; he only hinted that the cup might have been used in this manner.

Joseph was the first of the patriarchs to whom God didn't speak personally, but we know He communicated with him through his dreams. He therefore wouldn't have had any use for a divining cup, and we can safely assume it was used solely for drinking. As we shall see in the next few verses, this was all part of the complicated plot on Joseph's part to get his whole family down to Egypt.

VERSE 7

And they said unto him, Wherefore saith my lord these words? God forbid that thy servants should do according to this thing:

VERSE 8

Behold, the money, which we found in our sacks' mouths, we brought again unto thee out of the land of Canaan: how then should we steal out of thy lord's house silver or gold?

VERSE 9

With whomsoever of thy servants it be found, both let him die, and we also will be my lord's bondmen.

VERSE 10

And he said, now also *let* **it** *be* **according unto your words: he with whom it is found shall be my servant; and ye shall be blameless.**

VERSE 11

Then they speedily took down every man his sack to the ground, and opened every man his sack.

VERSE 12

> **And he searched, *and* began at the eldest, and left at the youngest: and the cup was found in Benjamin's sack.**

VERSE 13

> **Then they rent their clothes, and laded every man his ass, and returned to the city.**

VERSE 14

> **And Judah and his brothers came to Joseph's house, for he *was* yet there: and they fell before him on the ground.**

VERSE 15

> **And Joseph said unto them, What deed *is* this that ye have done? wot ye not that such a man as I can certainly devine?**

The rest of this chapter could easily have been one long verse. It's a good example of a narrative that has been broken up arbitrarily into short verses without really helping the flow of the story. It is the pleading of Judah to Joseph and is much easier read as one speech.

VERSE 16

> **And Judah said, What shall we say unto my lord? what shall we speak? or how shall we clear ourselves? God hath found out the iniquity of thy servants: behold, we *are* my lord's servants, both we and *he* also with whom the cup is found.**

VERSE 17

> **And he said, God forbid that I should do so: *but* the man in whose hand the cup is found, he shall be my servant; and as for you, get you up in peace unto your father.**

Joseph, knowing the truth, refused to impose the harsh punishment Judah expected.

VERSE 18

Then Judah came near unto him, and said, Oh my lord, let thy servant, I pray thee, speak a word in my lord's ears, and let not thine anger burn against thy servant: for thou *art* even as Pharaoh.

VERSE 19

My lord asked his servants, saying, Have ye a father, or a brother?

VERSE 20

And we said unto my lord, We have a father, an old man, and a child of his old age, a little one; and his brother is dead, and he alone is left of his mother, and his father loveth him.

VERSE 21

And thou saidst unto thy servants, Bring him down unto me, that I may set mine eyes upon him.

VERSE 22

And we said unto my lord, The lad cannot leave his father; for *if* he should leave his father, *his father* would die.

VERSE 23

And thou saidst unto thy servants, Except your youngest brother come down with you, ye shall see my face no more.

VERSE 24

And it came to pass when we came unto thy servant my father, we told him the words of my lord.

VERSE 25

And our father said, Go again, *and* **buy us a little food.**

VERSE 26

And we said, we cannot go down: if our youngest brother be with us, then will we go down: for we may not see the man's face, except our youngest brother *be* **with us.**

VERSE 27

And thy servant my father said unto us, Ye know that my wife bare me two *sons;*

VERSE 28

And the one went out from me, and I said, Surely he is torn in pieces; and I saw him not since:

VERSE 29

And if ye take this also from me, and mischief befall him, ye shall bring down my gray hairs with sorrow to the grave.

VERSE 30

Now therefore when I come to thy servant my father, and the lad *be* **not with us; seeing that his life is bound up in the lad's life;**

VERSE 31

It shall come to pass, when he seeth that the lad *is* **not** *with us,* **that he will die: and thy servants shall bring down the gray hairs of thy servant our father with sorrow to the grave.**

VERSE 32

For thy servant became surety for the lad unto my father, saying, If I bring him not unto thee, then I shall bear the blame to my father for ever.

VERSE 33

Now therefore, I pray thee, let thy servant abide instead of the lad a bondman to my lord; and let the lad go up with his brethren.

VERSE 34

For how shall I go up to my father, and the lad be **not with me? lest peradventure I see the evil that shall come on my father.**

I believe this offer from Judah took Joseph by surprise. Joseph had obviously hoped to keep Benjamin there with him and perhaps to get the rest of the family to join them later. Judah's offer to take Benjamin's place changed everything, and as we will see in the next chapter, Joseph decided to stop the charade and tell the brothers who he was and what he had in store for them.

CHAPTER FORTY-FIVE

VERSE 1

Then Joseph could not refrain himself before all them that stood by him; and he cried, Cause every man to go out from me. And there stood no man with him, while Joseph made himself known unto his brethren.

Joseph obviously didn't want to discuss his family business before the Egyptians who were present.

VERSE 2

And he wept aloud: and the Egyptians and the house of Pharaoh heard.

VERSE 3

And Joseph said unto his brethren, I am Joseph; doth my father yet live? And his brethren could not answer him; for they were troubled at his presence.

I believe "troubled at his presence" is more than an understatement; they were probably in utter disbelief and denial and speechless; no doubt some of it was due to fear.

VERSE 4

And Joseph said unto his brethren, Come near to me, I pray you. And they came near. And he said, I am Joseph your brother, whom ye sold into Egypt.

VERSE 5

Now therefore be not grieved, nor angry with yourselves, that ye sold me hither: for God did send me before you to preserve life.

VERSE 6

For these two years *hath* **the famine been in the land: and yet** *there are* **five years, in the which** *there shall* **neither** *be* **earing nor harvest.**

The word translated here as "earing" (used also in Exodus 34:21, Deuteronomy 21:4, 1 Samuel 8:12, and Isaiah 30:24) is the Hebrew *charash.* Earing is an Old English term for ploughing or tilling the soil. It has since fallen into disuse and is now primarily used in sailing to describe a line (rope) used to fasten the corners of a sail to a yard or gaff.

VERSE 7

And God sent me before you to preserve you a posterity in the earth, and to save your lives by a great deliverance.

VERSE 8

So now *it was* **not you** *that* **sent me hither, but God: and he hath made me a father to Pharaoh, and lord of all his house, and a ruler throughout all the land of Egypt.**

This might be a clue to the dates of Joseph's time in Egypt. The expression "made me a father to Pharaoh" perhaps indicated that the pharaoh in question was one of the very young boy pharaohs, the most notable of which was Tutankhamun. There were of course other young men and more than a few women pharaohs over the years, and the life span of most was relatively short, so it is still just speculation.

VERSE 9

Haste ye, and go up to my father, and say unto him, Thus saith thy son Joseph, God hath made me lord of all Egypt: come down unto me, tarry not:

VERSE 10

And thou shalt dwell in the land of Goshen and thou shalt be near unto me, thou, and thy children,

> **and thy children's children, and thy flocks, and thy herds, and all that thou hast:**

Goshen was a rich pastureland in an area apart from the rest of the country that was inhabited by the Egyptians. It was probably on the east side of the Nile between the Red Sea and the Mediterranean Sea. It was there that the Hebrews built the treasure cities of Rameses and Pithom for the new Pharaoh (Exodus 1:11).

VERSE 11

> **And there will I nourish thee; for yet** *there are* **five years of famine; lest thou, and thy household, and all that thou hast, come to poverty.**

VERSE 12

> **And, behold, your eyes see, and the eyes of my brother Benjamin, that** *it is* **my mouth that speaketh unto you.**

VERSE 13

> **And ye shall tell my father of all my glory in Egypt, and of all that ye have seen; and ye shall haste and bring down my father hither.**

VERSE 14

> **And he fell upon his brother Benjamin's neck, and wept; and Benjamin wept upon his neck.**

VERSE 15

> **Moreover he kissed all his brethren, and wept upon them: and after that his brethren talked with him.**

VERSE 16

> **And the fame thereof was heard in Pharaoh's house, saying, Joseph's brethren** *are* **come: and it pleased Pharaoh well, and his servants.**

VERSE 17

And Pharaoh said unto Joseph, Say unto thy brethren, This do ye; lade your beasts, and go, get you unto the land of Canaan;

VERSE 18

And take your father and your households, and come unto me: and I will give you the good of the land of Egypt, and ye shall eat the fat of the land.

VERSE 19

Now thou art commanded, this do ye; take your wagons out of the land of Egypt for your little ones, and for your wives, and bring your father, and come.

The Israelites hadn't brought wagons down to Egypt when they came to buy food; they had only asses and beasts of burden. As we shall see, the wagons were a present from Pharaoh.

VERSE 20

Also regard not your stuff; for the good of all the land of Egypt *is* yours.

VERSE 21

And the children of Israel did so: and Joseph gave them wagons, according to the commandment of Pharaoh, and gave them provisions for the way.

VERSE 22

To all of them he gave each man changes of raiment; but to Benjamin he gave three hundred *pieces* of silver, and five changes of raiment.

VERSE 23

And to his father he sent after this *manner*; ten asses laden with the good things of Egypt, and ten

she asses laden with corn and bread and meat for his father by the way.

VERSE 24

So he sent his brethren away, and they departed: and he said unto them, See that ye fall not out by the way.

VERSE 25

And they went up out of Egypt, and came into the land of Canaan unto Jacob their father,

VERSE 26

And told him, saying, Joseph *is* yet alive, and he *is* governor over all the land of Egypt. And Jacob's heart fainted, for he believed them not.

VERSE 27

And they told him all the words of Joseph, which he had said unto them: and when he saw the wagons which Joseph had sent to carry him, the spirit of Jacob their father revived:

VERSE 28

And Israel said, *It is* enough; Joseph my son *is* yet alive: I will go and see him before I die.

CHAPTER FORTY-SIX

VERSE 1

And Israel took his journey with all that he had, and came to Beersheba, and offered sacrifices unto the God of his father Isaac.

Beersheba, the site where Abraham had made a covenant with Abimelech (chapter 21) and the home of Isaac, was where Jacob had lived as a boy before journeying to Hebron. It is significant that he waited until he again reached this city before offering his sacrifices, no doubt in thanks and for a safe journey.[12]

VERSE 2

And God spake unto Israel in the visions of the night, and said, Jacob, Jacob. And he said, Here *am* I.

VERSE 3

And he said, I *am* God, the God of thy father: fear not to go down into Egypt; for I will there make of thee a great nation:

God reaffirmed the promise made to Abraham and Isaac. In retrospect, it's easy to see that the promise was more than fulfilled, but at the time, there must have been concerns about the journey into a foreign land ruled by people who may have been hostile.

VERSE 4

I will go down with thee into Egypt; and I will also surely bring thee up *again*: And Joseph shall put his hand upon thine eyes.

I believe the second part of this verse, "And Joseph shall put his hand upon thine eyes," was an idiom that referred to the act that would occur at Jacob's death and assured him Joseph would be there to comfort him in his old age and bury him.

VERSE 5

And Jacob rose up from Beersheba: and the sons of Israel carried their father, and their little ones, and their wives, in the wagons which Pharaoh had sent to carry him.

We're not told the exact number of people involved in the migration, but according to the listing in the verses to follow, there were sixty-six people named who were blood relatives of Jacob in the entourage that journeyed from Canaan to Egypt.[13]

And of course the men all had wives. Only two daughters were mentioned, but there must have been more, and they would presumably also have had husbands and children, so the total family involved could have been well over a hundred. We can also assume there were servants and herdsmen. Therefore, the entire entourage could very possibly have numbered several hundred, if not more. We know that in just the 430 years of captivity the number involved in the Exodus grew to what has been estimated at somewhere between one and a half million to as many as two and a half million people.

VERSE 6

And they took their cattle, and their goods, which they had gotten in the land of Canaan, and came into Egypt, Jacob, and all his seed with him:

VERSE 7

His sons, and his sons' sons with him, his daughters, and his sons' daughters, and all his seed brought he with him into Egypt.

VERSE 8

And these are the names of the children of Israel, which came into Egypt, Jacob and his sons: Reuben, Jacob's firstborn.

VERSE 9

And the sons of Reuben; Hanoch, and Phallu, and Hezron, and Carmi.

VERSE 10

And the sons of Simeon; Jemuel, and Jamin, and Ohad, and Jachin, and Zohar, and Shaul the son of a Canaanitish woman.

VERSE 11

And the sons of Levi; Gershon, Kohath, and Merari.

VERSE 12

And the sons of Judah; Er, and Onan, and Shelah, and Pharez, and Zerah; but Er and Onan died in the land of Canaan. And the sons of Pharez were Hezron and Hamul.

Numbers 26:19 also mentions the deaths of Er and Onan as having occurred in Canaan. We were given the account of their deaths in 38:7–10, where we were told they were slain by God for their treatment of Tamar.

VERSE 13

And the sons of Isachar; Tola, and Phuvah, and Job, and Shimron.

VERSE 14

And the sons of Zebulun; Sered, and Elon, and Jahleel.

VERSE 15

These *be* the sons of Leah, which she bare unto Jacob in Padanaram, with his daughter Dinah: all the souls of his sons and his daughters *were* thirty and three.

VERSE 16

> **And the sons of Gad; Ziphion, and Haggi, Shuni, and Ezbon, Eri, and Arodi, and Areli.**

VERSE 17

> **And the sons of Asher; Jimnah, and Ishuah, and Isui, and Beriah, and Serah their sister: and the sons of Beriah; Heber, and Malchiel.**

Note the mention of a woman here. This Sera was mentioned in Numbers 46:26 and in 1 Chronicles 7:30 but has no place in any other narrative. Because of this and the fact that she was listed at all has given rise to several legends called *midrashim.* They make for interesting reading.

VERSE 18

> **These** *are* **the sons of Zilpah, whom Laban gave to Leah his daughter, and these she bare unto Jacob,** *even* **sixteen souls.**

VERSE 19

> **The sons of Rachel Jacob's wife; Joseph, and Benjamin.**

VERSE 20

> **And unto Joseph in the land of Egypt were born Manasseh and Ephraim, which Asenath the daughter of Potipherah priest of On bare unto him.**

VERSE 21

> **And the sons of Benjamin** *were* **Belah, and Becher, and Ashbel, Gera, and Naaman, Ehi, and Rosh, Muppim, and Huppim, and Ard.**

Muppim and Huppim sound like names for twins.

VERSE 22

These *are* the sons of Rachel, which were born to Jacob: all the souls *were* fourteen.

VERSE 23

And the sons of Dan; Hushim.

To have only one son was very uncommon. It's probable that Dan had many daughters. We know there became a tribe of Dan who were very idolatrous. It's possible the daughters all married men outside their religion. The tribe of Dan is known as one of the lost tribes, and there is much speculation as to where they went and what people are their descendants.

VERSE 24

And the sons of Naphtali; Jahzeel, and Guni, and Jezer, and Shillem.

VERSE 25

These *are* the sons of Bilhah, which Laban gave unto Rachel his daughter; and she bare these unto Jacob: All the souls *were* seven.

VERSE 26

All the souls that came with Jacob into Egypt, which came out of his loins, besides Jacob's sons' wives, all the souls *were* threescore and six;

VERSE 27

And the sons of Joseph, which were born him in Egypt, *were* two souls: all the souls of the house of Jacob, which came into Egypt, were threescore and ten.

Jacob himself, Joseph, and Joseph's two sons would make up the difference between sixty-six and seventy. Acts 7:14 mentions seventy-five; I won't go into the number of explanations for the difference. I believe the larger number included members of the family who had been born later.

VERSE 28

> **And he sent Judah before him unto Joseph, to direct his face unto Goshen; and they came into the land of Goshen.**

VERSE 29

> **And Joseph made ready his chariot, and went up to meet Israel his father, to Goshen, and presented himself unto him; and he fell on his neck, and wept on his neck a good while.**

VERSE 30

> **And Israel said unto Joseph, Now let me die, since I have seen thy face, because thou *art* yet alive.**

VERSE 31

> **And Joseph said unto his brethren, and unto his father's house, I will go up, and shew Pharaoh, and say unto him, My brethren, and my father's house, which *were* in the land of Canaan, are come unto me;**

VERSE 32

> **And the men *are* shepherds, for their trade hath been to feed cattle; and they have brought their flocks, and their herds, and all that they have.**

VERSE 33

> **And it shall come to pass, when Pharaoh shall call you, and shall say, What *is* your occupation?**

VERSE 34

> **That ye shall say, Thy servants trade hath been about cattle from our youth even until now, both we, *and* also our fathers: that ye may dwell in**

the land of Goshen; for every shepherd *is* an abomination unto the Egyptians.

As mentioned before, Goshen was separated from the part of Egypt inhabited by the Egyptians and so would not have been a cause for contention or strife. By locating his people in Goshen, Joseph kept his family together and separate from the Egyptians' influence, with their idolatrous ways, which might in some way have corrupted the Israelites.

CHAPTER FORTY-SEVEN

VERSE 1

Then Joseph came and told Pharaoh, and said, My father and my brethren, and their flocks, and their herds, and all that they have, are come out of the land of Canaan; and, behold, they *are* in the land of Goshen.

VERSE 2

And he took some of his brethren, *even* five men, and presented them to Pharaoh.

We aren't told why he took only five. It may have been to keep from seeming too large an invasion.

VERSE 3

And Pharaoh said unto his brethren, What *is* your occupation? And they said unto Pharaoh, Thy servants *are* shepherds, both we, *and* also our fathers.

VERSE 4

They said moreover unto Pharaoh, For to sojourn in the land are we come; for thy servants have no pasture for their flocks; for the famine *is* sore in the land of Canaan: now therefore, we pray thee, let thy servants dwell in the land of Goshen.

VERSE 5

And Pharaoh spake unto Joseph, saying, Thy father and thy brethren are come unto thee:

VERSE 6

> **The land of Egypt** *is* **before thee; in the best of the land make thy father and brethren to dwell; in the land of Goshen let them dwell; and if thou knowest** *any* **men of activity among them, then make them rulers over my cattle.**

The word translated as "cattle" here is the Hebrew word *miqneh*, which more properly can be translated as "livestock" as it would include cattle, sheep, goats, horses, asses and oxen. And while the Egyptians considered shepherds an abomination, they still kept and used sheep for wool and meat. They also kept cattle, but the tending was left chiefly to women and children. So Pharaoh saw an opportunity to have his own flocks and herds tended by these newcomers who didn't share the Egyptians' repugnance at herding. He was wise enough to settle them in Goshen, an area away from the Nile Valley where the Egyptian cattlemen were.

VERSE 7

> **And Joseph brought in Jacob his father, and set him before Pharaoh: and Jacob blessed Pharaoh.**

VERSE 8

> **And Pharaoh said unto Jacob, How old** *art* **thou?**

The ancient Egyptians rarely lived to one hundred years of age. The average was much less, perhaps as low as forty to fifty; some estimates are as low as thirty-three for men and twenty-nine for women. So the question is understandable considering Jacob was much older than anyone Pharaoh was likely to have ever seen. And, Pharaoh may have been still a very young boy.

VERSE 9

> **And Jacob said unto Pharaoh, The days of the years of my pilgrimage** *are* **an hundred and thirty years: few and evil have the days of the years of my life been, and have not attained unto the days**

of the years of the life of my fathers in the days of their pilgrimage.

Since the flood, the average age had been declining for each generation. Jacob was no doubt aware that his forefathers had lived to be much older than he was, and he was aware his time was coming to an end.

VERSE 10

And Jacob blessed Pharaoh, and went out from before Pharaoh.

The blessings Jacob gave would have been ones according to his own faith, not those of Pharaoh. Pharaoh obviously didn't take offense, however, and accepted them in the spirit in which they were offered.

VERSE 11

And Joseph placed his father and his brethren, and gave them a possession in the land of Egypt, in the best of the land, in the land of Rameses, as Pharaoh had commanded.

The "land of Rameses" and the "land of Goshen" are the same. It was in the northeastern Nile Delta region, where the Nile flows into the Mediterranean Sea. It's west of the Sinai Peninsula and north of the Valley of the Kings and its famous pyramids.

VERSE 12

And Joseph nourished his father, and his brethren, and all his father's household, with bread, according to *their* families.

VERSE 13

And *there was* no bread in all the land; for the famine *was* very sore, so that the land of Egypt and *all* the land of Canaan fainted by reason of the famine.

VERSE 14

And Joseph gathered up all the money that was found in the land of Egypt, and in the land of Canaan, for the corn which they bought: and Joseph brought the money into Pharaoh's house.

VERSE 15

And when money failed in the land of Egypt, and in the land of Canaan, all the Egyptians came unto Joseph, and said, Give us bread: for why should we die in thy presence? For the money faileth.

VERSE 16

And Joseph said, Give your cattle; and I will give you for your cattle, if money fail.

This was a brilliant strategy for Joseph to adopt. By accepting cattle in payment for food, he would be able to feed both the people and the cattle, since they were a possession of Pharaoh. Otherwise, the cattle would have starved along with the people.

VERSE 17

And they brought their cattle unto Joseph: and Joseph gave them bread *in exchange* for horses, and for the flocks, and for the cattle of the herds, and for the asses: and he fed them with bread for all their cattle for that year.

VERSE 18

When that year was ended, they came unto him the second year, and said unto him, We will not hide *it* from my lord, how that our money is spent; my lord also hath our herds of cattle; there is not aught left in the sight of my lord, but our bodies, and our lands:

VERSE 19

Wherefore shall we die before thine eyes, both we and our land? buy us and our land for bread, and we and our land will be servants unto Pharaoh: and give *us* seed, that we may live, and not die, that the land be not desolate.

VERSE 20

And Joseph bought all the land of Egypt for Pharaoh; for the Egyptians sold every man his field, because the famine prevailed over them: so the land became Pharaoh's.

VERSE 21

And as for the people, he removed them to cities from *one* end of the borders of Egypt even to the *other* end thereof.

Joseph's wisdom was becoming evident; he was taking care of the people and vastly increasing the wealth and power of Pharaoh, to whom he owed so much. Moving the people to the cities to be nearer the storage centers was his final stroke of genius; the rural areas couldn't produce anything anyway.

VERSE 22

Only the land of the priests bought he not; for the priests had a portion *assigned them* of Pharaoh, and did eat their portion which Pharaoh gave them: wherefore they sold not their lands.

The priests were like our government workers. They got their food and keep from Pharaoh; they didn't have to produce it themselves.

VERSE 23

Then Joseph said unto the people, Behold, I have bought you this day and your land for Pharaoh: lo, *here is* seed for you, and ye shall sow the land.

VERSE 24

And it shall come to pass in the increase, that ye shall give the fifth *part* **unto Pharaoh, and four parts shall be your own, for seed of the field, and for your food, and for them of your households, and for food for your little ones.**

VERSE 25

And they said, Thou hast saved our lives; let us find grace in the sight of my lord, and we will be Pharaoh's servants.

VERSE 26

And Joseph made it a law over the land of Egypt unto this day, *that* **Pharaoh should have the fifth** *part***, except the land of the priests only,** *which* **became not Pharaoh's.**

VERSE 27

And Israel dwelt in the land of Egypt, in the country of Goshen; and they had possessions therein, and grew, and multiplied exceedingly.

There are several theories about just how many people this entailed. That is partly due to the uncertainty of the length of the captivity. Although some scholars have placed it at about 215 years, I'll stick with the number listed in Exodus 12:40, which is 430 years. In Exodus 38:26 and in Numbers 1:46, it is stated that there were 603,550 men twenty years and older who could serve as fighters. (Numbers lists a complete breakdown by tribe.) That would put the total number of Israelites somewhere between 1.5 and 2.5 million. While this is a staggering number, it's certainly possible given the time frame and the normal population growth over approximately fifteen generations. And it would seem to confirm the longer time (430 years) of the stay in Egypt.

VERSE 28

**And Jacob lived in the land of Egypt seventeen
years: so the whole age of Jacob was an hundred
forty and seven years.**

VERSE 29

**And the time drew nigh that Israel must die: and he
called his son Joseph, and said unto him, If now I
have found grace in thy sight, put, I pray thee, thy
hand under my thy, and deal kindly and truly with
me; bury me not, I pray thee, in Egypt:**

VERSE 30

**But I will lie with my fathers, and thou shalt carry
me out of Egypt, and bury me in their buryingplace.
And he said, I will do as thou hast said.**

VERSE 31

**And he said, Swear unto me, And he sware unto
him. And Israel bowed himself upon the bed's
head.**

The beds used at that time were mostly mats placed on the floor.
They didn't have beds with headboards, so Jacob would have been
merely bowing on his mat. The word used for "bed" is *mittâh*, which
can have several meanings, including a bier or coffin, but the most
common usage is simply a bed.

CHAPTER FORTY-EIGHT

VERSE 1

And it came to pass after these things, that *one* told Joseph, Behold, thy father *is* sick: and he took with him his two sons, Manasseh and Ephraim.

VERSE 2

And *one* told Jacob, and said, Behold, thy son cometh unto thee: and Israel straightened himself, and sat upon the bed.

VERSE 3

And Jacob said unto Joseph, God Almighty appeared unto me at Luz in the land of Canaan, and blessed me,

VERSE 4

And said unto me, Behold, I will make thee fruitful, and multiply thee, and I will make of thee a multitude of people; and will give this land to thy seed after thee *for* an everlasting possession.

VERSE 5

And now thy two sons, Ephraim and Manasseh, which were born unto thee in the land of Egypt before I came unto thee into Egypt, *are* mine; as Reuben and Simeon, they shall be mine.

VERSE 6

And thy issue, which thou begettest after them, shall be thine, *and* shall be called after the name of their brethren in their inheritance.

VERSE 7

And as for me, when I came from Padan, Rachel died by me in the land of Canaan in the way, when yet *there was* **but a little way to come unto Ephrath: and I buried her there in the way of Ephrath; the same** *is* **Bethlehem.**

VERSE 8

And Israel held Joseph's sons, and said, Who *are* **these?**

VERSE 9

And Joseph said unto his father, These *are* **my sons, whom God hath given me in this** *place.* **And he said, Bring them, I pray thee, unto me, and I will bless them.**

VERSE 10

Now the eyes of Israel were dim with age, *so that* **he could not see. And he brought them near unto him; and he kissed them, and embraced them.**

VERSE 11

And Israel said unto Joseph, I had not thought to see thy face: and, lo, God hath shewed me also thy seed.

VERSE 12

And Joseph brought them out from between his knees, and he bowed himself with his face to the earth.

VERSE 13

And Joseph took them both, Ephraim in his right hand toward Israel's left hand, and Manasseh in his left hand toward Israel's right hand, and brought *them* **near unto him.**

VERSE 14

And Israel stretched out his right hand, and laid *it* upon Ephraim's head, who *was* the younger, and his left hand upon Manasseh's head, guiding his hands wittingly; for Manasseh *was* the firstborn.

VERSE 15

And he blessed Joseph, and said, God, before whom my fathers Abraham and Isaac did walk, the God which fed me all my life long unto this day,

VERSE 16

The angel which redeemed me from all evil, bless the lads; and let my name be named on them, and the name of my fathers Abraham and Isaac; and let them grow into a multitude in the midst of the earth.

VERSE 17

And when Joseph saw that his father laid his right hand upon the head of Ephraim, it displeased him: and he held up his father's hand, to remove it from Ephraim's head unto Manasseh's head.

VERSE 18

And Joseph said unto his father, Not so, my father: for this *is* the firstborn; put thy right hand upon his head.

VERSE 19

And his father refused, and said, I know *it*, my son, I know *it*: he also shall become a people, and he also shall be great: but truly his younger brother shall be greater than he, and his seed shall become a multitude of nations.

VERSE 20

And he blessed them that day, saying, In thee shall Israel bless, saying, God make thee as Ephraim and as Manasseh: and he set Ephraim before Manasseh.

Paul mentioned this blessing in Hebrews 11:21. It's yet another instance where a happening in Genesis was confirmed in the New Testament, further proof that the Genesis record was known and accepted by the apostles of Christ.

VERSE 21

And Israel said unto Joseph, Behold, I die: but God shall be with you, and bring you again unto the land of your fathers.

VERSE 22

Moreover I have given to thee one portion above thy brethren, which I took out of the hand of the Amorite with my sword and my bow.

The portion mentioned here is probably a portion of land as opposed to money or other types of inheritance. The New International Version translates this passage as "And to you I give one more ridge of land than to your brothers, the ridge I took from the Amorites." The New Living Translation also uses the phrase "an extra portion of land," and the Darby Bible Translation says "one tract (of land)." The Holman Christian Standard Bible states, "I am giving you the one mountain slope I took from the hand of the Amorites." The Net Bible also mentions a mountain slope, though I really don't see the source for that. Other translations also either agree with the portion consisting of land or don't define it at all and just leave it as a portion of the inheritance.

CHAPTER FORTY-NINE

And Jacob called unto his sons, and said, Gather yourselves together, that I may tell you *that* **which shall befall you in the last days.**

Jacob knew he was dying. He called his sons together to tell them what was to befall them in the future not for themselves only but for their descendants, who would become the twelve tribes of Israel.

The Bible doesn't tell us how Jacob got this information. It may have been insight based on what he knew of his sons' natures, or it may have been divinely inspired, perhaps through a dream. However he came by the knowledge, the prophecies have proven to be accurate. Later books of Scripture as well as secular histories confirm their accuracy so far.

Some prophesies deal with the end times that have yet to be fulfilled (for example, what would happen to the nations of Ephraim and Manasseh if they turned their backs to God and refused to obey Him).

VERSE 2

Gather yourselves together, and hear, ye sons of Jacob; and harken unto Israel your father.

While the descendants of the twelve tribes together made up the nation of Israel, remember that each tribe and its descendants had separate destinies and have at times gone their separate ways. Some have fared better than others, and some have nearly been destroyed.

As with the stories with morals, I won't attempt to interpret or explain here the meaning of Jacob's message for his sons. There are many good works available concerning all the biblical prophecies, those that have been fulfilled and those that concern the future. Suffice it to say there are enough that have been proven true to establish the veracity of the Bible to all but the absolute, die-hard nonbeliever. And for those I believe no evidence would be sufficient.

VERSE 3

Reuben, thou *art* my firstborn, my might, and the beginning of my strength, the excellency of dignity, and the excellency of power:

VERSE 4

Unstable as water, thou shalt not excel; because thou wentest up to thy father's bed; then defiledst thou *it*: he went up to my couch.

VERSE 5

Simeon and Levi *are* brethren; instruments of cruelty *are in* their habitations.

VERSE 6

O my soul, come not thou into their secret; unto their assembly, mine honour, be not thou united: for in their anger they slew a man, and in their selfwill they digged down a wall.

VERSE 7

Cursed *be* their anger, for *it was* fierce, and their wrath, for it was cruel: I will divide them in Jacob, and scatter them in Israel.

VERSE 8

Judah, thou *art he* whom thy brethren shall praise: thy hand *shall be* in the neck of thine enemies; thy father's children shall bow down before thee.

VERSE 9

Judah *is* a lion's whelp: from the prey, my son, thou art gone up: he stooped down, he couched as a lion, and as an old lion; who shall rise him up?

VERSE 10

The scepter shall not depart from Judah, nor a lawgiver from between his feet, until Shiloh come; and unto him *shall* **the gathering of the people** *be.*

The word translated "Shiloh" is *shîylôh*, used here as an epithet for the Messiah.

VERSE 11

Binding his foal unto the vine, and his ass's colt unto the choice vine; he washed his garments in wine, and his clothes in the blood of grapes:

VERSE 12

His eyes *shall be* **red with wine, and his teeth white with milk.**

VERSE 13

Zebulun shall dwell at the haven of the sea, and he *shall be* **for an haven of ships; and his border** *shall be* **unto Zidon.**

VERSE 14

Isachar *is* **a strong ass couching down between two burdens:**

VERSE 15

And he saw the rest *was* **good, and the land that it** *was* **pleasant; and he bowed his shoulder to bear, and became a servant unto tribute.**

VERSE 16

Dan shall judge his people, as one of the tribes of Israel.

VERSE 17

> Dan shall be a serpent by the way, an adder in the path, that biteth the horse heels, so that his rider shall fall backward.

VERSE 18

> I have waited for thy salvation, O Lord.

VERSE 19

> Gad, a troop shall overcome him: but he shall overcome at the last.

VERSE 20

> Out of Asher his bread *shall be* fat, and he shall yield royal dainties.

VERSE 21

> Naphtali *is* a hind let loose: he giveth goodly words.

VERSE 22

> Joseph *is* a fruitful bough, *even* a fruitful bough by a well; *whose* branches run over the wall:

VERSE 23

> The archers have sorely grieved him, and shot *at him*, and hated him:

VERSE 24

> But his bow abode in strength, and the arms of his hands were made strong by the hands of the mighty *God* of Jacob; (from thence *is* the shepherd, the stone of Israel;)

VERSE 25

> *Even* by the God of thy father, who shall help thee; and by the Almighty, who shall bless thee with

blessings of heaven above, blessings of the deep that lieth under, blessings of the breasts, and of the womb:

VERSE 26

The blessings of thy father have prevailed above the blessings of my progenitors unto the utmost bound of the everlasting hills: they shall be on the head of Joseph, and on the crown of the head of him that was separate from his brethren.

VERSE 27

Benjamin shall ravin *as* a wolf: in the morning he shall devour the prey, and at night he shall divide the spoil.

The word *ravin* means to "plunder" or "pillage," the act of preying on something or someone.

VERSE 28

All these *are* the twelve tribes of Israel: and this *is it* that their father spake unto them, and blessed them; every one according to his blessing he blessed them.

Actually, as mentioned previously, these are not so much blessings as prophecies.

VERSE 29

And he charged them, and said unto them, I am to be gathered unto my people: bury me with my fathers In the cave that *is* in the field of Ephron the Hittite.

VERSE 30

In the cave that *is* in the field of Machpelah, which *is* before Mamre, in the land of Canaan, which Abraham bought with the field of Ephron the Hittite for a possession of a buryingplace.

VERSE 31

There they buried Abraham and Sarah his wife; there they buried Isaac and Rebekah his wife; and there I buried Leah.

VERSE 32

The purchase of the field and of the cave that *is* therein *was* from the children of Heth.

VERSE 33

And when Jacob had made an end of commanding his sons, he gathered up his feet into the bed, and yielded up the ghost, and was gathered unto his people.

CHAPTER FIFTY

VERSE 1

And Joseph fell upon his father's face, and wept upon him, and kissed him.

VERSE 2

And Joseph commanded his servants the physicians to embalm his father: and the physicians embalmed Israel.

The ancient Egyptians believed that preservation of the mummy empowered its soul after death, which would return to the preserved corpse. This was undoubtedly not Joseph's belief, but the process would have made it easier to transport the body to Canaan. And the time taken for the process would provide a suitable mourning period.

Embalming was practiced in ancient times by many cultures throughout the old and new world. Some examples have been discovered dating back to 5000 BC and earlier, but Egypt was the forerunner in developing the process of embalming and mummification.

VERSE 3

And forty days were fulfilled for him; for so are fulfilled the days of those which are embalmed: and the Egyptians mourned for him three score and ten days.

The total embalming process took seventy days. The first fifteen days were for cleaning and purifying. Then forty days were required for the corpse to completely dry out. The last fifteen days were for wrapping and painting. This also corresponded to the seventy days of mourning.

VERSE 4

And when the days of his mourning were past, Joseph spake unto the house of Pharaoh, saying, If now I have found grace in your eyes, speak, I pray you, in the ears of Pharaoh, saying,

Interesting that Joseph sent word to Pharaoh rather than speaking to him directly.

VERSE 5

My father made me swear, saying, Lo, I die: in my grave which I have digged for me in the land of Canaan, there shalt thou bury me. Now therefore let me go up, I pray thee, and bury my father, and I will come again.

VERSE 6

And Pharaoh said, Go up, and bury thy father, according as he made thee swear.

VERSE 7

And Joseph went up to bury his father: and with him went up all the servants of Pharaoh, the elders of his house, and all the elders of the land of Egypt,

VERSE 8

And all the house of Joseph, and his brethren, and his father's house: only their little ones, and their flocks, and their herds, they left in the land of Goshen.

VERSE 9

And there went up with him both chariots and horsemen: and it was a very great company.

We can only imagine what this procession looked like. It must have been several miles long and would have moved very slowly, much as any funeral procession today. We aren't told whether they took provisions for the entire company for the whole trip or whether they lived off the land, but either scenario would have included a multitude of problems.

The military escort of chariots and horsemen also supports the theory that the pharaoh at the time was a Hyksos king, not an Egyptian, as it's highly doubtful that an Egyptian pharaoh would accord such an honor to a Semite.

VERSE 10

And they came to the threshingfloor of Atad, which *is* beyond Jordan, and there they mourned with a great and very sore lamentation: and he made a mourning for his father seven days.

This might provide the answer to the question of provisions. The phrase "beyond Jordan" usually referred to the land on the east side of the river, which would have been out of the way for a direct journey to Jacob's burial place.[14] So it may be that the caravan traveled in a circuitous route to acquire provisions along the way.

VERSE 11

And when the inhabitants of the land, the Canaanites, saw the mourning in the floor of Atad, they said, This *is* a grievous mourning to the Egyptians: wherefore the name of it was called Abelmizraim, which *is* beyond Jordan.

The Hebrew word for mourning is *aveil*, which translates into English as "Abel." Mizraim is the Hebrew word for Egypt. Hence the name Abelmizraim translates as "the mourning of Egypt."

VERSE 12

And his sons did unto him according as he commanded them:

VERSE 13

For his sons carried him into the land of Canaan, and buried him in the cave of the field of

Machpelah, which Abraham bought with the field for a possession of a buryingplace of Ephron the Hittite, before Mamre.

Judaism and Islam agree that entombed within the cave at Mamre are the biblical and Qur'anic patriarchs—Abraham, Isaac, and Jacob—as well as three matriarchs—Sarah, Rebekah, and Leah. Their graves are made inaccessible by the cenotaphs that cover them. Jews are not permitted to visit Isaac and Rebekah's tomb in Isaac Hall except for about nine or ten days a year on special Jewish days because Muslims control 81 percent of the building.

One of these days is the Sabbath of Haye Sarah. The Israeli authorities (who are mainly Jewish secular authorities) also don't allow Jewish religious authorities the right to maintain the site and allow only Muslims to do so. The tombs of Abraham and Sarah are synagogues, whereas the tomb of Isaac and Rebekah is a mosque. Many Israeli tour buses escort tourists there daily. Over 300,000 people annually visit the building and the Jewish section of Hebron. The Cave of the Patriarchs is considered the spiritual center of the ancient city. It lies in the southwest part of the West Bank, in the heart of ancient Judea. In Hebrew, it is called Me'arat HaMakhpela, ("The Cave of the 'double' caves or tombs"). It is the second holiest site in Judaism (after the Temple Mount) and holds considerable theological significance for Islam and Christianity as well as Judaism.

VERSE 14

And Joseph returned into Egypt, he, and his brethren, and all that went up with him to bury his father, after he had buried his father.

VERSE 15

And when Joseph's brethren saw that their father was dead, they said, Joseph will peradventure hate us, and will certainly requite us all the evil which we did unto him.

VERSE 16

And they sent a messenger unto Joseph, saying, Thy father did command before he died, saying,

VERSE 17

So shall ye say unto Joseph, Forgive, I pray thee now, the trespass of thy brethren, and their sin; for they did unto thee evil: and now, we pray thee, forgive the trespass of the servants of the God of thy father. And Joseph wept when they spake unto him.

Joseph probably knew this whole story was a lie. It would have caused him to weep for several reasons: first, because his brothers still didn't recognize that he was a compassionate man who didn't hold a grudge, and second, because his brothers were still involved in trying to deceive him.

VERSE 18

And his brethren also wept and fell down before his face; and they said, behold, *we be* thy servants.

VERSE 19

And Joseph said unto them, Fear not: for *am* I in the place of God?

VERSE 20

But as for you, ye thought evil against me; *but* God meant it unto good, to bring to pass, as *it is* this day, to save much people alive.

VERSE 21

Now therefore fear ye not: I will nourish you, and your little ones. And he comforted them, and spake kindly unto them.

VERSE 22

And Joseph dwelt in Egypt, he, and his father's house: and Joseph lived an hundred and ten years.

VERSE 23

And Joseph saw Ephraim's children of the third *generation*: **the children also of Machir the son of Manasseh were brought up upon Joseph's knees.**

VERSE 24

And Joseph said unto his brethren, I die: and God will surely visit you, and bring you out of this land unto the land he sware to Abraham, and Isaac, and to Jacob.

VERSE 25

And Joseph took an oath of the children of Israel, saying, God will surely visit you, and ye shall carry up my bones from hence.

VERSE 26

So Joseph died, *being* **an hundred and ten years old: and they embalmed him, and he was put in a coffin in Egypt.**

Joseph's bones were preserved in Egypt until the Exodus, when Joshua 24:32 tells us, "The bones of Joseph, which the children of Israel brought up out of Egypt buried they in Shechem, in a parcel of ground which Jacob bought of the sons of Hamor the father of Shechem for an hundred pieces of silver; and it became the inheritance of the children of Joseph."

And so ends the book of Genesis. The accuracy and historicity is still being confirmed by archaeologists today. However, according to a recent survey, 23 percent of US adults think of themselves as atheists, agnostics, or "nothing in particular." And that figure is increasing every year. We have lost a lot of our faith since this country was founded. But of one thing I am certain: nearly all the people who don't accept

Genesis as the Word of God and as fact haven't read the book. They have taken someone else's opinion with such lame criticisms as "The book was written by mortal men," or "There were several different writers," or "The facts don't fit with science," or any number of other arguments put forth by unbelievers for their own purposes to support their own agendas and to deny the truth of the book.

Those who wrote the Old and New Testaments didn't question the truth of Genesis. Jesus Himself quoted Genesis many times, and that's all the proof I need. I believe you accept Genesis or you reject the entire Bible and with it the whole of Christianity.

ENDNOTES

1   For a detailed description of the condition of the earth prior to the flood, I recommend Alfred M. Rehwinkel, *The Flood*, Concordia Publishing House (St. Louis, Mo.,1951)

2   See Jay Green, general editor and translator, *The Interlinear Hebrew/Greek English Bible*, four volumes, volume 1 (Lafayette, IN: Publishers and Authors, 1979)

3   The term *Fertile Crescent* was first used in 1916 by James Henry Breasted in *Ancient Times: A History of the Early World* (Ginn and Company, Boston, New York, etc., 1916)

4   H. S. Bellamy in *Moons, Myths and Men* (Faber & Faber, London, 1936) estimates that altogether there are over 500 flood legends worldwide. See "Flood Legends From Around the World—Northwest Creation" at www.nwcreation.net/noahlegends.html.

5   John Morris, *Noah's Ark: The Search Goes On* (Institute for Creation Research, 2007).

6   For a more detailed explanation of this and other customs as they are mentioned throughout the Bible, I recommend *Commentary on the Whole Bible* by Jamieson, Fausset and Brown, (Zondervan Publishing House, Grand Rapids, MI:, 1961).

7   It's believed the locations of Sodom and Gomorrah have been positively identified. See Bryant G. Wood, "The Discovery of the Sin Cities of Sodom and Gomorrah," *Bible and Spade* (Summer 1999): 67–80.

8   W. H, Mare, "Gerar," *The Zondervan Pictorial Encyclopedia of the Bible*, Merrill C. Tenney, editor, five volumes (Grand Rapids, MI: Zondervan, 1976).

9   For more on this incident, google "The hollow of the thigh." There are many interesting articles to research.

10   Bethel and Ephrath (originally called Ephratah) are two of the cities the serious student would do well to research. In fact, an investigation of all the cities and kingdoms mentioned in Genesis

will help in understanding the history of the people and therefore the veracity of the narrative itself. The places are real; the people were real.

11 From Book of Yasher, chapter 10.

12 Maps are a requisite for me during my Bible study. They help me understand the geography and the significance of historical backgrounds, and give me insight into the problems of travel to the places mentioned in the Bible as well as furthering my understanding of the migrations of all the ancient peoples. For excellent maps of this journey as well as other biblical locations and journeys, I suggest Biblos.com.

13 Sixty-six is an interestingly significant number in biblical history. Among other things, it's the number of books in the Bible.

14 See chapter 23 for the description of the cave in the field of Machpelah. Abraham buried Sarah there, and Abraham himself was buried there (Genesis 25:8–10), then Isaac (Genesis 35:27–29), and then Rebekah and Leah (Genesis 49:31). Rachel of course had her own tomb just outside Bethlehem.

Printed in the United States
By Bookmasters